Eastward on Five Sounds

Eastward on Five Sounds

CRUISING FROM NEW YORK TO NANTUCKET

By Morten Lund

 Walker and
Company, New York

THIS BOOK
IS DEDICATED TO
BEA

 THE AUTHOR WISHES TO ACKNOWLEDGE

the help of the three professional photographers who
came on the cruise and shot the pictures for the book;
Barry Stott of Vail, Colorado; George Wilkinson (Wilk)
of Aspen, Colorado and Kim Massie of Brooklyn Heights,
New York City. He also wishes to thank the amateurs
who contributed their pictures: Bea Williams and Sid
Reichman; further, Evinrude Motors for supplying the
technical know-how and advice for the engine installation. Lastly, Bea Williams for typing the manuscript and
providing valuable advice and aid in getting the manuscript into publishable shape.

Cover: *Shenandoah,* by Barry Stott

First published in the United States of America in 1971 by
the Walker Publishing Company, Inc.

Published simultaneously in Canada by The Ryerson Press,
Toronto.

Library of Congress Catalogue Card Number: 74-142834
ISBN: 0-8027-0338-0

Designed by Carl Weiss

Printed in the United States of America.

CONTENTS

CAUTIONARY NOTE ON THE MAPS

These maps are not charts.

That is to say: the maps are designed to give the skipper an over-all view of the situation, to help him decide on a quick course change in the large sense of deciding to go to one port ten miles away, rather than the one abeam. The maps are *not* designed for close navigation, or for laying out exact compass courses or negotiating a harbor entrance. The only good navigational *charts* for these waters are those supplied by the Coast and Geodetic Survey, available at all sizeable marine stores and most large marinas. These charts tend to sell out early in the season, so buy in the spring, if you are planning to cruise.

Just as the maps are not charts, so the numbers on the maps do *not* indicate anchorages. They merely indicate entire places: harbors, bays, ports of call, points of interest. When it comes to actually anchoring the skipper again must consult the Geodetic charts. He must *not* anchor in traffic channels marked by channel buoys, nor in obvious access channels because in case of a night collision, a skipper whose yacht is anchored in the traffic channel is going to be held liable for damages.

Thirdly, the inlets and harbor entrances in these waters have been dredged quite extensively in recent years. Therefore, only the latest Geodetic charts will have the right depths marked. Any changes from the most recent chart will be noted in Notices to Mariners, put out by the Geodetic Survey Office.

INTRODUCTION TO THE MAPS, NEW YORK TO NANTUCKET

The New York to Nantucket cruise runs past an exceptional coast. The historical bedrock of the nation lies here, now a most industrialized and opulent shore, yet one which is full of magnificent cruising possibilities. There are plenty of harbors that remain nearly empty all summer and many anchorages that are still secluded. There are harbors and beaches along the Connecticut shore that are serene and wholly delightful. And further out there are the harbors of the Elizabeths, utterly remote, the untouched shores of Gardiners Island, the myriad gunkholes of Peconic Bay and the equally lovely small river and bays that can be found along the Cape's south shore.

The cruising generally offers shelter on two opposite shores, an estimable advantage, because there is nearly always a lee harbor and a choice of routes.

The challenge is there, too: the winds are notoriously unpredictable. Storms can arrive with nearly tropical rapidity and violence. There are occasions, many of them, therefore, when a yachtsman needs to know—immediately—just what his alternatives are. In the ten maps that follow, all available ports along any portion of the route from New York to Nantucket are indicated by dotted lines leading away from the solid line of the cruise. Weather coming in or a new breeze coming gives rise nearly every day of the cruise to the question, "Go here or go there?"

IX

The answer can make or break a cruise.

A glance at the right map and a second quick glance at the descriptive captions that follow each map will tell a skipper what his options are at any given moment, without having to unwrap a big four-by-four navigation chart or puzzle over long printed texts.

The itinerary of the model cruise set forth in the maps courses over five sounds: Inner, Middle, and Outer Long Island Sound, Block Island Sound, Rhode Island Sound, Vineyard Sound and Nantucket Sound. It often behooves a skipper to alter strategy as he goes from one to the other, as will be suggested in the text of the book: the tide in the Elizabeths floods north, not west, and in parts of Vineyard and Nantucket Sounds, the tide floods directly east, toward the sea, exactly opposite of the Long Island Sound tides.

The text of the book, besides describing advantageous courses, is an historical and ecological commentary dovetailed into the log of an actual cruise over the itinerary, taken by the author.

There is still peace to be found on the water, in spite of the extraordinary number of boats (probably near a quarter of a million) berthed along the shores. Any given day's traffic is spread over a surface of thousands of square miles. Crowds of boats condense on a very small portion of the whole. The rest is yours.

Eastward on Five Sounds

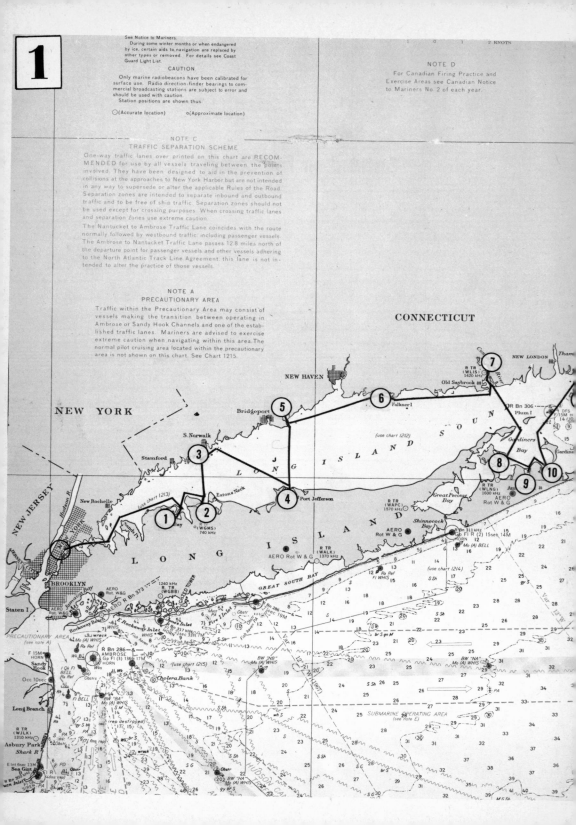

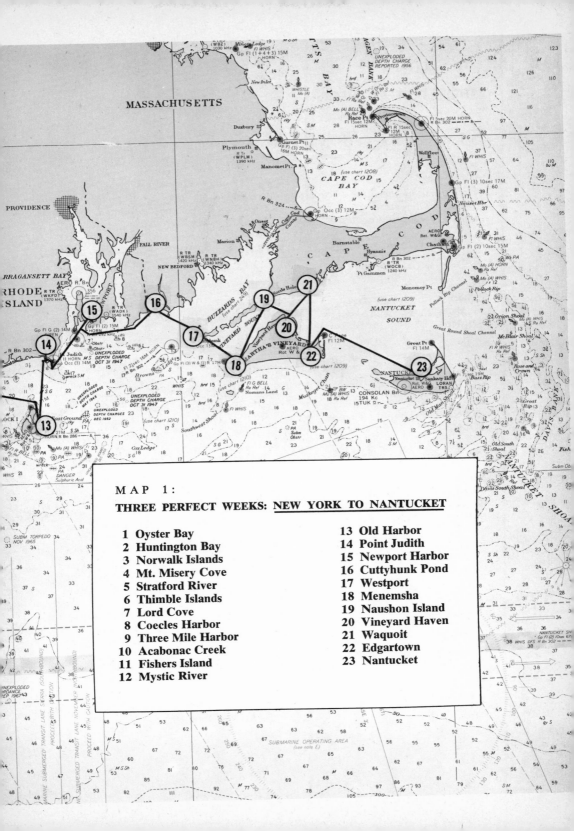

MAP 1:

THREE PERFECT WEEKS: <u>NEW YORK TO NANTUCKET</u>

1 Oyster Bay	**13** Old Harbor
2 Huntington Bay	**14** Point Judith
3 Norwalk Islands	**15** Newport Harbor
4 Mt. Misery Cove	**16** Cuttyhunk Pond
5 Stratford River	**17** Westport
6 Thimble Islands	**18** Menemsha
7 Lord Cove	**19** Naushon Island
8 Coecles Harbor	**20** Vineyard Haven
9 Three Mile Harbor	**21** Waquoit
10 Acabonac Creek	**22** Edgartown
11 Fishers Island	**23** Nantucket
12 Mystic River	

THREE PERFECT WEEKS:

NEW YORK TO NANTUCKET

The course of the three-week cruise described in this book is given in the second column. The cruise might be extended to four weeks, or contracted to two, by adding or omitting certain stops as indicated in columns 1 and 3.

	TWO-WEEK CRUISE (16 stops)	THREE-WEEK CRUISE (23 stops)	FOUR-WEEK CRUISE (30 stops)
INNER LONG ISLAND SOUND	DAY 1 Oyster Bay 2 Norwalk Islands	DAY 1 Oyster Bay 2 Huntington Bay 3 Norwalk Islands	DAY 1 Oyster Bay 2 Huntington Bay 3 Norwalk Islands 4 Southport
MIDDLE LONG ISLAND SOUND	3 Mt. Misery Cove 4 Stratford River 5 Thimble Islands	4 Mt. Misery Cove 5 Stratford River 6 Thimble Islands	5 Mt. Misery Cove 6 Stratford River 7 Thimble Islands 8 Branford
OUTER LONG ISLAND SOUND	6 Lord Cove 7 Three Mile Harbor 8 Fishers Island 9 Mystic River	7 Lord Cove (Connecticut River) 8 Coecles Harbor (Shelter Island) 9 Three Mile Harbor (East Hampton) 10 Acabonac Creek 11 Fishers Island 12 Mystic River	9 Lord Cove (Connecticut River) 10 Selden Cove 11 Mattituck 12 Coecles Harbor (Shelter Island) 13 Sag Harbor 14 West Neck Bay (Shelter Island) 15 Three Mile Harbor (East Hampton) 16 Acabonac Creek 17 Fishers Island 18 Mystic River

	TWO-WEEK CRUISE (16 stops)	THREE-WEEK CRUISE (23 stops)	FOUR-WEEK CRUISE (30 stops)

RHODE
ISLAND
SOUND
	10 Old Harbor
	11 Newport Harbor
	12 Cuttyhunk Pond
		13 Old Harbor
		  (Block Island)
		14 Point Judith
		15 Newport Harbor
		16 Cuttyhunk Pond
		17 Westport
			19 Old Harbor
			  (Block Island)
			20 Point Judith
			21 Newport Harbor
			22 Padanarum
			23 Cuttyhunk Pond
			24 Westport

VINE- **YARD** **SOUND/** **NAN-** **TUCKET** **SOUND**	13 Menemsha 14 Naushon Island 15 Edgartown 16 Nantucket	18 Menemsha 19 Naushon Island 20 Vineyard Haven 21 Waquoit 22 Edgartown 23 Nantucket	25 Menemsha 26 Naushon Island 27 Vineyard Haven 28 Waquoit 29 Edgartown 30 Nantucket

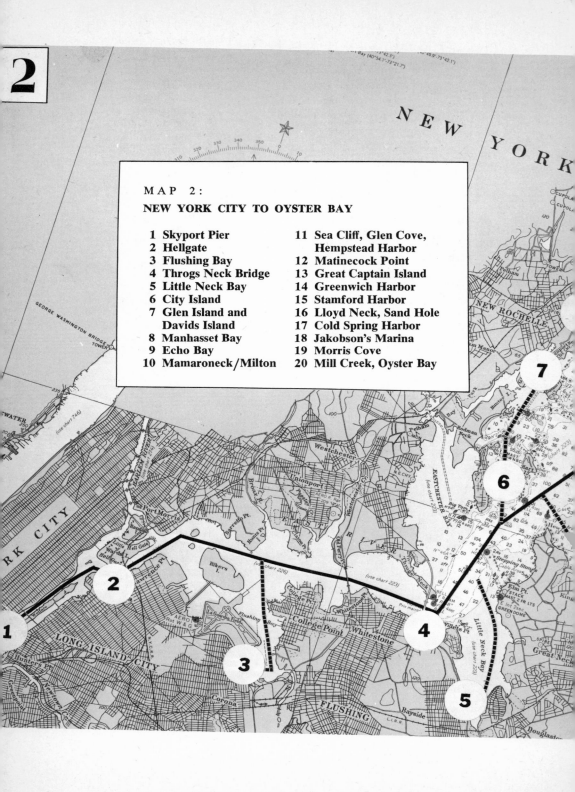

2

MAP 2:

NEW YORK CITY TO OYSTER BAY

1 Skyport Pier
2 Hellgate
3 Flushing Bay
4 Throgs Neck Bridge
5 Little Neck Bay
6 City Island
7 Glen Island and
 Davids Island
8 Manhasset Bay
9 Echo Bay
10 Mamaroneck/Milton
11 Sea Cliff, Glen Cove,
 Hempstead Harbor
12 Matinecock Point
13 Great Captain Island
14 Greenwich Harbor
15 Stamford Harbor
16 Lloyd Neck, Sand Hole
17 Cold Spring Harbor
18 Jakobson's Marina
19 Morris Cove
20 Mill Creek, Oyster Bay

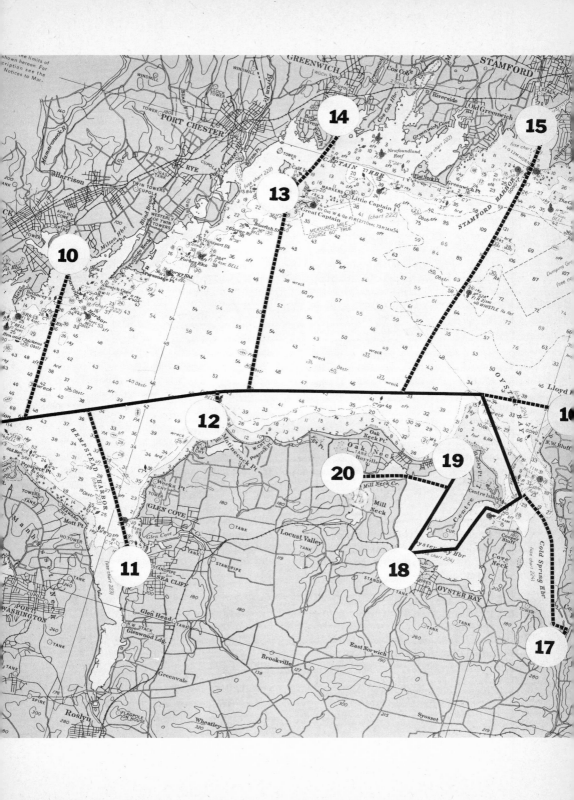

NEW YORK CITY TO OYSTER BAY

The Inner Sound is the most crowded and citified part of the cruise itinerary. Only the interior of Oyster Bay is relatively lightly used. This bay is incomparably the best harbor in this part of Long Island Sound. The relatively quiet stretches of its broad surface are an unexpected blessing.

1—*Skyport Pier,* East River, Manhattan: if you're going to leave from Manhattan, this is the best place. It's just north of the East Village at Twenty-third Street and northeast of Greenwich Village. Skyport is the only yacht basin on Manhattan's East River.
2—*Hellgate:* under the Triboro Bridge are the strongest tides encountered on the whole itinerary, with the possible exception of those at Woods Hole, Massachusetts. The tide can bury buoys and carry injurious flotsam. Go with it, not against it.
3—*Flushing Bay:* situated between the World's Fair grounds, La Guardia Airport and the Mets' Stadium, it contains Nichols World's Fair Marina, the largest within city limits. Recommended for emergency stops.
4—*Throgs Neck Bridge:* the entrance to the Inner Sound.
5—*Little Neck Bay:* on the border of New York City proper. Great Neck, on the far side of the bay, is in suburbia. There's a nice marina and an anchorage at the bottom of Little Neck.
6—*City Island:* more boats per shore foot than any place else on the East Coast; ringed with marinas, shipyards, yacht clubs and moorings.
7—*Glen Island and Davids Island:* these two hide Travers Island; Travers is part of the mainland. Here the New York Athletic Club has its moorings. North of Travers is New Rochelle Harbor well-protected in a slot behind Davenport Neck.

8—*Manhasset Bay:* the busiest bay of the itinerary, having more yacht hulls in its confines than exist within any other harbor in the East. Port Washington is the major city on the shores. Club Capri here is the most fashionable commercial marina on the Inner Sound.
9—*Echo Bay, New Rochelle:* good protection for yachts caught short in this part of the Sound. Crowded, but usually with a mooring or slip to spare in one of the two yacht clubs or the commercial marina. Larchmont, next harbor north, is shallow and difficult to enter. Stay away. Go north into Mamaroneck-Milton—see below.
10—*Mamaroneck-Milton:* reasonably easy access. Slips are available sometimes at Nichols Yacht Yard in the West Basin of the Mamaroneck Harbor. Mamaroneck-Milton Harbor. Both are harder to get into Club is in East Basin at Mamaroneck, and American Yacht Club is at the mouth of Milton Harbor. Both are harder to get into and have little room for visitors.
11—*Sea Cliff, Glen Cove, Hempstead Harbor:* the easiest place to tie up in the large expanse of Hempstead Harbor is behind the breakwater at Sea Cliff Yacht Club or Glen Cove Yacht Club on the eastern shore. Both are well protected. Down at the bottom of the harbor, there's a gunkhole on the east shore behind Bar Beach, but that's a long way in.
12—*Matinecock Point:* the J. P. Morgan estate. Watch for the reef off the point.

Just beyond is Peacock Point, with a nice beach and a tide creek for dinghying.

13—*Great Captain Island, Captains Harbor:* real islands, scattered, and kind of fun for an afternoon's visit. The largest, Great Captain, has seventeen acres. The anchorage behind Calf Island is least crowded. Port Chester Harbor is just west of Great Captain; it offers a small gunkhole behind Manursing.

14—*Greenwich Harbor:* the easiest harbor to get into in a hurry of those around Captains Islands, it's a straight shot from Little Captain to Indian Harbor Yacht Club at the entrance. Cos Cob Harbor is next east from Greenwich but it is an unprepossessingly long and busy creek (Mianus); next east again is Greenwich Cove, with a moored fleet belonging to Old Greenwich Yacht Club. There's a deep anchorage beside the moorings.

15—*Stamford Harbor:* another easy, straight-shot entrance, well protected behind double breakwaters. West branch has a marina and boat basin. East branch has Yacht Haven, the largest marina in the Sound—guest slips available. Next harbor east is Westcott Cove, not as simple to enter.

16—*Lloyd Neck Sand Hole, Oyster Bay:* first of the five or six nice anchorages in Oyster bay. There is no landing on the beach but, as a consequence, there are usually not many yachts in here. The shore is clean of people and homes; normally there is a remote feeling hard to find this far west on the Sound.

17—*Cold Spring Harbor:* down behind Cold Spring Beach, is a relatively quiet gunkhole, opposite The Moorings, which is one of the better Sound waterside restaurants.

18—*Jakobsons Marina, Oyster Bay Harbor:* the finest of the Inner Sound yacht yards. A good rendezvous for the start of any cruise in these waters. The anchorage off the yard is protected from southerlies.

19—*Morris Cove, Oyster Bay Harbor:* up behind Oak Beach and Centre Island, there's a small notch in the shore with five feet of water, protected except for strong southerlies. Seawanhaka Corinthian Yacht Club is on the east side of Centre Island. Teddy Roosevelt's estate is on Cove Neck.

20—*Mill Creek, Oyster Bay Harbor:* great dinghying or shoal draft (two feet) in rather fresh surroundings: summer homes, small craft and tide runs. North branch has Seaman Seacraft, a high-tide shipyard open on Sundays.

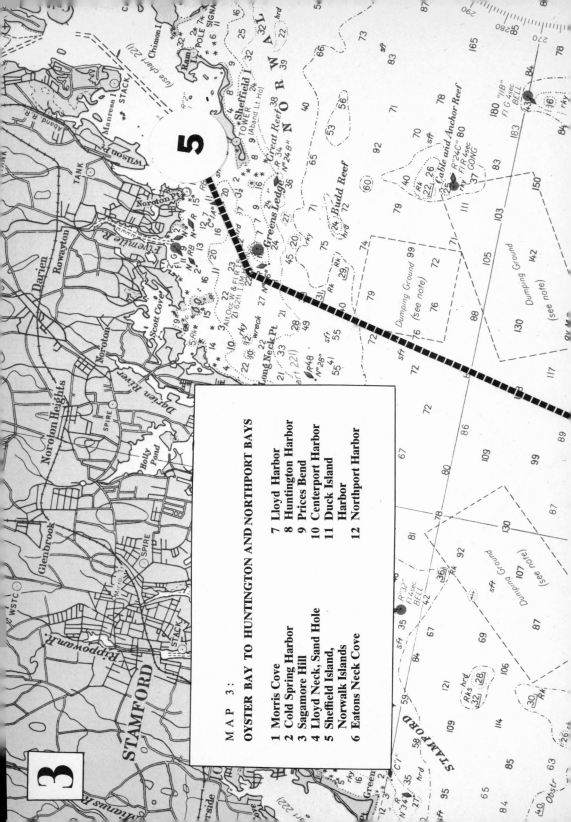

MAP 3:

OYSTER BAY TO HUNTINGTON AND NORTHPORT BAYS

1 Morris Cove
2 Cold Spring Harbor
3 Sagamore Hill
4 Lloyd Neck, Sand Hole
5 Sheffield Island,
  Norwalk Islands
6 Eatons Neck Cove

7 Lloyd Harbor
8 Huntington Harbor
9 Prices Bend
10 Centerport Harbor
11 Duck Island
   Harbor
12 Northport Harbor

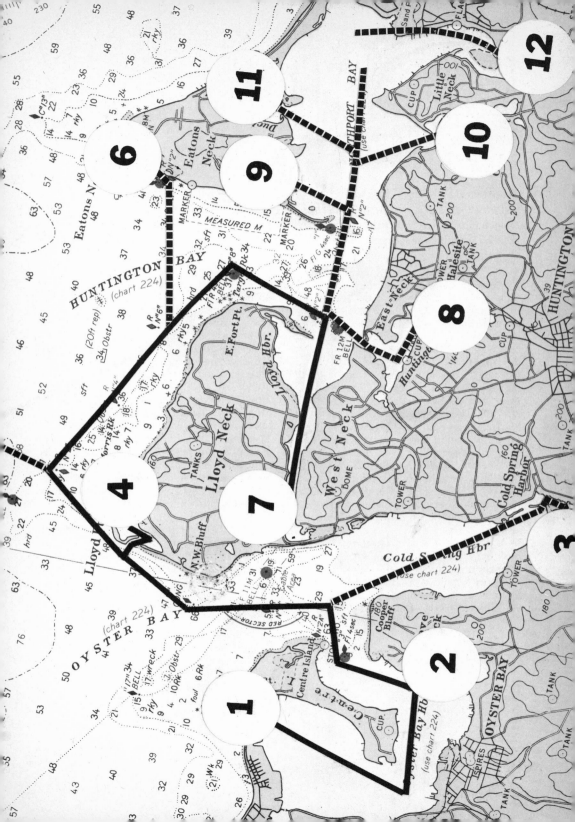

OYSTER BAY TO HUNTINGTON AND NORTHPORT BAYS

The second section of excellent cruising in Inner Long Island Sound is the huge connected complex consisting of Huntington and Northport bays. From Lloyd Harbor on the northwest to Northport on the southeast is nearly twenty miles. Busy places are interspersed with get-away-from-it places all through these bays

1—*Morris Cove, Oyster Bay Harbor:* a nick in the back of Oak Neck Beach, well protected from all but strong southerlies.

2—*Cold Spring Harbor, Oyster Bay:* it has a nice small anchorage behind its beach, opposite The Moorings restaurant.

3—*Sagamore Hill, Oyster Bay:* Teddy Roosevelt's estate museum. Can be visited on foot from a landing on Cove Neck.

4—*Lloyd Neck Sand Hole, Oyster Bay Harbor:* a small beach-encircled cove, dug by dredging. You can't land on the beach; in compensation, there are only a few boats in here at any one time.

5—*Sheffield Island, Norwalk Islands:* if the tides and winds stand fair for the north, you might want to go off and visit the Norwalk Islands instead of Huntington Bay, hoping for a boost down to Huntington later.

6—*Eatons Neck Cove, Huntington Bay:* a busy but interesting gunkhole: many yachts at anchor; encircled by the beach—landing and fires permitted ashore. A Coast Guard Station lies on the northern shore.

7—*Lloyd Harbor, Huntington Bay:* a long, narrow, nearly perfectly protected natural harbor.

8—*Huntington Harbor, Huntington Bay:* a busy, busy place: four active yacht clubs in the harbor hold incessant races.

9—*Prices Bend, Northport Bay:* a very sheltered natural anchorage, nearly land-locked if you go in far enough: five feet at low tide.

10—*Centerport Harbor, Northport Bay:* even busier than Huntington Harbor, with fewer moorings available. Stay out.

11—*Duck Island Harbor, Northport Bay:* a small slot extending just beyond the entrance between Duck Island and Eatons Neck has depths of eight feet at the entrance, shoaling rapidly. Gives protection all around. Swimming at Asharoken Beach on the Sound side.

12—*Northport Harbor, Northport Bay:* If you need repair or supplies in Huntington-Northport, head right down to the bottom where the Northport Boat Yard and Marina lies. The William K. Vanderbilt museum, Eagle's Nest, on Little Neck opposite Northport town, can be reached by taxi.

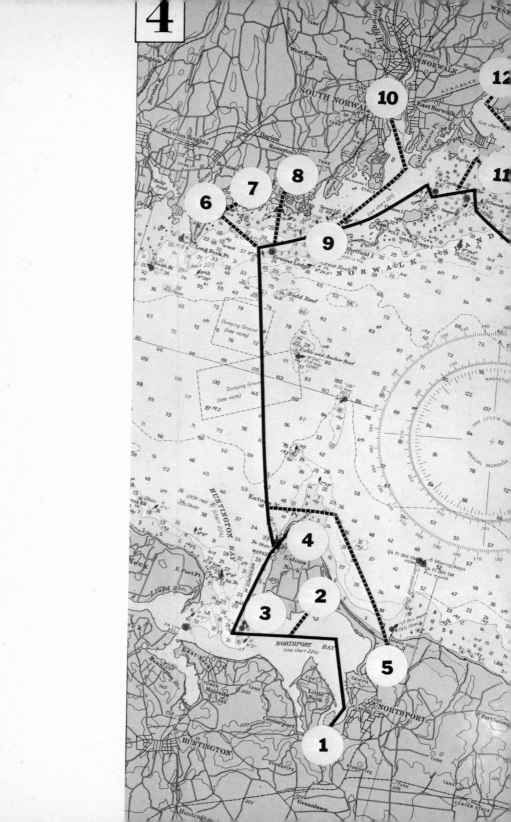

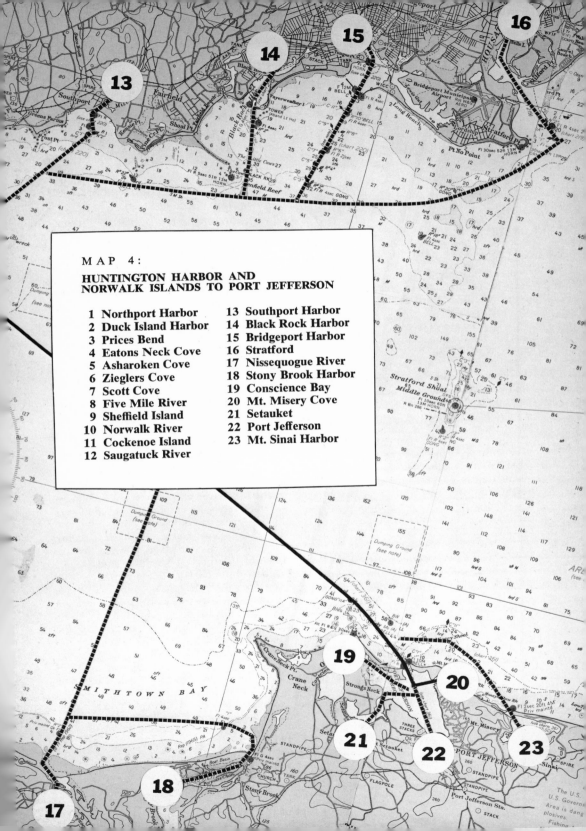

MAP 4:

**HUNTINGTON HARBOR AND
NORWALK ISLANDS TO PORT JEFFERSON**

1 Northport Harbor	13 Southport Harbor
2 Duck Island Harbor	14 Black Rock Harbor
3 Prices Bend	15 Bridgeport Harbor
4 Eatons Neck Cove	16 Stratford
5 Asharoken Cove	17 Nissequogue River
6 Zieglers Cove	18 Stony Brook Harbor
7 Scott Cove	19 Conscience Bay
8 Five Mile River	20 Mt. Misery Cove
9 Sheffield Island	21 Setauket
10 Norwalk River	22 Port Jefferson
11 Cockenoe Island	23 Mt. Sinai Harbor
12 Saugatuck River	

HUNTINGTON HARBOR AND NORWALK ISLANDS TO PORT JEFFERSON

A good way to enter the Middle Sound is to cross from Huntington to the intriguing Norwalk Islands and then go on to the sand walls of Mt. Misery Cove in Port Jefferson. A trip to the beautiful Stratford Shakespeare Theatre up the Housatonic is in order.

1—*Northport Harbor, Northport Bay:* the repair and shopping stop in Huntington Bay-Northport Bay cruising grounds. Northport Boat Yard and Marina is one of the best.

2—*Duck Island Harbor, Northport Bay:* a slot in the entrance of the harbor holds boats with up to eight feet draft—good protection.

3—*Prices Bend, Northport Bay:* another well-protected spot; you can carry five feet right up to the northern cove of the harbor.

4—*Eatons Neck Cove, Huntington Bay:* a small beach-encircled harbor where you can light fires ashore and cook out; usually very crowded, but always room for one more in the anchorage inside. The only installation is a Coast Guard station at the north end.

5—*Asharoken Cove, Northport Bay:* a small dredged channel with good protection next to a big power plant. A harbor of refuge but not of beauty.

6—*Zieglers Cove, Darien:* just off the port bow when you turn the corner at Greens Ledge Light to enter the channel into Sheffield Harbor is Zieglers Cove, a nice but fairly popular spot. On the near side of Long Neck Point is Noroton Harbor at Darien, where neither the Noroton Yacht Club nor the Darien River afford room for transients.

7—*Scott Cove, Darien:* you can go in a short way drawing five feet, all the way drawing three. A neat hole for shallow draft craft.

8—*Five Mile River, Rowayton:* easiest harbor to get into in the vicinity: a straight shot from Greens Ledge Light. Carry seven feet to Nun 6 and three feet beyond. A series of marinas along the river will take care of your needs.

9—*Sheffield Island, Norwalk Islands:* a relatively sheltered harbor behind a picturesque lighthouse. Further east on the island is an interesting mansion ruin. Landing permitted on the eastern end of the island.

10—*Norwalk River, Norwalk:* first cove on the right is Norwalk Cove Marina, excellent service and reputation. Further up, the river is heavy with commercial traffic, not worth a trip unless you want to try one of the oyster bars—they're great. Just east of the river entrance is Village Creek, a gunkhole with room for a couple of boats—eight feet at low.

11—*Cockoenoe Island, Norwalk Islands:* pronounced Ko-Keé-Nee. Owned by the town of Westport. All right to land. A nice shallow-draft harbor on the north.

12—*Saugatuck River, Westport:* a couple of small yacht basins with marinas in them on each side of the mouth of the river. Don't expect overnight room. Rest of the river is crowded, but interesting for its yacht basins and good restaurants.

13—*Southport Harbor, Fairfield:* a pretty harbor, but the Pequot Yacht Club and some municipal facilities offer only the occasional slip or mooring. You're now headed down the Connecticut shore, with a chance for a run to Port Jefferson in favoring winds.

14—*Black Rock Harbor, Bridgeport:* If you need rest or shelter between the Norwalk Islands and Stratford on the Housatonic, Black Rock is the best bet. The Fayerweather Yacht Club and the Bridgeport Marina both provide moorings.

15—*Bridgeport Harbor, Bridgeport:* good protection behind double breakwaters; there's an anchorage next to a good swimming beach (on the east side, just after the breakwaters). Further up, the river is full of commercial craft, no place for a yacht. Ferry to Port Jefferson leaves from here.

16—*Stratford, Housatonic River:* the Shakespeare Theatre has tree-shaded picnic grounds by the river. Stratford Marina, just upriver from the theatre, has ample room. A snug, protected river.

17—*Nissequogue River, Smithtown:* five miles down from Asharoken Cove, not pretty, but serviceable. You can carry eight feet inside; there are facilities, but not much overnight space, sometimes none. The beach east of the entrance is terrific and usually rather untenanted.

18—*Stony Brook Harbor, Smithtown:* can take only about four feet in here at low, but five at mid-tide. Stony Brook is an idyllic village with a good restaurant, village green, horse carriage museum. It's

worth waiting for a high tide to take you to the western end of the harbor if you can't make it at low. Here the boats thin out.

19—*Conscience Bay, Port Jefferson Harbor:* possible anchorage to both sides of small islands at the entrance to Conscience Bay: five to eight feet depths at low. You will have only one or two neighbors, usually.

20—*Mt. Misery Cove, Port Jefferson Harbor:* high, hundred-foot sand walls make this a snug, if popular, place. Lots of yachts share the anchorage. Great fun climbing the walls and running down. Warm swimming.

21—*Setauket, Port Jefferson Harbor:* winding narrow channel but you can get marine supplies here without going into town. No groceries.

22—*Port Jefferson, Port Jefferson Harbor:* somewhat depressing town with handy grocery three blocks off. Plenty of dockside space for shopping or overnight. Bridgeport ferry berths here. For privacy from sightseers, use Setauket Yacht Club dock—the furthest east in the harbor.

23—*Mt. Sinai Harbor, Mt. Sinai:* if you need supplies, you might stop here rather than Port Jefferson. It's prettier, has plenty of water within red stakes marking its anchorage. It has a grocery and a boat yard.

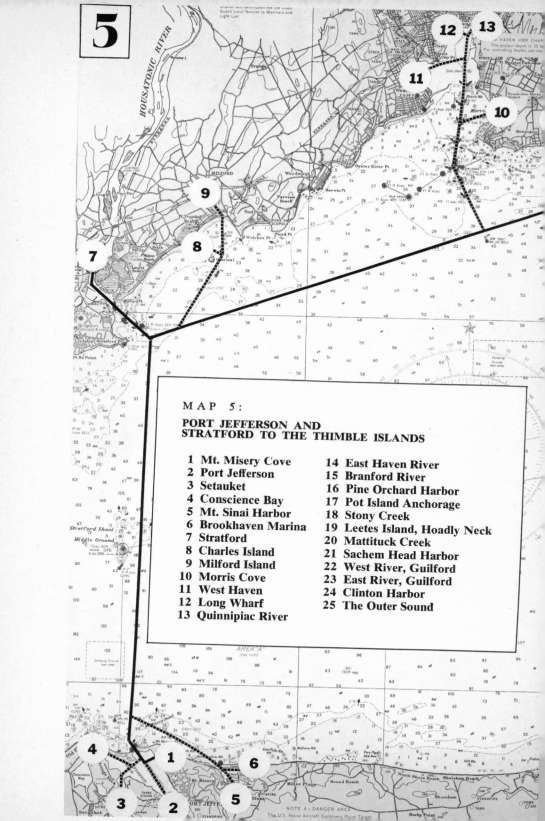

5

MAP 5:

PORT JEFFERSON AND STRATFORD TO THE THIMBLE ISLANDS

1 Mt. Misery Cove
2 Port Jefferson
3 Setauket
4 Conscience Bay
5 Mt. Sinai Harbor
6 Brookhaven Marina
7 Stratford
8 Charles Island
9 Milford Island
10 Morris Cove
11 West Haven
12 Long Wharf
13 Quinnipiac River
14 East Haven River
15 Branford River
16 Pine Orchard Harbor
17 Pot Island Anchorage
18 Stony Creek
19 Leetes Island, Hoadly Neck
20 Mattituck Creek
21 Sachem Head Harbor
22 West River, Guilford
23 East River, Guilford
24 Clinton Harbor
25 The Outer Sound

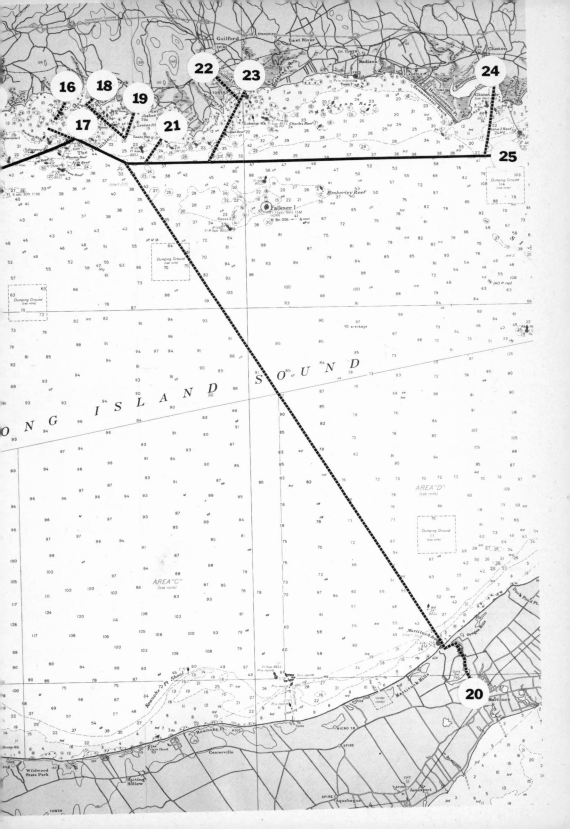

PORT JEFFERSON AND STRATFORD TO THE THIMBLE ISLANDS

After you enjoy the sand walls of Mt. Misery Cove and the Shakespeare festival at Stratford on the Housatonic, the itinerary clearly lies along the Connecticut shore to the Thimble Islands. The Long Island shore is barren of shelter, even a marsh. Conversely, the Thimbles are the best set of small islands on the whole cruise. The Middle Sound is wider and winds are stronger than in the Inner Sound. Make sure you know where harbors of refuge are.

1—*Mt. Misery Cove, Port Jefferson Harbor:* an anchorage for fun, in Port Jefferson Harbor. High sand walls are a delight.

2—*Port Jefferson, Port Jefferson Harbor:* has plenty of dockside space and supplies, including groceries, nearby.Bridgeport ferry lands here. Not very pretty; for privacy, use the Setauket Yacht Club dock farthest east if you can.

3—*Setauket, Port Jefferson Harbor:* winding channel, and narrow. If you want to go ashore without getting into a crowd, this is it. Has marine supplies, no food.

4—*Conscience Bay, Port Jefferson Harbor:* for privacy, anchor at the mouth of the bay on either side of small islands here.

5—*Mt. Sinai Harbor, Mt. Sinai:* red stakes mark deep water anchorage. You can come shoreside at high tide.

6—*Brookhaven Marina, Mt. Sinai Harbor:* lots of boats, but you can anchor off either end of the marina in deep water or outside the marina. Beach is great.

7—*Stratford, Housatonic River:* home of the Shakespeare Theatre, which has tree-shaded picnic grounds by the river; Stratford Marina just upriver from the theatre, has room for you. A snug, protected river.

8—*Charles Island, Milford:* an out-of-the-way anchorage just behind the island—a nice stopover place.

9—*Milford Harbor, Milford:* you can buy a mooring for overnight at the Milford Yacht Club, but this is a narrow, busy harbor and recommended only in an emergency.

10—*Morris Cove, New Haven Harbor:* an anchorage where you miss most of the business of the channel to New Haven. There are a couple of marinas here.

11—*West Haven, New Haven Harbor:* two boat yards and a good restaurant—Adams and Podoloff.

12—*Long Wharf, New Haven Harbor:* if you want to go to town, go no further. Take the dinghy ashore, eat at the Long Wharf Restaurant, attend the Long Wharf Theatre, walk into town, see Yale.

13—*Quinnipiac River, New Haven:* you can go under the New England Turnpike and past the main part of town to a couple of anchorages upriver, but there's only three feet at low tide. A great hurricane hole. You can buy lobsters and fish ashore.

14—*East Haven River, East Haven:* a possible refuge in a hurry. It has a couple of marinas, nice countryside on the banks.

15—*Branford River, Branford:* best harbor and marina facilities between Stratford and the Connecticut River. Branford Yacht Club has fore-and-aft moorings at stakes. Johnson's Branford Boat Yard, further upriver, is outstanding. Nice-looking country, handsome yachts.

16—*Pine Orchard Harbor, Pine Orchard:* rather exposed anchorage. If you like swank, there's the Pine Orchard Yacht Club.

17—*Pot Island anchorage, Thimble Island:* the best seascape in the Sound. Anchor anywhere off the western Pot Island shore. Good protection in all but strong westerlies. Further down, there's another anchorage off Money Island—a whole island world, with kids, prams, a ferry.

18—*Stony Creek, Thimble Islands:* if you need supplies while in the islands, this is the nearest village.

19—*Leetes Island, Hoadly Neck, Thimble Islands:* if a strong westerly gets uncomfortable out in the islands, the anchorage east of Leetes and Hoadly Neck is protected—three-foot draft craft can stay back of the point; with more draft, you will have to go east of Wayland Island by Nun "4."

20—*Mattituck Creek, Long Island:* across from the Thimbles, this is the only port for some forty miles along the nothern Long Island shore. It is a great favorite with fishing parties but the docks are a long way in. Be leery of trying to reach Mattituck at night, when no one can see you if you have troubles. Mattituck has lots of supplies, repairs.

21—*Sachem Head Harbor, Sachem Head:* exposed to prevailing southwesterlies that are likely to make you roll.

22—*West River, Guilford:* a shallow river with a high-tide shipyard, Browns.

23—*East River, Guilford:* a pretty town. Come only in good weather because it is not an easy entrance. A number of homes were built here in the 1600's and 1700's.

24—*Clinton Harbor, Clinton:* much easier access than at Guilford's East River. A straight shot in and then plenty of protection, eight feet deep. Cedar Island Marina in the Hammonassett River inside has three hundred slips, but it's busy on weekends.

25—*The Outer Sound:* once past Falkner Island, the skipper is in a narrower part of the Sound again, with a sea swell starting to roll in from the sea outside. Start paying attention to your tide current charts. A strong tide will slow you down much more than its indicated speed—due to turbulence, increased drag on the hull and difficulty of holding proper course.

PART 6

SOUNDINGS IN FEET
AT MEAN LOW WATER

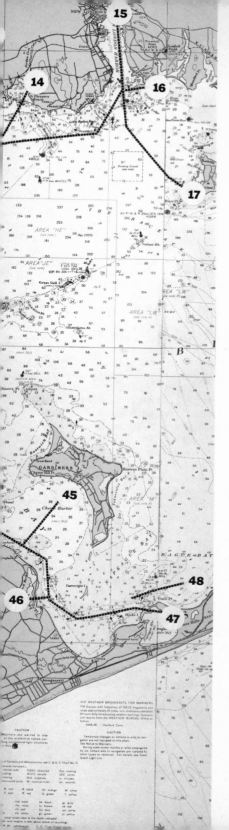

MAP 6:

CONNECTICUT RIVER TO GARDINERS BAY

1 Middle Sound
2 Clinton Harbor
3 Duck Island Roads
4 Westbrook Harbor
5 Old Saybrook
6 Lord Cove, Old Lyme
7 Saybrook
8 Nott Island
9 Essex, Conn. River
10 Upper Connecticut River
11 Rocky Neck, Niantic Bay
12 Giants Neck
13 Niantic River
14 Millstone Harbor
15 New London
16 Pine Island
17 Silver Eel Pond,
   Fishers Island
18 Orient Point, Plum Gut
19 Coecles Harbor
20 Long Beach
21 Orient
22 Gull Pond
23 Greenport
24 Dering Harbor
25 Mill Creek
26 Town Creek and
   Jockey Creek
27 Corey Creek
28 Wooley Pond
29 Cutchogue Harbor
30 North Sea Harbor
31 Deep Hole Creek
32 Bullhead Bay
33 Flanders Bay
34 Shinnecock Canal
35 Noyack Creek,
   Noyack Bay
36 Noyack Harbor
37 West Neck Bay
38 North Haven Harbor
39 Cedar Point
40 Mashomack Creek
41 Northwest Creek
42 Northwest Creek
43 Sag Harbor
44 Three Mile Harbor
45 Cherry Harbor
46 Acabonac Creek
47 Napeague Harbor
48 Block Island Sound

CONNECTICUT RIVER TO GARDINERS BAY

The Outer Sound's initial outstanding cruising grounds are, first, the Connecticut River with its many upriver hideouts and, second, Peconic Bay, Shelter Island Sound and Gardiners Bay, with a total of fifty ports and anchorages.

1—*Middle Sound:* just west of the Outer Sound, it is wider than the Outer Sound and less friendly along the Long Island shore, where there is only one port, Mattituck, in its entire length.

2—*Clinton Harbor, Clinton:* an easy port to get into, with a big marina, Cedar Island, at the yachtsman's disposal.

3—*Duck Island Roads, Westbrook:* a double breakwater built as a harbor of refuge. Not a very good place to spend the night if it blows up, since the ocean rolls heavily in here. Better try Westbrook, below.

4—*Westbrook Harbor, Westbrook:* two rivers, the Patchogue and the Menunketesuck, have been well dredged and fenced with marinas. There's no reason to stay outside in Duck Island Roads. Groceries, repairs, etc.

5—*Old Saybrook, Connecticut River:* right on Saybrook Point are Hull Harbor Marina and just above that, the flashiest marina on the Sound, Terra Mar, with 125 slips, pools, cocktail lounge with live rock bands, motel, etc. Just north of Saybrook Point is a small secure dredged anchorage, North Cove, if you want something less artificial.

6—*Lord Cove, Old Lyme, Connecticut River:* branch east behind Calves Island, and you can go up into Lord Cove, completely wild, and across it into Lord Creek, even wilder. You'll have the creek to yourself, normally.

7—*Saybrook, Connecticut River:* several marinas around the bridge here, but the best is Ferry Point Marina, in behind the bulge of Ferry Point. There are also repairs to be had here.

8—*Nott Island, Connecticut River:* there is a quiet anchorage in eight feet of water between Nott Island and the mainland. Enter only from the south .

9—*Essex, Connecticut River:* this town is one of the most beautiful on the trip: anchor in front or land at Steamboat Dock Marina and have lunch at the Griswold Inn. Just a bit south is a six-foot channel into Middle Cove with Essex Marine Railway Marina, and a bit north is a channel into the second North Cove, with three big marinas inside. Go to town, walk around Essex.

10—*Upper Connecticut River:* the river is navigable to Hartford. Along this forty-mile stretch you can anchor in seclusion at Hamburg Cove, a mile north from Essex; Seldon Creek, another mile or so north; and Whalebone Creek, another couple of miles upriver.

11—*Rocky Neck, Niantic Bay:* one of the best beaches in the cruise, usually with only a few bathers.

12—*Giants Neck, Niantic Bay:* an anchorage here, between Griswold Island and a breakwater ashore at the mouth of the Patguansett River, makes for a nice secluded evening.

13—*Niantic River, Niantic Bay:* not an easy entrance, with swift tides and two drawbridges, but, once inside, there's a long, winding channel inland to a couple of miles of peaceful shoreline.

14—*Millstone Harbor, Niantic Bay:* a somewhat sheltered get-away daytime anchorage, just east of Millstone Point. Open to the south.

15—*New London, Thames River:* here's where the ferries come from Orient Point, Long Island, and Fishers Island. The Fishers Island ferry and the New York to New London train and bus stations are on the same block. You can pull in at the Fishers Island ferry dock and wait for the train to come in. A prime rendezvous point for picking up a new crew.

16—*Pine Island, Thames River:* a handy overnight place at the mouth of the river, just west of Bushy Point Beach; rather busy and with some roll in southerlies. Showers, laundry available.

17—*Silver Eel Pond, Fishers Island:* this is where the Fishers Island ferry lands. No place for overnighting but you can sneak in to pick up crew and save yourself the trip up the river to New London.

18—*Orient Point, Plum Gut:* the New London ferry lands here, and there's a marina and a gas dock and an inn as well.

19—*Coecles Harbor, Shelter Island, Gardiners Bay:* (pronounced "cockles" harbor) through Plum Gut from the Sound into Gardiners Bay, this is the nearest prime anchorage; large, relatively unused, pretty.

20—*Long Beach, Orient Harbor:* the outer part is a beautiful, wild beach with lots of birds, quite protected and deep water—ten feet.

21—*Orient, Orient Harbor:* this neat little village has a harbor protected from the north and east (in southern winds, get behind Long Beach, above) plus a couple of very well set-up museums of old farm and sailing days.

22—*Gull Pond, Shelter Island Sound:* this is at the beginning of Shelter Island Sound which girdles Shelter Island. Gull Pond is a dredged gunkhole with two small lonely creeks going inland from it.

23—*Greenport, Shelter Island Sound:* the biggest commercial fishing port on Long Island, lots of jagged pilings, artistic-looking tumble-down piers, commercial fishing trawlers, fish factories, etc. For good shelter, get inside Stirling Basin.

24—*Dering Harbor, Shelter Island Sound:* here the Shelter Island Yacht Club is home port for some outstanding sailing yachts, and there are marinas and a charter fishing dock. The flounder in the bottom of the bay are yours for the fishing.

25—*Mill Creek, Southold Bay, Shelter Island Sound:* very much taken up by marinas, slips, etc.—good shelter. Upper end of Hashamomuck Pond, beyond the creek, goes to within a hundred yards of the Sound to the north.

26—*Town Creek and Jockey Creek, Southold Bay, Shelter Island Sound:* more marinas; visit Southold Library and the N.Y. Archaeological Museum for Indian lore.

27—*Corey Creek, Little Peconic Bay:* a possible emergency anchorage in the dredged pond outside Minitos Marina. You are now headed down Peconic Bay toward the Shinnecock Canal.

28—*Wooley Pond, Little Peconic Bay:* home of Peconic Bay Marina with fifty-five slips and thirty-three moorings, some available on guest basis.

29—*Cutchogue Harbor, Little Peconic Bay:* there are four creeks and coves off the harbor: Wickham Creek, with a marina; East Creek, with an anchorage; Mud Creek, with an anchorage; and Haywater-Broadwater Cove, with an anchorage—is the easiest to get into.

30—*North Sea Harbor, Little Peconic Bay:* anchor in three feet or use one of the two marinas; this is the port for the village of Southampton.

31—*Deep Hole Creek, Great Peconic Bay:* carry five feet into Strong's Mattituck Marina and you are on the back side of the Sound port of Mattituck, only half a mile by land from the end of Mattituck Creek to the north.

32—*Bullhead Bay, Great Peconic Bay:* Ram Island is inside and there's a yacht club, but no commercial marinas. You are on the edge of the National Golf Course; there's a small anchorage up Little Sebonac Creek for four-foot-draft.

33—*Flanders Bay, Great Peconic Bay:* a smaller bay at the end of the Peconic River at Riverhead, off the present map.

34—*Shinnecock Canal, Great Peconic Bay:*

go by locks (maximum depth 4½ feet) and under a couple of bridges (clearance twenty feet) into Shinnecock Bay behind Westhampton Beach on the South shore of Long Island—an inland waterway goes from there all the way back to New York City.

35—*Noyack Creek, Noyack Bay, Shelter Island Sound:* continuing around Shelter Island again: shallow draft boats can come in; it is at the base of Jessup Neck, a lovely public wildlife bird refuge.

36—*Noyack Harbor, Noyack Bay, Shelter Island Sound:* you can carry six feet in here and anchor behind Noyack Beach; private marinas only inside.

37—*West Neck Bay, West Neck Harbor, Shelter Island Sound:* West Neck Harbor has a creek that empties two miles up into West Neck Bay, a wonderful anchorage.

38—*North Haven Harbor, Shelter Island Sound:* a usually uncrowded, small slot in North Haven Peninsula.

39—*Cedar Point, North west Harbor, Shelter Island Sound:* a state park, a lovely beach.

40—*Mashomack Creek, Mashomack Point, Shelter Island Sound:* a small tidal creek, warm on the ebb, on the southeastern end of Shelter Island. Great dinghying.

41—*Northwest Creek, Northwest Harbor, Shelter Island Sound:* another anchorage that is snug; there's a rowboat rental in here.

42—*Majors Harbor, Shelter Island Sound:* an anchorage protected against easterlies. Nice beach.

43—*Sag Harbor, Shelter Island Sound:* hard to get into, but once in it's a sort of crinkly historical town with a whaling museum, lots of old homes, and reasonable anchorage behind the breakwater. Check your chart for the unbuoyed rocks just outside the lighthouse. They are really there.

44—*Three Mile Harbor, Gardiners Bay:* the most renowned of the Outer Long Island Sound harbors, the port for East Hampton; Dick Sage's Maidstone Boat Yard and other marinas; plenty of anchoring room inside behnd Sammys Beach. Watch the channel markers closely until past Maidstone Boat Yard.

45—*Cherry Harbor, Gardiners Island, Gardiners Bay:* no landing, but nice swimming off the eastern shore—very wild, rather untouched. Mansion of the present Gardiner is up on hill above windmill on Cherry Harbor. Island held by the Gardiners since 1600.

46—*Acabonac Creek, Gardiners Bay:* largest of the East Hampton creeks, "Bonak Creek" has anchorage inside the mouth, lots of calm—only a few fishing boats and rowboats.

47—*Napeague Harbor, Napeague Bay, Block Island Sound:* once past Gardiners Island, you are in Block Island Sound. Napeague has anchorage inside; carry five feet down to the far end, a mile away, and walk over to glorious Amagansett Beach facing the open Atlantic to the south. It's a twenty-minute walk.

48—*Block Island Sound:* as you go out toward Montauk Point the only harbor on the island is Lake Montauk; next is Block Island, about twenty miles out from Napeague.

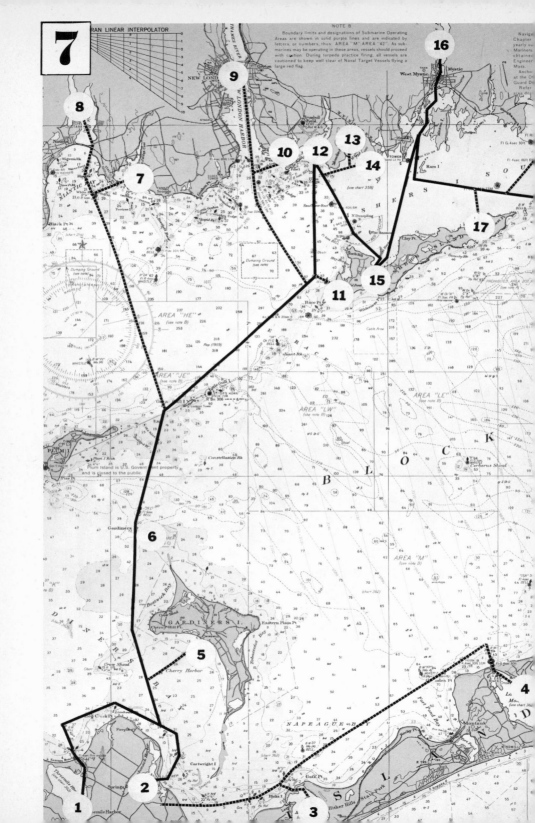

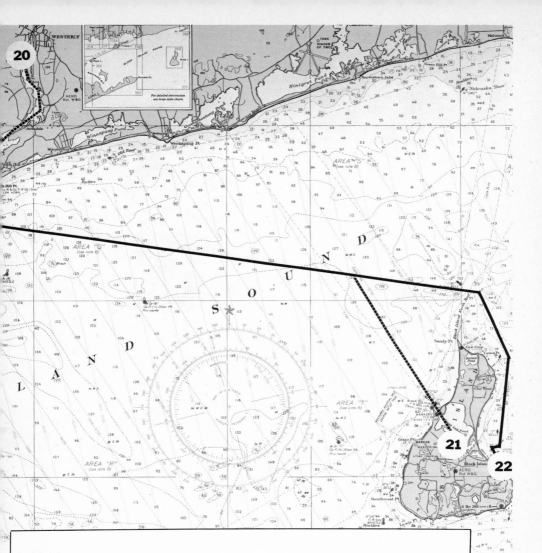

MAP 7:

GARDINERS BAY AND FISHERS ISLAND SOUND TO BLOCK ISLAND

1 Three Mile Harbor
2 Acabonac Creek
3 Napeague Harbor
4 Lake Montauk
5 Cherry Harbor
6 Gardiners Point
7 Millstone Harbor
8 Niantic River
9 New London
10 Pine Island
11 Silver Eel Pond,
   Fishers Island

12 Bushy Point Beach
13 Mumford Cove
14 Venetian Harbor
15 West Harbor
16 Mystic Seaport
17 East Harbor
18 Stonington
19 Watch Hill Harbor
20 Pawcatuck River
21 New Harbor
22 Old Harbor, Block Island

GARDINERS BAY AND FISHERS ISLAND SOUND TO BLOCK ISLAND

This is the transition from the Outer Sound to the first of the sounds beyond—Block Island Sound, and it brings us to Rhode Island. Fishers Island is relaxed and New England; Mystic Seaport is fantastic and Block Island an experience. Any journey to Block Island is a trip on the open sea where precise navigation becomes important.

1—*Three Mile Harbor, Gardiners Bay:* the port of East Hampton, a lovely anchorage behind sand bars, after the narrow channel passes Dick Sage's Maidstone Boat Yard.

2—*Acabonac Creek, Gardiners Bay:* the choice of the creeks in the area, quiet, with an anchorage just inside the mouth for up to five feet.

3—*Napeague Harbor, Napeague Bay, Block Island Sound:* an anchorage inside the mouth of the harbor for five-foot-deep yachts; a big lake with a channel going a mile down to the back of the famous Amagansett Beach on the Atlantic.

4—*Lake Montauk, Montauk Point, Block Island Sound:* sticking out into Block Island Sound and the Atlantic, Montauk Point is the easternmost point of New York State. Montauk Lake, just inside it, has a channel and slips for visitors among the big charter fishing fleet on Star Island. These are turbulent waters with very strong tides. There is also a channel four feet deep to the bottom of the lake where there's an anchorage.

5—*Cherry Harbor, Gardiners Island, Gardiners Bay:* above the windmill is the Gardiner mansion; the Gardiners have held this island since the 1600's; no landing without permission.

6—*Gardiner Point, Gardiners Bay:* you may think you can sneak between this little bit of land, a mile north of Gardiners Island, and the island itself, but the tide runs very fast over the slots in the sand bank and may wash you aground.

7—*Millstone Harbor, Niantic Bay:* a sheltered day-anchorage; open to the south; good overnight only in northerly winds.

8—*Niantic River, Niantic Bay:* a hard-to-make fast-tide entrance with two bridges to get opened but once inside, you have a couple of miles of protected water, lots of nice shores to anchor off.

9—*New London, Thames River:* a prime rendezvous place. Ferries come to town from Orient Point on Long Island and Fishers Island; the New York and New Haven trains and Greyhound buses come to dockside at the Fishers Island ferry landing.

10—*Pine Island, Thames River:* a handy spot by the mouth of the Thames to wait for someone coming into New London by train or bus.

11—*Silver Eel Pond, Fishers Island, Fishers Island Sound:* the New London ferry comes in here. Don't tie up inside except to pick up crew members coming from New London. In an emergency, tie off private pier furthest east.

12—*Bushy Point Beach, Fishers Island Sound:* a great daytime anchorage for a swim. Unspoiled beach, deserted except on weekends.

13—*Mumford Cove, Fishers Island Sound:* a dredged channel and a couple of dredged anchorages, the upper one very often containing only a couple of boats.

XL

14—*Venetian Harbor, Fishers Island Sound:* a small yacht harbor chock full of private floats; could be used as a harbor of refuge.

15—*West Harbor, Fisher Island, Fishers Island Sound:* the main town on the island is around the harbor; the yacht club slips make this the place to land to see Fishers.

16—*Mystic Seaport, Mystic River, Fishers Island Sound:* the most visited port on the Connecticut coast. A restoration of a seaport of the 1600's, with full-scale whaling ships, a square rigger, old hulls of all sorts. A must stop on any cruise. Berths available by reservation, some shoal draft anchorage room at the end of the dredged channel.

17—*East Harbor, Fishers Island, Fishers Island Sound:* a small anchorage open to the north, no docks, just big homes ashore.

18—*Stonington, Little Narragansett Bay:* a pretty colonial town with a yachty waterfront protected by breakwaters; also the entrance to Little Narragansett Bay. The only channel runs north of Sandy Point. You can't go between Sandy Point and Napatree to the south. You have to go via Stonington.

19—*Watch Hill Harbor, Little Narragansett Bay:* Watch Hill Yacht Club here, and some fine homes. Open to the north.

20—*Pawcatuck River, Little Narragansett Bay:* leads up to the town of Westerly via a buoyed channel; there is a Westerly Yacht Club with some moorings for guests, very protected.

21—*New Harbor, Great Salt Pond, Block Island Sound:* once you leave Fishers Island Sound headed east, you have to either go fifteen miles to Block Island Sound, or twelve to Lake Montauk or sixteen to Point Judith (see map 8). New Harbor is at the inner end of Great Salt Pond, and has several restaurants ashore. It is further from the center of things than Old Harbor (below) but has lots more room. Anchor out in the pond, but not in the ferry channel.

22—*Old Harbor, Rhode Island Sound:* a couple of breakwaters sticking out from shore make a snug crowded harbor: usually room for a few visitors, either at anchor or dockside. Lots of restaurants with bars, a night spot or two, a clutch of Victorian hotels. Rent bikes and explore Block Island. It's a fine sea island.

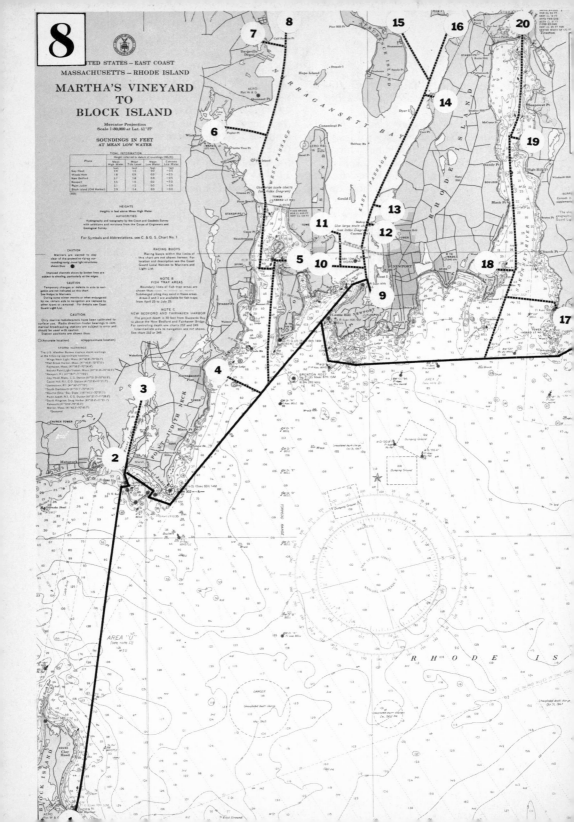

MAP 8:

BLOCK ISLAND AND NARRAGANSETT BAY TO BUZZARDS BAY

1 Old Harbor, Block Island
2 Galilee, Pt. Judith Pond
3 Wakefield, Pt. Judith Pond
4 Narragansett Pier
5 Dutch Island Harbor, West Passage
6 Wickford
7 Allen Harbor
8 Upper West Passage
9 Newport, East Passage
10 Jamestown, East Passage
11 Potter Cove
12 Coasters Harbor
13 Coddington Harbor
14 Melville
15 Upper East Passage
16 Passage to Mt. Hope Bay
17 Sakonnet Point, Sakonnet Passage
18 Sachuest
19 Fogland Point
20 Tiverton
21 Acoaxet
22 West Branch,
   Westport River
23 Westport Harbor
24 East Branch,
   Westport River

BLOCK ISLAND AND NARRAGANSETT BAY TO BUZZARDS BAY

This is the transition from Block Island Sound to Rhode Island Sound. The great north-reaching bay of Narragansett cuts the state of Rhode Island right in two. It's the only part of the cruising grounds with no land to the south. You have to "go down east" or "west'ard." (First land due south is Haiti.)

1—*Old Harbor, Block Island, Rhode Island Sound:* opens toward Rhode Island waters. It is perfectly possible to jump straight east to the Elizabeth Islands (See map 9), but you'll miss some pleasant cruising and a safer route along the Rhode Island shore.

2—*Galilee, Point Judith Pond, Rhode Island Sound:* north-northeast from Old Harbor, thirteen miles up, through a couple of outside breakwaters, is Point Judith Harbor of refuge—but don't anchor here because it's rolling water; go inside to Galilee, a fishing town which has good dockside space.

3—*Wakefield, Point Judith Pond, Rhode Island Sound:* a quiet anchorage up Point Judith Pond if you don't want dockside at Galilee.

4—*Narragansett Pier, Rhode Island Sound:* a possible do-or-die refuge against westerly storms—an old casino, a couple of docks —this was once the "middle-class Newport."

5—*Dutch Island Harbor, West Passage, Narragansett Bay:* first refuge if you have to run up West Passage into the bay in front of a southerly.

6—*Wickford, West Passage, Narragansett Bay:* the supply and repair shop of the bay. Anchor off from the crowd in one of the creeks to the north.

7—*Allen Harbor, West Passage, Narragansett Bay:* used by the Navy but open to pleasure yachts. Dredged to ten feet.

8—*Upper West Passage, Narragansett Bay:* there are a couple more good harbors north of here, and then Providence River leading to Providence, capital of Rhode Island.

9—*Newport, East Passage, Narragansett Bay:* if you want to anchor off and walk into the great mansions on Newport Neck, hook a right and anchor in Brenton Cove off the Ida Lewis Yacht Club on Ida Lewis Rock. For supplies, proceed straight ahead to the docks of the town. The homes on Newport Neck are the most impressive sight in these waters. The town has the beginnings of resort life: antique stores, etc. and the shipyards are great spectator stuff.

10—*Jamestown, East Passage, Narragansett Bay:* a Navy port, but with an active yacht club and available repair and moorings.

11—*Potter Cove, East Passage, Narragansett Bay:* Navy place, not for you.

12—*Coasters Harbor, East Passage, Narragansett Bay:* Navy only.

13—*Coddington Harbor, East Passage, Narragansett Bay:* Navy only.

14—*Melville, East Passage, Narragansett Bay:* Navy only.

15—*Upper East Passage, Narragansett Bay:* goes to beautiful Potter Cove on Prudence Island, a rather busy (on weekends) harbor. North of Prudence Island the passage joins West Passage and Providence River.

16—*Passage to Mt. Hope Bay:* west of Hog

Island, you go through north of Aquidneck into Mt. Hope Bay, joining the Sakonnet River at the same time.

17—*Sakonnet Point, Sakonnet River Passage:* port of refuge along in the route east to the islands and the Cape. Some slips, a restaurant here.

18—*Sachuest, Sakonnet River:* mansions ashore—otherwise a nice secluded anchorage open only to the northeast.

19—*Fogland Point, Sakonnet River:* another secluded harbor, a good stop on the way up the river, open to the northwest.

20—*Tiverton, Sakonnet River:* a lively harbor, yacht club, marina and restaurant. Next north is Mt. Hope Bay, then Fall River, Mass., clear through Rhode Island.

21—*Acoaxet, Westport River:* at the edge of Buzzards Bay, a fairly protected anchorage for yachts enroute to the islands. Don't come in if the surf is heavy, though. Once inside, try Horseneck Beach for swimming on the Sound.

22—*West Branch, Westport River:* shallow, but great for dinghy exploring.

23—*Westport Harbor, Westport River:* moorings, Westport Yacht Club here.

24—*East Branch, Westport River:* can be navigated with four-foot-deep vessel with care. But more fun to take in a dinghy—get the tide with you both going and coming back.

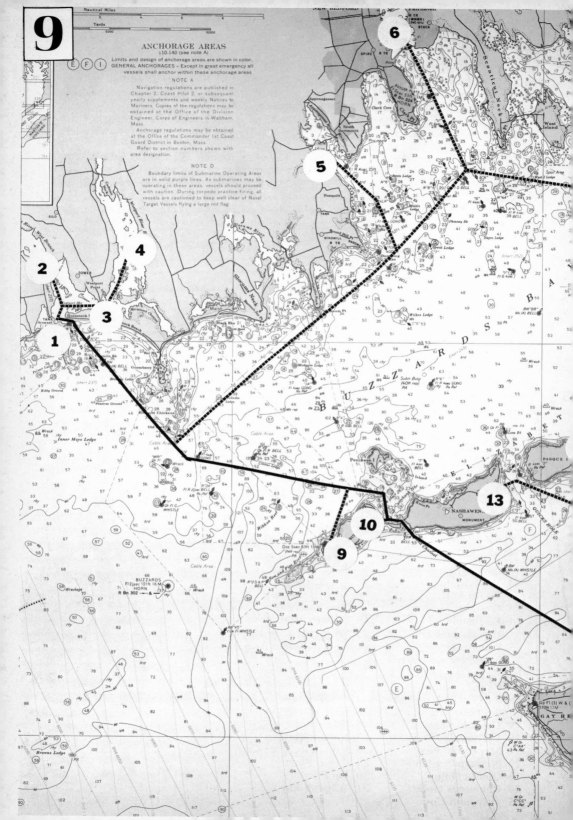

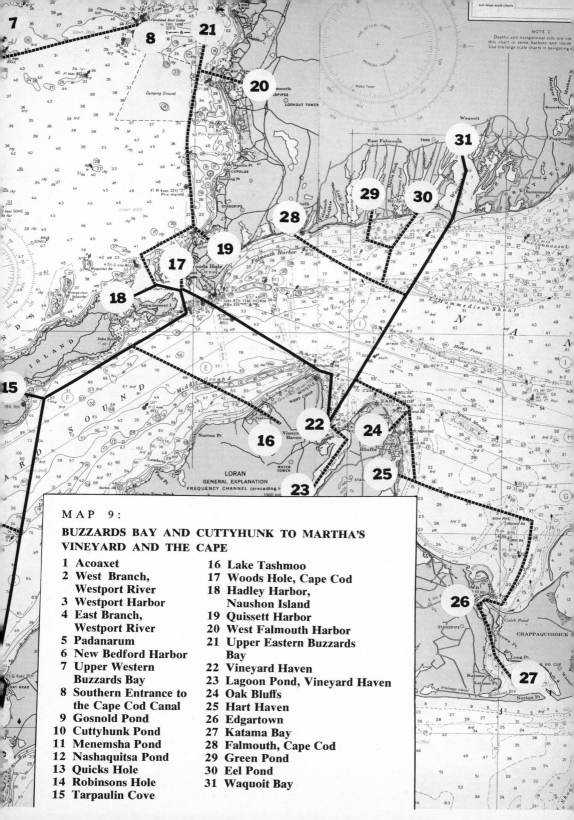

MAP 9:

BUZZARDS BAY AND CUTTYHUNK TO MARTHA'S VINEYARD AND THE CAPE

1 Acoaxet
2 West Branch, Westport River
3 Westport Harbor
4 East Branch, Westport River
5 Padanarum
6 New Bedford Harbor
7 Upper Western Buzzards Bay
8 Southern Entrance to the Cape Cod Canal
9 Gosnold Pond
10 Cuttyhunk Pond
11 Menemsha Pond
12 Nashaquitsa Pond
13 Quicks Hole
14 Robinsons Hole
15 Tarpaulin Cove
16 Lake Tashmoo
17 Woods Hole, Cape Cod
18 Hadley Harbor, Naushon Island
19 Quissett Harbor
20 West Falmouth Harbor
21 Upper Eastern Buzzards Bay
22 Vineyard Haven
23 Lagoon Pond, Vineyard Haven
24 Oak Bluffs
25 Hart Haven
26 Edgartown
27 Katama Bay
28 Falmouth, Cape Cod
29 Green Pond
30 Eel Pond
31 Waquoit Bay

BUZZARDS BAY AND CUTTYHUNK TO MARTHA'S VINEYARD AND THE CAPE

This area takes us from Rhode Island Sound across Buzzards Bay, through the Elizabeth Islands and down to Vineyard Sound. The Vineyard is one of the world's most beautiful islands. Along either side of Vineyard Sound there are plenty of good harbors. The tides are almost opposite from those in the rest of the cruising grounds. Generally the tide in Vineyard Sound goes east toward the open Atlantic on the flood, while off the Elizabeths it goes north; read your Eldridge tide tables carefully.

1—*Acoaxet, Westport River:* a relatively snug anchorage just inside the mouth of the river (do not enter if there's a surf).

2—*West Branch, Westport River:* great dinghying but shoal sailing.

3—*Westport Harbor, Westport River:* the town and the yacht club are here.

4—*East Branch, Westport River:* there's a channel here that is a fathometer test to follow. Better dinghy it.

5—*Padanarum, South Dartmouth, Buzzards Bay:* heading up into the bay this is the first port. A jumping-off place for the islands; snug anchorage behind a breakwater; home of the New Bedford Yacht Club.

6—*New Bedford Harbor, Buzzards Bay:* an historic town, with a busy commercial fishing harbor, the busiest on the whole cruising grounds, lots of fishing boats. Melville Reading Room in the library ashore has extraordinary whaling lore. Fairhaven across the harbor is where Joshua Slocum started his epochal 'round the world trip, single-handed, in the last century.

7—*Upper Western Buzzards Bay:* the bay gets shallow up here and very choppy. Winds are steady and heavy. No place to get caught out in a heavy southwester if you can avoid it. Ports along the shore, in order, are Mattpoisett, Marion, Wareham, Onset, then Buzzards Bay. Out in the middle, the Cape Cod Canal begins—see below.

8—*Southern Entrance to the Cape Cod Canal:* it is six miles through Cape Cod Canal to Cape Cod Bay north of the cape. Best approach to the canal is along east shore. The water on the west and in the middle is usually rough and choppy.

9—*Gosnold Pond, Cuttyhunk, Elizabeth Islands:* entrance not navigable, but a small interesting pond with warm swimming and mussels in the tide creek. On an island in the pond is a statue to Bartholomew Gosnold, on the site of the first white man's habitation on the northeast coast.

10—*Cuttyhunk Pond, Cuttyhunk Island, Elizabeth Islands:* a sheltered, usually crowded harbor where cruising yachts and tuna fishermen meet. The town is small, delightful. The whole island is unspoiled. Watch tricky approach along Jogleg Channel to pond.

11—*Menemsha Pond, Martha's Vineyard:* the harbor at Menemsha's entrance is very small and has nearly no room for visitors. But at low tide, you can carry 3½ feet up the creek from the harbor to Menemsha pond if you do it carefully. Best come in and out during high slack tide. The pond is terrific, set in typical moorland.

12—*Naquashita Pond, Martha's Vineyard:* "Quitsa Pond" can be reached by shoal draft yachts. The channel in the creek between Menemsha is unmarked, but three feet even can be carried through. Best of all, make it a dinghy trip. Stonewall Pond lies beyond, nearly on South Beach, the famous Vineyard sand coast.

13—*Quicks Hole, Elizabeth Islands:* coming into Vineyard Sound from Buzzards, this is the easiest of the passages, although Canapitsit, on the itinerary, just west of Nashawena, is certainly possible (with care and favorable conditions plus high tide). Nashawena Beach in Quicks Hole is a fine beach, but landings are technically not allowed above high tide, although people do land. There's an ample anchorage off Neshawena at the southern end.

14—*Robinsons Hole, Elizabeth Islands:* third of the four holes through these islands, good but tight shelter from southwesters. Anchor fore and aft between Nuns 3 and 4.

15—*Tarpaulin Cove, Naushon Island, Elizabeth Islands:* the most famous beach in the islands; landings and small fires allowed. Not so good for overnight anchoring—open to the south and east and ferry wakes.

16—*Lake Tashmoo, Martha's Vineyard:* you can get three feet in through the entrance at low tide, four at mid-tide; the lake is secluded; a good place to get away from everyone but just a few shoreside residents. James Cagney summers inside.

17—*Woods Hole, Cape Cod:* the ferries to Martha's Vineyard and Nantucket come in here; there is the oceanographic institute and a good aquarium. Snuggest anchorage is under draw into Eel Pond. Other places tend to roll with the wind, tide, and ferry wakes.

18—*Hadley Harbor, Naushon Island, Elizabeth Islands:* across Woods Hole is the entrance to this harbor, the prettiest and best known of the Elizabeth harbors. Expect lots of company, even though it is a somewhat intricate entrance. Read directions for entering carefully and don't fight the tides unless you are sure you want to; they run up to five or six knots and bury some of the buoys. Use power except at slack tide.

19—*Quissett Harbor, Buzzards Bay:* narrow winding entrance, but a prime place to anchor for the beauty of it all.

20—*West Falmouth Harbor, Buzzards Bay:* room for six feet just inside, three feet further in. A fine shoal draft anchorage.

21—*Upper Eastern Buzzards Bay:* the right way to approach the entrance to the Cape Cod Canal; next anchorages north are Fiddler Cove and Pocasset Harbor.

22—*Vineyard Haven, Martha's Vineyard:* well filled with yachts usually, but with a few moorings available. The place to meet incoming ferry boats from Woods Hole.

23—*Lagoon Pond, Vineyard Haven, Martha's Vineyard:* an inner harbor, reached via a drawbridge. Carry six feet inside—very calm with rather elegant shores. Secluded except for motorboats running under the bridge.

24—*Oak Bluffs, Martha's Vineyard:* the country's first vacation town, worth a walk through to see the old-fashioned cottages. Harbor usually too full to hold visitors, but has a fine grocery-liquor store with its own dock.

25—*Hart Haven, Martha's Vineyard:* you can carry four feet in here in relative quiet and find a place to anchor.

26—*Edgartown, Martha's Vineyard:* the anchorage is just behind the Chappaquiddick Beach opposite the town. Edgartown is the liveliest port on the Vineyard, with the streets of the town jammed on weekends. Good restaurants, supplies, old captains' homes, inns, singles' night life.

27—*Katama Bay, Martha's Vineyard:* get away from the crowd at Edgartown, go down here and make sure your anchor is in solid because tides run rather strongly.

28—*Falmouth, Cape Cod:* a swinging singles town. Lots of bars and restaurants and the famous playhouse. Meet a nice Boston girl here. No anchoring; dock space is very much in demand; try reserving your space at a marina by phone ahead of time.

29—*Green Pond, Cape Cod:* a harbor of refuge, lots of boats inside, but you can find a spot if you have to.

30—*Eel Pond, Cape Cod:* another place for quick shelter; it will take you into Waquoit Bay by a back route.

31—*Waquoit Bay, Cape Cod:* the roomiest of the south shore Cape Cod anchorages. Head of the harbor is the best place to anchor to allow Edgartown and Falmouth to wear off.

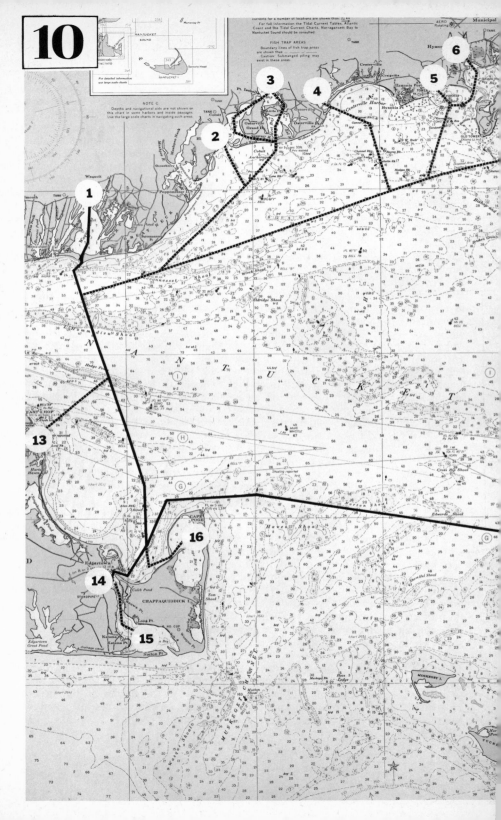

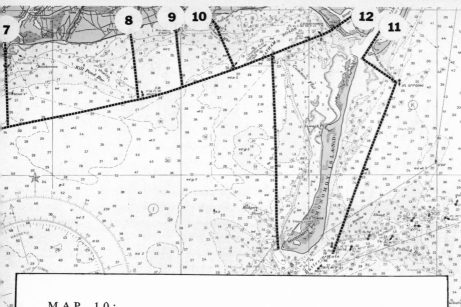

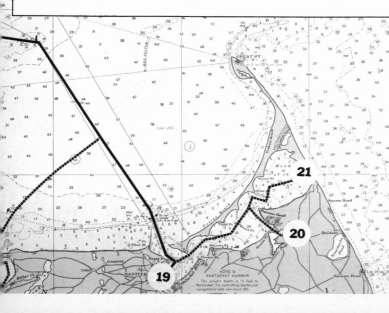

MAP 10:

CAPE COD AND MARTHA'S VINEYARD TO NANTUCKET

1	Waquoit, Cape Cod	12	Stage Harbor
2	Cotuit Bay	13	Oak Bluffs
3	North Bay	14	Edgartown
4	East Bay	15	Katama Bay
5	Hyannis Port	16	Cape Poge Bay
6	Hyannis Harbor	17	Tuckernuck Island
7	Bass River	18	Madaket Harbor
8	Herring River	19	Nantucket Town, Nantucket
9	Allen Harbor	20	Polpis Harbor
10	Wychmere Harbor	22	Wauwinet
11	Chatham Harbor		

CAPE COD AND MARTHA'S VINEYARD TO NANTUCKET

This is the final leg of most cruises: beyond Nantucket there is only the Atlantic. The tides run east on the flood in Nantucket Sound. Along the Cape shores the sands are shifty—best make sure by phone you can clear the entrance you pick. Beyond Monomoy on the Cape are some of the most vicious tides and shoals in the world—they deflected the New York-bound Mayflower toward Boston. Nantucket is historically a unique island, the colonial equivalent of Texas—whale oil instead of petroleum.

1—*Waquoit, Cape Cod:* biggest, most protected pond on the inner shore of the Cape, a few homes ashore.

2—*Cotuit Bay, Cape Cod:* part of the three-bay system surrounding Osterville Grand Island.

3—*North Bay, Cape Cod:* a nice inside bay, north of Osterville Grand Island, can be reached from Cotuit or West Bay below it. Above it, a narrow channel leads even further inland to Prince Cove.

4—*East Bay, Cape Cod:* you can carry four feet in here to a pond used only by a few small hulls.

5—*Hyannis Port, Cape Cod:* secure anchorage in a southwester behind the breakwater, exposed to the southeast. Ashore is the Kennedy compound.

6—*Hyannis Harbor, Lewis Bay, Cape Cod:* if you go all the way up Lewis Bay in to the marinas at the end, you can walk up into the considerable town of Hyannis; passenger ferries for the Vineyard and Nantucket; the famous music tent. Less citified anchorages in the southwest corner of the bay are behind Pine Island and way inside the southern cove, Uncle Roberts Cove, but you have to sound the narrow channel yourself.

7—*Bass River, Cape Cod:* can take six feet up to the bridge; after that it is downhill; you can high-tide-it into Grand Cove below the second bridge at South Dennis—the bridge is a fifteen-foot clearance. Above that you can dinghy up to Follins Pond, where there are ancient mooring holes attributed to the Vikings.

8—*Herring River, Cape Cod:* carry four feet upriver and anchor in among a fleet of locals—hardly any cruising yachtsmen.

9—*Allen Harbor, Cape Cod:* there's a slough off the main part of the round crowded harbor where you may be able to be off by yourself; plenty of water going in.

10—*Wychmere Harbor, Cape Cod:* a little round jewel of a harbor but nearly all moorings likely to be taken; yacht club or boat yard may have one to rent.

11—*Chatham Harbor, Cape Cod:* this is a long long harbor behind Nauset Beach—goes for miles and miles, not always well marked. To get there by water, you have to go around Monomoy Island, which is for expert sailors only. When you get there, it is best to follow a local boat up to Tern Island for your first landing at Nickerson's East Dock.

12—*Stage Harbor, Cape Cod:* a newly dredged entrance through Harding Beach takes you into an outer harbor back of the beach or an inner one behind Morris Island. Great place to go ashore; rent a bike and tour the beach country.

13—*Oak Bluffs, Martha's Vineyard:* a crowded harbor, but with good store—groceries and liquor—at the water's edge with its own dock. An historic cottage community lies ashore.

14—*Edgartown, Martha's Vineyard:* anchor behind Chappaquiddick Beach, hail the yacht club tender or dinghy ashore to the Chappaquiddick Beach and take the Chappaquiddick ferry a hundred yards to Edgartown. Divide your time between visiting old whaling captains' mansions and sampling the life on the main street—bars, restaurants, antiques, paintings.

15—*Katama Bay, Martha's Vineyard:* to get away from the heavily populated harbor at Edgartown, swing down to the Katama Bay anchorage and have it by yourself, or nearly so.

16—*Cape Poge Bay, Martha's Vineyard:* a nice dinghy trip or for a shoal draft power-boat. A lovely pond.

17—*Tuckernuck Island:* a tortuous channel leads you past Madaket Harbor to this shore of Tuckernuck. Some shelter here from southerlies due to Smith Point, but not an overnight anchorage. An unusually isolated island, worth hiking.

18—*Madaket Harbor, Nantucket Island:* a charming shoal-draft harbor—all local fishermen and summer yachts. You can go up Hither Creek and find room at the boat yard there.

19—*Nantucket Town, Nantucket Island:* a new system of pilings protects the renovated Nantucket Island Marina. There is usually guest space. Walk to Nantucket town and get a view of the costly main street restoration; the rest of the town has naturally aged, mellow, two-hundred-year-old houses. Take a cab out to Siasconset, the charming summer village with houses tracing back to the 1600's.

20—*Polpis Harbor, Nantucket Island:* carry three feet at low tide into the East Branch as an alternative to tying up at the marina.

21—*Wauwinet, Nantucket Island:* carry four feet to the head of the harbor, beach your dinghy and explore the splendid beach here on the Atlantic side. Good shelter behind the beach, except in strong north-easters.

CHAPTER ONE

~~~~~~

START OF THE CRUISE—NEW YORK CITY

~~~~~~

Across the horizon lies an immense, blinding canyon wall of pure ice, stretching east and west to vanishing points. The wall gronds monstrously forward, spilling icebergs down its face like drops down a windshield. At the base, icewater rivers cascade over a mountain range of broken trees, boulders and earth. The great blade advances, shoving the earth-mountains ahead in shattering landslides. The behemoth front of ice-rock-earth drives across New England. It reaches the sea.

A thousand rivers now foam down the face, spreading earth into the sea. The rising and foaming waters of the sea part as a crescent of flat islands and promontories forms—and slowly this land gains grass,

1

bushes and trees.

The prehistoric turmoil subsides. Harbors and lakes fringe the land; under the force of a storm, some harbors close to become lakes; lakes break open to join the sea.

A species of man appears. He camps by the shore, makes his openings in the ponds, fishes, hunts and grows easy crops on a fertile soil. The ice wall retreats out of sight and mind; the prehistoric Indian settles down to his coast and tells tales of the old days when a giant forbear Indian named Maushop created these lands, pouring sand out of his moccasins into the sea.

These islands and shores become what we now know as Long Island, Shelter Island, Gardiners Island, Fishers Island, Cape Cod, Martha's Vineyard and Nantucket. They were, and are, unique—soft, fertile, easily changed by currents and storms, maintaining a constant give and take with the sea.

The Indians on these lands whaled, netted, farmed, clammed and grew corn. When white men arrived, they did the same. The shore was hospitable, nurturing. Man did not work for other men; he worked nature for himself.

This self-reliance—this nurturing coast—gave birth to a nation of enterprising men. History was not prepared for the United States; nothing like the eastern seaboard of the original thirteen American colonies had yet happened or is likely to happen again. There was never a welcome such as that given by the eastern fringe of this continent.

The welcome is now a bit worn out by man's excessive use; nevertheless, it is still there. A man may still sustain himself on this coast, even if he were denied its civilized supply centers. The fish are here and the oysters and clams; there are sweet fruits still growing wild. There is sweet water still in the glacier-formed ponds. The climate in the summer months is such that man could go without clothing, if need be—a nurturing coast.

It is, as well, a coast of great respite.

There are hundreds of small islands, as well as miles of beachfront, which man has not yet closed off in little patches.

There are innumerable small villages along this coast where the past is still in the present and where trees mean something, and grass is not cut into square lots and where the creek that runs is protected and the bay in which only one or two anchor at a time is not seen as a waste.

There are creeks and ponds, interlaced fresh and salt existences that can be walked, dug into, explored. There are the birds—osprey, gull, tern, swan and wild duck—and estuarine marshes where the land and the water intermingle inextricably to feed an ocean.

And there are some notable works of man on this coast, as well.

The homes at Newport are a rich legacy of architecture; there is a stateliness at Oyster Bay in Teddy Roosevelt's Sagamore Hill, at Huntington in Vanderbilt's Eagles Nest and in the vastness of Forbes' island estates. There are neatly preserved colonial societies hiding along the shores—Fishers Island, Southport, Essex, Cold Spring Harbor, Orient. And there are fishing villages true to their origins still—Cuttyhunk, Menemsha, Montauk. The smell of the sea is in them.

On these shores the yachtsman can have meals at excellent restaurants without taxis, traffic or smog. He can have a civilized drink at a relaxed yacht club without dues or meetings.

An auto trip around this coast is an exercise in frustration. By water it is a wholly different experience: one can stay on one's own course, pick one's own time and destination. There is only the sky to consult. It is an exercise in individualism.

There is companionship.

There are tens of thousands of accomplished cruising men in these waters, normally communicative with their fellows. The sea lore accumulated in the heads of these yachtsmen matches that accumulated by those on any other stretch of coast. And the coast's yachts are, as a result, among the world's most exquisite and best equipped.

No one can cruise these waters without becoming a better sailor; the challenge is as extreme as anywhere except in mid-ocean. There are as many quick storms in the Sound as in the tropics, as many fogs as are necessary to sharpen navigation, enough unmarked harbors to challenge one's skill at water-reading and dead-reckoning, enough creeks up which to row a dinghy to keep one healthily exercised and enough water worth swimming to cleanse your soul of the city.

The cruffise log which follows is intended to illustrate all this and more.

Our first leg of the cruise is to be Inner Long Island Sound, where the three great Long Island harbors are: Oyster Bay, Huntington, and Northport bays.

THE START

The Marine and Aviation Department's pier at Twenty-third Street in Manhattan, technically known as Skyport Pier, was where I brought my thirty-foot trimaran sloop *Nimble* for provisioning. Oyster Bay was thirty miles off, so *Nimble* was loaded and debarked early.

The onloaders were, first of all, two New Yorkers—myself and Bea Williams, tall, blonde and fiery, our galley captain. Then there was George Wilkinson of Aspen, Colorado, who had signed on as one of the cruise photographers. Rickie Williams of Aspen, skier extraordinaire, made four.

Just a few blocks from where we were starting our cruise, one Adraien Block, Dutchman, having had his first ship *Tiger* burn on shore, built a new one. He cut his wood in what is now Greeenwich Village. Calling his new ship *Onrust*, he set sail up the East River into Long Island Sound in 1613, the first white man to sail the course we would now take.

9:00 A.M.: The skies were blue-gray over the East River. We cast off. A red-superstructured tug came streaming up with a sponge-like bumper over her bows and bulging wake. Before us was the two hundred-mile-long cruising ground to Nantucket.

We had the tide with us. It isn't a good idea to buck the Hellgate tide because it runs well over six knots, literally burying East River buoys. We were timing our run to pass Hellgate on the last of the northward flood tide and to catch the beginning of the eastward ebb in the Sound to help run us out to Oyster Bay.

We throbbed under Hellgate (point 2, map 2) nearly at slack tide. The currents oiled this way and that, not powerfully, but playfully. Then we proceeded under Whitestone Bridge, leaving Flushing Bay with its World's Fair Marina, 90 percent powerboats, to starboard.

A comfortable day's sail and a comfortable day's powering are not necessarily all that different: the usual distances on the cruise plan we had worked out were ten to twenty miles.

I have found that, after a couple of hours powering through twenty miles of chop in a powerboat, you have felt vibrations long enough to welcome a respite.

Likewise, after four or five hours under sail (you've traveled as far as the powerboat in two), you begin to lose the sharpness indispensable to good sailing; it becomes tedious.

Applied with some sense, our twenty-three-day itinerary would work for power and sail, both. It's possible to make marathon runs under either power or sail but we were traveling for fun.

9:40 A.M.: We hit Throgs Neck Bridge. It springs out of the Bronx like an elegant Gila monster, curving up from a long tail to legs that stilt their way across the river, subsiding into Queens. We passed under.

We were in the Sound.

We hoisted sail a few hundred yards beyond Throgs Neck; we had timed it right and had caught the ebb. The wind was from the west. We slid the big Genoa jib up and cranked up the main; the creak of line was sublimely heard. The silencing of the engine was like a cocktail after work, an easing into a better life.

10:00 A.M.: To the left was the upper Bronx, to the right Long Island and ahead, Stepping Stones with the Victorian lighthouse on it.

The Coast Guard reports that nearly a hundred boats actually *hit* Stepping Stones every year (sort of like hitting the side of your house with the car).

The sad truth is that only a few people in boats know what those symbols on Geodetic Charts are all about. The Coast Guard estimates that about 10 per cent of the people who sail know how to use the charts; half the rest don't even carry them.

10:20 A.M.: We had but to look north to see Orchard Beach, Hart Island and City Island (point 6, map 2). At City Island, I had often boarded *Foto* to cruise with the late Morris Rosenfeld—Rosie—of the technically flawless photography, the Bachrach of boating.

Rodman's Neck leads from City Island to the rest of the Bronx. The British under General William Howe once attempted to cut off George Washington's retreat from Manhattan at Rodmans Neck. Washington had fled from Brooklyn and was in retreat once more. (Things were not going well for our Revolution.) Marblehead sailors and fishermen, under Colonel Glover—750 Marbleheaders against four thousand British—kept Howe from cutting off Washington's retreat. They laid down a withering fire that got Washington free.

North of Rodmans Neck is Hunter Island; behind that is Travers Island, the New York Athletic Club yacht station. North of Travers, connected to New Rochelle by bridge, is Glen Island, home of Glen Gray in the Era of Big Bands (Glen Miller and Benny Goodman played there).

10:30 A.M.: South of us was Great Neck, the East's first "exurb." The word was coined by A. C. Spectorsky in *The Exurbanites*—he now directs the fortunes of *Playboy* magazine. Concerning Great Neck, he wrote, "Its nights were riotous and its days were hung over."

Scott Fitzgerald rented on Great Neck while beginning *The Great Gatsby*. Great Neck in those days was a garden paradise. Whiskey, for those inclined, made it definitely paradise. As marijuana is bootlegged today, so whiskey was then. Deliciously illegal. Fitzgerald and his wife, Zelda, staged parties that would have called for the Tactical Police Force today in New York City.

In *The Great Gatsby,* Fitzgerald, however, captured Long Island accurately, poetically:

" . . . gradually I became aware of the old island here that flowered once for Dutch sailors' eyes . . . for a transitory enchanted moment man must have held his breath in the presence of this continent, compelled into an aesthetic contemplation he neither understood nor desired, face to face for the last time in history with something commensurate to his capacity for wonder."

On *Nimble,* the waters before us were like an azure sheet bounded by green shores. Fresh-looking yacht harbors alternated with smoking spurts from industrial towns. Sea haze lay like photographic grain across a horizon specked with the white flicker of sails. Bright triangles paraded like myriad, swarming, minute butterflies; exotic, full-rounded spinnakers ran like strange moths in unpredictable directional migrations.

To the south, Manhasset Bay (point 8, map 2) was alive with the movement of the most numerous fleet within the confines of a local body of water on this coast. Sailing into Manhasset Bay today would have been like flying down the throat of a snowstorm and trying to avoid the flakes.

Inside Manhasset were the masts of yachts at Club Capri, one of the Sound's most ornate marinas. The club is the whole bit: pool, kiddie pool, electric go-cart to take you down to the sea, dance band at the pool on Saturday night. It usually has guest space if you need to run in for shelter, making Manhasset the best of the Inner Sound Long Island ports in an emergency.

11:00 A.M.: Execution Rock to the south (captured pirates were once tied to the rock to await the engulfing tide). North was Larchmont Harbor and Mamaroneck-Milton Harbor, the home of the Larchmont, Orienta and American Yacht Clubs, respectively; hot-beds of yachtsmanship, one-design racing and social sailing. The best and easiest of all the harbors to the north for a quick run to safety is Mamaroneck, to Nichols Boat Yard in the west basin.

1:00 P.M.: *Nimble* was now about a third of the way down the "Inner Sound," the narrow busy part. Beyond this, the Sound widens; you can't as easily hop from shore to shore. In compensation, it gets progressively cleaner.

Fifteen years ago, no one had any worries about swimming in the Inner Sound. Today, in this part of the Inner Sound, swimming is inadvisable except at high tide or with knowledge of local conditions. Shellfish in the Inner Sound are either polluted or in danger of pollution.

Not only the towns' industrial wastes but the farmers' pesticides are polluting the Sound. DDT has been detected in enough concentration in birds and fish to make them unable to reproduce. Birds' eggs lose their thickness and don't hatch. DDT accumulates in fish eggs and kills the fry after they have hatched. Man, the final link in the food chain, gets the cumulative concentration of the other links' ingestion of DDT. Right now, there is more DDT in mothers' milk along the Eastern Seaboard than the Public Health people are willing to allow in cow's milk sold to the public. No one knows what effect DDT has on people in the long run. We do know it affects birds and fish.

The federal authorities (Federal Water Pollution Control Administration) keep a watch on the Sound's pollution indexes, they now report that the cumulative concentration is double what it was ten years ago. Nuclear plants (five) scheduled for the Sound will warm the waters and increase the growth of polluting algae. The Sound is headed for the fate of Lake Erie, where you can neither swim nor drink the water. It stinks.

A number of colleges have banded together to form a million-dollar study station for pollution prevention at Fort Pond, Montauk. It is already very late for studies. Marine biologists feel that fish may simply die out in a generation, if not by DDT then by rot. Fish near New York City are coming down with "fin rot" caused by excessive concentration of pollution products.

In addition to complete pollution, Long Island Sound is under threat of bridges. Two bridges all the way across the Sound from Connecticut are being planned tentatively—the "tentative" way that nearly always seems to lead to execution. No one really *has* to have these bridges.

Manhattan voters managed to kill the Lower Manhattan Expressway; they finally got the authorities to concede they could perhaps turn their attention to the problem of public transportation, which has languished without funds for so long, instead of burying us all in cement once again. Crowded in places as it may be, the Sound is still the best recreation that the whole New York-Connecticut urban complex has to offer. To throttle the recreation potential by bottling up the Sound with bridges would be a criminal act. It would also cause to disappear that sanity still left to outer Long Island in the way of undeveloped countryside.

And now, proceeding with the cruise again:

2:00 P.M.: We were pressing outward with Sea Cliff (point 11, map 2) in Hempstead Harbor to starboard.

Hempstead Harbor is the third of the large, long harbors to the south of us, just as Larchmont-Mamaroneck-Milton is the third harbor of small, ragged, rather short harbors to the north. Long Island is basically a huge dump-pile of topsoil pushed ahead of the great glacier, but the Connecticut shore was carved out of the bedrock by rivers. The Connecticut shore is thus full of reefs and islands—ragged, difficult, cranky, underwater terrain—while the Long Island shore has almost no reefs and not a single island until you get past Orient Point.

We were making a good seven knots on our Omni speed indicator, passing Hempstead Harbor. Sea Cliff, lying halfway down Hempstead Harbor, is the best known of the Hempstead Harbor yacht clubs. North of Sea Cliff is Morgan Park, an open space preserved from housing developments by the J. P. Morgan family.

J. P. Morgan, the elder, was the proud owner of the super-yacht *Cor-*

sair, which occasioned the single most famous remark in yachting: asked how much it cost to own such a yacht, J.P.'s deathless reply was, "If you have to ask, you can't possibly afford it."

Morgan also expressed the opinion that when you have more than four guests aboard, "there's no real cruising." He wasn't counting the *Corsair*'s crew of eighty-five, naturally.

2:20 P.M.: *Nimble* was now starting to get the kind of breeze that sets her apart from single-hull craft. It was blowing nine by the Danforth wind speed indicator and *Nimble* was doing nine, not unusual when the wind is on the beam. We went creaming past East Island on Matinecock Point, as I consulted my "Wilensky."

Julius Wilensky has written two books of harbor charts covering nearly every harbor from New York to Block Island and, omitting the Rhode Island shore, from Cuttyhunk to Nantucket. The titles are: *Long Island Sound: Where to Go, What to Do, and How to Do It*, and ditto for Cape Cod. They show boat yards, docks, marinas, rocks, restaurants, museums and more—they are an immense resource.

2:30 P.M.: The sun was high but going. We decided to stop a bit and take a swim at Peacock Point. There's a beach, clean water and lots of people swimming. We swung *Nimble* up until we were within striking distance of the beach and dropped anchor. Bea, Wilk and Rickie dived in and swam ashore to the beach while I took the dinghy up the fast-running tidal creek that comes to a stop at a dam. It felt good to row again.

4:30 P.M.: After two luxurious hours, we left. We let the wind gently blow our skin dry. The breeze was coming down and it was warm. The Long Island shore was delightful, beginning to get a bit wild here. Abeam was Oak Neck. Off to our left on the Connecticut shore at this point was Captain Harbor (point 13, map 2), containing a number of small bays and a number of islands. Great Captain, the largest and most popular, is 17 acres in extent.

North of Captain Islands lie the cities of Rye, Port Chester and Greenwich (point 14, map 2) and Stamford. Of thirteen miles of mainland shoreline here, only two thirds of a mile is public. On weekends such as this, therefore, Captain Harbor contains a good percentage of the yachts that come out of Rye, Port Chester, Greenwich and Stamford. They surround the islands like the Persian fleet protecting the shore of Asia Minor. It is possible on such a day to go ashore and, with a sort of minimal privacy, lie on the beach at Great Captain Island.

I once tried to sail the newly purchased *Nimble* off the anchor in the crowd around Great Captain Island and, getting into a tight spot, turned the wheel, which had been hooked up in reverse of the normal way. An entirely inoffensive sailboat at anchor was heavily nudged by our bows three times. (When you get a hit from a tri, it's liable to be a triple.) We staved off the worst of it; we had time to get forward because our speed was low. Shortly thereafter I took the wheel off and substituted a tiller, which gave quicker control and surer steering and served well on this cruise.

Author and first mate on the cruise. (BARRY STOTT)

On Long Island Sound: Nimble *under sail.* (RAFAEL MACIA)

CHAPTER TWO

~~~~~~

THE INNER SOUND—OYSTER BAY

~~~~~~

(DAY 1)

We came tacking down into Oyster Bay against the dying west wind, still relaxed from our swim. A flight of gulls came off Centre Island. They drifted casually back toward a yacht astern and then disappeared over Centre Island.

Oyster Bay has three good anchorages. The first (point 17, map 2) lay dead ahead of us at the end of Cold Spring Harbor, the eastern branch of Oyster Bay. The second good anchorage, Morris Cove (point 19, map 2), is in Oyster Bay Harbor (the western branch of Oyster Bay), snug behind Oak Neck Beach.

The third anchorage is Sand Hole or Sand Diggers (point 16, map 2) and is out at the lip of Oyster Bay, a terrific spot enclosed in a cir-

11

cular beach. On *Nimble,* our first anchorage was to be Morris Cove.

At Jakobson's Marina, just past the entrance to Oyster Bay Harbor (point 18, map 2), we waited the arrival of Kim Massie and a friend of his, Greg Bourassa, coming out on the Long Island Railroad. One great advantage of a cruise in the Sound is the Long Island Railroad and likewise, on the other side, the New York, New Haven and Hartford. Planes are all right but, for this cruise, trains work much better because they go right out to the end of the Sound on both sides. That makes the Sound the only cruise grounds I know served by two parallel railroads as well as two parallel bus systems. To top it off, two ferries connect between.

Nimble has been to Jakobson's before, as a casualty. The original owner had chartered her to someone who put a hole in one hull in Oyster Bay and claimed he'd never heard it happen. There are two things to be said about that. First, if you hit anything with a plywood-and-fiberglass hull, it sounds like a bull butting a bass drum. Secondly, a hole in one hull of a tri is a lot less serious than a hole in a monohull. Therefore, the hulls can be built lighter without sacrificing the safety margin.

6:00 P.M.: Kim arrived with Greg. We promptly motored up behind Oak Neck Beach, across the expanse of the harbor—there were only three or four other yachts at anchor in the Morris Cove vicinity.

Kim was our second photographer. Greg was plainly a hippie.

I have absolutely nothing against hippies. That is, I watch them carefully to see if they conform to my expectations of type, and then— if they do—dismiss them. Seriously, Bourassa was a fine addition to the crew, and his drolleries had a way of helping the rest of us enjoy things.

In Oyster Bay we enjoyed the wide welcome look of the harbor, dined lightly swinging at anchor, and then, the summer sun still up, Bea and I went dinghying up Mill Neck Creek (point 20, map 2). There were two sets of yachts nesting in Oyster Bay and we inspected those on the way, wondering how they had come to meet each other. We were tempted to ask if theirs was a long-term relationship or a pick-up. If there were nesting damage, who would pay for it? Were they happy with their nest mates? And so on.

As we headed the dink up Mill Neck Creek we were powered by the little Evinrude folding 3½-horse engine; it pushed us along at a really good rate. There are times when a dinghy outboard saves a hell of a lot of rowing. We kept the little outboard folded up forward in the port pontoon, where it got in nobody's way.

One of the big advantages of a tri is storage space. In the port hull, in addition to the dinghy motor, I had three anchors with anchor lines, a spare 100-foot line, scrub brushes, chemical toilet (spare), lobster-cooking pot (large), spare ice chest (picnic type), plus miscellaneous fenders and deck swabs.

In the starboard hull I kept a complete spare Evinrude 9-hp engine (in an emergency it could be dropped in the well to replace the 18-hp Evinrude that rode there), an Aqua Barbecue charcoal broiler, bilge pumps, wood for miscellaneous repairs, spare plexiglass in case we broke a window, five-gallon reserve gas can, oil, boat hooks, cockpit tarpaulin, working jib and oddments. All this without taking up any space in the cabins or on deck.

Mill Neck Creek was great dinghying. It ran first under the bridge between Mill Neck and the beach at Oak Neck, where the swirl of the outgoing tide made the little motor whirr. Then we were in "lake country": little outboards at bouys, kayaks with kids aboard, canoes ashore, small modest cottages behind the beaches. Mill Neck was settled long before the waterfront got expensive.

Beyond this, Mill Neck Creek narrows and becomes marshy. "Wetland" ecology takes over. An osprey sailed overhead, probably to a nearby nest.

People used to insist on filling in as much swampland like this as they could, making houses rise on it, putting in solid roads. Today, the attitude of enlightened people toward marshlands has been reversed. We know now that tidal marshes are all that stand between man and a radical subversion of the water environment. The disappearance of marsh leads to the disappearance of birds, fish, animals, flood control and the shore itself.

A ten-acre marsh can absorb three million gallons of water in a one-foot abnormal rise caused by unusual wind or tide. The huge floods that recently washed over several million dollars of priceless art in Venice were the result of filling in the marshes on the outskirts of Venice, adjacent to the sea. These marshes used to absorb abnormal tides. Now the city does.

A salt marsh is a food factory. It produces plankton and shellfish, lower links in the food chain that goes through both fish and waterfowl to man.

The production of protein (complex food molecules) from an acre of marsh has been calculated to be seven times the protein production from an acre of wheatfield in Kansas. Nearly two thirds of all fish and shellfish taken commercially in the U.S. depend on these estuarine marshes. As the marshes have dwindled, so has the catch of fish. Commercial catches of some species of fish have been halved. The croaker, a common food fish, has disappeared from Long Island Sound; each year it disappears along another stretch of coast to the south along the Atlantic.

The coastal marshes which still remain are in imminent danger. New Jersey has filled in thirty-five thousand acres in fifteen years. In the Bronx, where there were two thousand acres fifteen years ago, only fifty remain.

The counterattack has been slow in coming: the State of New York passed an act by which it will share the cost of setting aside and maintaining wetlands within a municipality. Under this act, Hempstead has set aside ten thousand acres and Oyster Bay five thousand. Lloyd Harbor, next door, has a local ordinance that says that anyone filling in a marsh must put in ten feet of fill; this has discouraged the developers there.

The State of Connecticut allows filling only by permit and will fine violators $1,000 a day. Rhode Island fines at a rate of $100 a day. Massachusetts has a Coastal Wetlands Act in which all the wetlands are classified either as fillable, or as too valuable to fill; the latter may *never* be destroyed by fill.

The State of Maryland calculates that the value of an acre of tidal marsh in money generated by sale of fishing tackle, guns and ammunition, plus the value of the edible seafood and fowl produced in an acre, comes out to be $4,000. At that price, marshland is valuable to give away at wasteland prices. There is a move on to turn the whole of Oyster Bay into a federal land reserve and to stop all filling-in.

This would yield the dividend of discouraging the building of one of those infernal proposed Long Island Sound bridges. One plan calls for a terminal at Oyster Bay, which would ruin the nearest pretty harbor to New York City.

In our dinghy, Bea and I motored up Mill Neck Creek as far as the boatyard at its head. Seaman Seacraft is a high-tide shipyard (open on Sundays when sometimes no other yards are). Then we rejoined *Nimble* and her cargo of escapists.

Nimble has six berths: two in an aft cabin behind the cockpit, two in the main cabin, aft of the galley, and a double bunk forward, behind a partition. The privacy afforded by this arrangement would be outstanding in a forty-footer, let alone a thirty-foot yacht, and was a principal reason for my buying the boat.

There is no way to duplicate the rocking of the lulling waters of a good harbor. We got down to serious sleeping in record time.

Next morning the wind had shifted north. I padded around, delighted at the bare deck, slightly dewed, underfoot. No one else was up. The clouds on the horizon were like dark curly combers and not to my liking, but weather is something you bear on a cruise. Bea soon had the alcohol stove going, and we all sat around the cockpit to the luxury of toast, fresh scrambled eggs and fresh air.

We'd tacked into Morris Cove the day before; now on day one of the cruise proper, we would be tacking back out to Sand Hole, or Sand Diggers, seven miles off, an easy first day's run to a beautiful beach.

We rounded the shores of Centre Island in the morning sun. In the cross light, we got the full effect of the homes ashore. They are magnificent stuff, things most of us dream of owning. Today it costs a small fortune to run, let alone buy, one of these big rambling houses.

On *Nimble*, after turning north, we sailed past the cliffs of Sagamore Hill, where Teddy Roosevelt had his summer White House (point 2, map 3). It's a magnificent home, with some of the grand feeling of Teddy's own personality.

Teddy was a good "bayman." He admired the locals and would join them in their pursuit of clams, oysters, whitefish, bluefish and a solid draught at the local tavern thereafter.

We swung north in Oyster Bay proper, passing for this trip a chance to see Cold Spring Harbor (point 3, map 3). At the bottom of the harbor around Cold Spring Beach is a perfectly protected inner harbor. Opposite is a restaurant called The Moorings; it is one of the best of the Long Island seaside food places. It's a low, rambling building with its own dock, lots of non-nautical customers who arrive by car, a maitre d', a reservations list and—good food.

We were now closing on Sand Diggers (point 4, map 3), coasting along in an easy breeze. The hard-to-see entrance is marked by a low breakwater, not an easy entrance to navigate, so I took a good reading from Wilensky's book. You make an S-shaped course to keep from running onto the long breakwater underwater south of the entrance or the unmarked reef to the north.

Sailing successfully through Sand Diggers' entrance and turning north to get away from the houses at the south end, we passed through the narrow channel, past a cluster of dolphins—a sort of A-frame of pilings at the middle of it. A fine fiberglass outboard was tied to the dolphins, every occupant fishing hard. They had a whole netful of whitefish, which they held up when we asked how fishing was.

The northern end of Sand Diggers is completely untenanted and large enough so that the question of lee shore did come in. We searched away, testing here and there to get out of the freshening wind, and found a spot that seemed to promise a good calm night's rest. Bea made it the official lunch hour with some handsome sandwiches, after which the photographers got busy shining their lenses. They put Rickie and Bea in the dinghy and went ashore to do or die photographically. Because some of our fellow yachtsmen had been so callow as to leave trash on the shore, the local residents had posted the shore conspicuously with "no trespassing" signs.

But, being couthless photographers, Kim and Wilk ignored these, hoping to photograph Rickie and Bea as Oceanids. The police quickly descended. Our party of lawbreakers were herded off the beach in short order.

Sand Diggers is hauntingly beautiful. Its shore is wild. There are rarely more than a few boats in Sand Diggers. That, in a perverse way, makes yachting at Sand Diggers better. We saw only two other craft in here, in twelve hours, at the height of the cruising season.

We swam, and the water was reasonably warm. We watched the oyster dredge come in the narrow entrance, feel around the bottom of the entrance, make four or five passes and head back out for the Sound.

The beach lay as the sachems and their tribes knew it (except for the "keep off" signs). The beach grass bent in the breeze very much as it had for centuries, small rifles on the surface ran regularly against the sides of our boat—the different drummer that we all came to hear.

Greg in the pulpit, leaving Oyster Bay. (KIM MASSIE)

Greg and Wilk strike the genny en route to Lloyd Neck. (KIM MASSIE)

Headed for Lloyd Neck in a gale. (GEORGE WILKINSON)

CHAPTER THREE

≈≈≈≈≈≈≈≈≈≈≈≈≈≈≈≈≈≈≈≈≈≈≈≈≈≈≈

THE INNER SOUND—
HUNTINGTON AND NORTHPORT BAYS

≈≈≈≈≈≈≈≈≈≈≈≈≈≈≈≈≈≈≈≈≈≈≈≈≈≈≈

(DAY 2)

We set sail at seven in the morning, headed for Huntington and Northport—two huge connected bays, each with a half dozen estimable anchorages in the wide expanses of their interiors. The wind was veering east, which was convenient, but also a warning. The barometer on the mast in the main cabin had made a significant dip. We had only eight miles to Lloyd Neck Harbor, which we planned as a breakfast stop before going to Northport for supplies and a visit to the fabulous Eagle's Nest.

The short first leg to Lloyd Neck Harbor proved to be the toughest sail of the trip. The easterly gusts started coming on strong, stirring the instinctive depths of my sailing soul. I got the main roller-reefed, took

17

in the genny, and set the working jib. We hadn't poked our nose out of Oyster Bay into Long Island Sound proper a quarter mile when the nor'easter came lashing down with harrying squalls. Under thunderous claps of wind, *Nimble* leapt ahead like a struck cat. The Danforth wind speed indicator read something above forty-five—full-gale treatment.

Nimble went boiling around Lloyd Neck like a motor cruiser with her diesel turned up. Our speed indicator intermittently read 15 and I believed it. It would have taken a Coast Guard boat full of young men to move this rate under power. Wilk had the helm, and was whooping through splattering rain squalls in the same way he shouts skiing three feet of powder snow.

We surged down into outer Huntington Bay and coasted between the abandoned lighthouse and the flasher at the entrance to the harbor at Lloyd Neck (point 7, map 3), a green harbor not quite so remote-looking as Sand Diggers, but nevertheless, acceptably unspoiled.

Our swift little nor'easter was left behind outside, subsiding, and we were in the peace of coming in. On the far side of the harbor a young man was operating a clam rake, a business which had given him Atlas-like shoulders and arms; I could see the muscle definition at well over a hundred yards. Ashore in $40,000 homes, as the sky cleared, the young rich and becoming rich were waking. Some were soon stretching their Sunday legs behind power mowers, whose song was beginning to be heard in the land. Cars were beginning to come across the causeway from Lloyd Neck to West Neck, cars headed for church with the wife and kids—the husband presumably still behind his mower. Other Sunday signs were about; a babysitter appeared down on the Lloyd Neck pier in charge of small kids.

After breakfast, to rouse the crew for the run to Northport and Vanderbilt's place, I summarized the facts of the once-famous Collings murder mystery, recalled by the late Fessenden Blanchard in his book *Long Island Sound* (now out of print, but available from Sailing Book Service, 34 Oak Street, Tuckahoe, New York). Benjamin Collings and his wife were moored in Northport Bay one day in 1931. Two individuals came aboard at night, tied Collings up, dumped him into the bay to drown, set his boat adrift with his five-year-old daughter aboard and left his wife bound in another boat in Oyster Bay. No one ever came up with a plausible suspect or motive.

The wayward wind of the morning had gone west, giving us a steady, obedient breeze of six to eight knots, ready to nudge us on our way.

Once out of Lloyd Neck Harbor and into Huntington Bay, we passed the entrance to Huntington Harbor (point 8, map 3) between East Neck and West Neck, a narrow entrance behind a lighthouse that marks the harbor.

West Neck and East Neck probably were the literal inspiration for the names "West Egg" and "East Egg" in Fitzgerald's *The Great Gatsby*. A fertile literary air hangs over Long Island Sound. In one way or another, it nurtured poet Walt Whitman, playwright Eugene O'Neill, and Herman Melville, as well as Fitzgerald.

Whitman's family owned five-hundred acres just south of Huntington Harbor. The house, on Route 110, is now a public museum. Whitman, like Teddy Roosevelt, qualified as a "bayman." He did his share of clamming and fishing and bringing in the hay from the salt marshes. Whitman wove Long Island country into the very fabric of his works."When Lilacs Last in the Dooryard Bloom'd" was not only the finest poem on the death of President Lincoln, but a fine poem on Long Island.

In *Song of Myself*, Whitman wrote, "I lean and loafe at my ease, observing a spear of summer grass . . ." followed by "the sniff of green leaves and dry leaves, and of the shore and dark color'd sea-rocks . . ."

The country around Huntington, where Whitman grew up, was never far below the surface of his writing.

The long, inland-pointing stretch of Huntington Harbor is not a likely tie-up spot. All moorings are liable to be taken. There is a seafood restaurant on the right, with a bulkhead that is worth getting up onto for taking pictures of the harbor. The town itself is even farther down toward the bottom, inshore from Knutsen Marine, too far up the road for an easy walk. Beyond the town is the highest point on Long Island, Dix Hills, a magnificent 426 feet above sea level.

We on *Nimble* passed the entrance of Huntington Harbor as it was disgorging a fleet at sail. We moved nicely along West Neck, west of the entrance, past the point where young Nathan Hale, a Yale graduate and the country's first martyr, landed after his sail over from Connecticut to spy on the British during the Revolutionary War. He was trapped before he could return to Washington's headquarters, but left us with that fine exit line, "I only regret I have but one life to lose for my country." Back then we were underdeveloped, and it was the British who were insistent on supplying us the benefits of advanced technology.

Now we were headed across Huntington Bay into the connected interior bay, Northport Bay, equally large and complex. We picked up our Coast and Geodetic Small Craft Chart, on which we could plot the entire course.

The Coast and Geodetic people have finally recognized that the average small-boat cockpit does not have a four foot by four foot chart table, and have reduced a number of their charts to an approximately eight- by fifteen-inch, fold-out format. (Get your SC charts early. They go fast, they're so handy.)

Inset 13 on our 117SC showed us we had to head about 90° true to get past West Neck and under the long finger of West Beach into Northport Bay.

There's yet another magnificent source for cruising guidance, the MacMillan *Marine Atlas for Long Island Sound and South Shore*. Here the Geodetic charts are placed right on handy atlas-sized book pages. This and the map atlas for Long Island and New England, also published by MacMillan (866 3rd Avenue, N.Y., N.Y., or at the Hammond's Map Store in N.Y.C.), will cover most of what you need. One nice feature of the MacMillan charts is that they have mark-to-mark courses plotted on them, with magnetic compass bearings. The process of laying your own bearings can be quickly checked and MacMillan becomes a welcome timesaver. A final resource is *Soundings*, a yachting newspaper devoted to Long Island sailing—a sort of up-to-date fact sheet. For a copy, write Box 26, Wethersfield, Conn.

Nimble now ran past Prices Bend (point 9, map 3), an undeveloped anchorage with excellent protection.

To starboard, *Nimble* passed Centerport (point 10, map 3). Poor little old Centerport; Duncan and Ware's *Cruising Guide to New England* doesn't even mention the place; Wilensky gives it only a scant quarter-column. Not terribly protected and open to the north winds, it has so many of its own boats that there are few moorings available (in a pinch, Simpson's Boat Yard might have some). While it's small and congested, it is pretty, and there are lots of yachty things going on.

We doused sail off Duck Island Harbor (point 11, map 3), a shallow and well-protected harbor on the north shore of Northport Bay. The breeze was coming up to about 15; we went piling down into Northport Harbor itself and ran into about eight fleets of Sunday racing hulls—there was simply no way around. They had the entire harbor. Short of buying a sky hook, there wasn't anything to do but try and cause as little disturbance as possible.

We lowered sail way up the harbor and proceeded under power down into Northport Harbor, dodging as best we could, catching several uncomplimentary shouts from racing skippers, hyped-up in their drive to victory.

The shores of Northport Harbor are quite serene. There's none of the shoreside conglomeration of the Sound shore further in toward the city; the houses and shores seem quite 1915. The boats, whether racing or not, were elegant and attractive—an endless variation on the theme of sail and power afloat.

At this point, I was especially happy I had spent so much time on my auxiliary engine installation. The *Nimble* has a portside outboard well; in it the 18-horse Evinrude admirably filled the power needs of the boat. Besides the outboard's advantage of low initial cost for the power it gives, it makes carrying a usable spare engine possible. Nothing can be more lethal to a cruise than holing up in some dull anchorage while you fetch a mechanic to fix your engine. (As a matter of record, our 18-hp outboard functioned flawlessly throughout the cruise.)

The front of the engine abutted the after cabin bulkhead, so there was no chance to follow normal practice and put the controls forward of the engine. However, the cables are quite flexible, and I was able to bend them around and place the shift and speed controls up in the cockpit *behind* the engine. Now, as we moved through a crowded, busy, fast-moving, nearly-endless armada of yachts, this arrangement enabled me to maneuver the boat handily.

We sailed through fleets whose skippers were supremely well drilled. They held their courses, they trimmed their sails neatly; they allowed for the tide in making their marks; they fenced artfully with overtaking hulls and they gracefully gave way when overtaken. These intricacies and courtesies are a sight to warm the heart of any racing sailor.

Northport goes rather deeply into the shore. We persisted past the high legs of the municipal dock, cautiously following the buoyed path through the nearly endless corridors of pleasure craft anchored at the bottom of the harbor, and proceeded another mile or so through a privately buoyed channel. A sharp right turn at the bottom of the harbor fetched us into Northport Marina and Boat Yard, a copious facility where every berth has a float at dockside. After we tied up, Bea perched on top of the cabin behind my typewriter and typed a few memos to her boss. We swabbed down and then supped elegantly on small steaks.

The William K. Vanderbilt summer place, Eagle's Nest, is situated on the opposite shore.

Cornelius "Commodore" Vanderbilt got his start ferrying—to Staten Island from the Battery. Even before that he was a sailor. In his seventeenth year, his mother promised to finance a periouger—a flat bottom, two-masted scow—for him if he'd plow and plant eight of the Vanderbilt acres in corn on their modest Staten Island farm. "I didn't feel as much real satisfaction when I made two million in that Harlem corner as I did that morning sixty years before when I hoisted my own sail and put my hand on my own tiller."

The old Commodore reverted to the sea in his later days in style. He built himself a 270-foot yacht, *North Star*. It had room for the whole family—eight siblings and their spouses plus his in-laws—and took them to Europe. The boat cost a half million. He started Vanderbilt University in Nashville with the same amount.

He had four sons; two died, one was a mental case and the last, William Henry, the Commodore thought a weakling. However, he left

William Henry ninety million. Willliam Henry turned out to be better than weak, doubled the money and in turn passed on sixty million to Cornelius II, who built The Breakers in Newport and sixty million to William Kissam Vanderbilt, who used a good part of this to build Eagle's Nest, which we now visited.

Eagle's Nest is Spanish, elegant and overwhelming. It's got something for everyone: gold-fixtured marble bathtub, 1924 Lincoln limousine, a belltower, a thirteenth-century Portuguese sitting room, Napoleon's bed as bought by William K. Vanderbilt. In Vanderbilt's Hall of Fishes, there is his lifelong collection of marine and wildlife speciments is housed.

We returned to the boat, shopped on Main Street, bought the latest Soundings and made hardware purchases to effect a change in *Nimble*'s mainsheet installation. Northport Boatyard and Marina Store is one of the best on the Sound.

A sailor worth his salt is in a perpetual state of mild displeasure with his boat. If there's nothing to improve, it takes the fun out of it. I installed one block to rig the main so it wouldn't have to be tended when we came about close-hauled.

I managed to rig the lines before we took off so as to test it during the six miles out to the outer edge of Huntington Bay, where an evening at Eatons Neck Cove awaited us.

Nimble settled nicely against a freshening eight-knot breeze from the northwest, which lifted her hull and occasioned those surges of acceleration for which multi-hull are renowned. We were going to make it into Eatons Neck Cove by dark, easily.

We put *Nimble* about in the middle of Northport Bay. The main slammed over, gratifyingly automatic in its operation. Greg, Wilk and Kim took in the genny smartly with the winch, until it was like a board—no need for a belly in the sail in this wind. We were going like merry blazes. The wind direction indicator showed we were coming within 45 degrees of the relative wind as we went shooting past Duck Island Harbor. (It's a safe comfortable little harbor and you can dinghy to Asharoken Beach and go out over the high sand to the south side for a swim.)

There wasn't any wash from powerboats; they had gone home; there were only a few sails left. *Nimble* ran as if on rails. One of the remaining sails, a stout little thirty-five-footer, tried to come around and hold with us going out but gave up after *Nimble* took one gust under wing and surged ahead like a moonship coming out of parking orbit.

Here came West Beach; behind the beach is a small island (point 3, map 4) with a fork on it—another day and we'd have gone ashore and climbed the fort—great fun. Well out into Huntington Bay, we came about and took a course for the mouth of Eatons Neck Cove.

Eatons Neck Cove (point 4, map 4) has a tough little reef off the north side of the entrance (make sure you pass the little flasher on Can "1" to port, no matter how you approach the cove). We sliced in like a smoky blue racing machine. We kept the sail on as we went streaming up the channel. We were doing six knots, no trouble, against the current, close-hauled. We probably could have anchored without turning on the engine, but the Coast Guard had a place on the north end of the cove, and we didn't want to be giving them trouble right in front of their station. They have plenty to contend with outside. The rescue boat from Eatons Neck seems to cover everything that happens in the whole mid-Sound. One of the rescue boats—all lights and moving men in blue denims—came charging out past us, bent on an errand of mercy; it turned the flasher and then accelerated some more, doing belly-whoppers on every second wavetop. The boys would be tired before they got back.

Eatons Neck Cove is a circle of water, surrounded by low beach, a most crowded anchorage. The place was a net of anchor lines. Some of the small craft, in clever desperation, had anchored close to shore at high tide and let the tide go out under them. The beach was decorated with bright bottoms of careened small powerboat hulls lying at water's edge. Afloat, vessels were swinging side by side in a neighborliness not often demonstrated in anchorages. Luckily, the protection in the cove is excellent.

We motored to a spot just off the beach, set the anchor down, lit the galley fires and by dusk had a simple supper. Ashore, small bonfires were being lit and there was a soft murmur of radios and some bars of song up the beach. Bea and I took the dinghy in and walked the length of the beach, looking at the little tents put up by some of the powerboaters. We watched the lights flicker out on the Sound and stargazed. Somewhere out in the cove, a banjo and an accordian were playing *"Five Foot Two, Eyes of Blue."* Time to turn in; the cabin lights around the harbor shut down one by one and all that was left was a strand of mast lights.

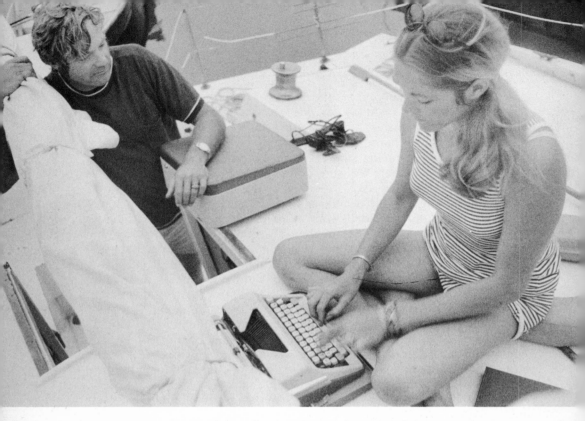

Bea typing on deck, Northport Marina and Boat Yard. (KIM MASSIE)

Engine well and control in Nimble: *the 18 hp Evinrude.* (BEA WILLIAMS)

Greg scrubs Nimble's *underside, Eatons Neck Cove.* (GEORGE WILKINSON)

~~~~~~~~~~~~~~~~~~~~~~~~~~~~~~~~~~

CHAPTER FOUR

THE MIDDLE SOUND—NORWALK ISLANDS, PORT JEFFERSON AND STRATFORD

~~~~~~~~~~~~~~~~~~~~~~~~~~~~~~~~~~

(DAYS 3, 4, 5)

The Inner Sound, where we had now been cruising two days, is the cozy part of the Sound. It's nothing to leap from one side to the other. As we lay in Eatons Neck Cove, it was a scant six miles across to Long Neck Point in Connecticut. The Inner Sound had only widened about a mile since we left Execution Rock.

Ahead of us was the Middle Sound, a thirty-five-mile stretch going out to Falkner Island off Connecticut. This section of the Sound is more adventuresome, less friendly. The distance between shores doubles. From the bottom of Smithtown Bay at Nissequogue, a few miles east of Eatons Neck, to the opposite Connecticut shore, it is easily twelve miles.

The Norwalk Islands lie eight miles across the Sound from Eatons Neck. The islands are a near thing to the islands off Maine. Our plan called for a hop up to the Norwalk Islands today.

The sky south of us made up into grayer and grayer layers, as we breakfasted on *Nimble* in Eatons Neck Cove on day three of the cruise.

After breakfast, we sidled *Nimble* over to a small scalloped indentation on one of the beach shores at Eatons. We wanted to ground her for a minute to take a look at the rudder, which had loosened. We ran softly into the sand, let ourselves down in the water, and I tightened the nuts with a vise grip while Greg, bless him, scrubbed the hulls, removing the sea growth. The Sound is so rich in nutrients provided by the decomposition of wastes, we could've gardened on *Nimble*'s bottom.

When we tried to push off, we found the outgoing tide had caught us. The tide *goes* when it goes in Eatons Neck. We shoved and rocked her—made frantic by visions of another twelve hours here. Happily, a crew of youngsters came across the sands to give us a needed hand. A final lurch and we were off.

Throwing our motor into full, we gunned out into the channel and into Huntington Bay with a blowy southeaster at our heels. We set sail and galloped off into the Sound with what looked like worse weather chasing us astern.

And we got worse weather. Rain.

We could have turned tail and gone into Asharoken Cove (point 5, map 4,) but instead doused sail, turned the engine on and proceeded through the slanting drizzle toward a gray spot in the gray in front of us which receded as we advanced.

We had been sailing only two days—seven miles the limit of our waters left and right; yet we weren't really distressed at our failure to round up a *New York Times* that morning. We were a bit more detached from our jobs left behind, people left behind, and shore things out of sight. We were on *Nimble* together, piercing a blank wall on a gray rippling surface, which heaved ever so slightly as if to remind us it too was part of that sea which ran to the Azores, to Cape Horn, and had known better sailors.

Long Island weather is very very fickle, it comes in strong with thunderstorms that hit with nearly no advance radio warning. Squalls get so fierce that you can sail bare poles and make considerable headway, while ten miles away sailors can be complaining about lack of wind. (The thermals that rise over the hot concrete of the cities on both sides makes the Inner Sound a place where good wind is less frequent than further out.) I've been hit hard enough by a squall to find myself standing, shaking with cold in a cockpit that looked hurricane-struck, just a scant twenty minutes after basking on deck in the sun.

The only real problem in a good Long Island storm is to stay away from shores, reefs or other vessels. (Keep two people on deck listening for horns or motors.) A squall is usually over in thirty minutes, but it can sure shake you up.

Other than collisions, the only real immediate danger in a squall is exposure. If you go overboard in May or even June, you may not be able to stand being immersed more than twenty minutes. The water is just that cold before July 4. Two friends of mine went over in a small planing hull in Glen Cove in May one year and drowned before anyone saw them, simply because they had no life jackets. They became too numb to hang on. That same squall tipped boats the whole length of the North Shore of the island, causing ten deaths.

In a squall, therefore, life jackets for all hands, at once, unless it's after July 4.

On *Nimble* this day, after a good hour and a half, the rain eased. We saw the ghost of Greens Ledge. The blotted line of the Connecticut shore appeared behind it.

Just behind Greens Ledge is Hay Island and in back of that is Zieglers Cove (point 6, map 4;) and Scott Cove (point 7, map 4). Both are worth a look if you come along the coast. They're two of the most popular gunkholes in the Sound.

Fessenden Blanchard, in *Long Island Sound*, published ten years ago, noted, "Greeenwich Cove is a good bet for the night, among the less well-known anchorages. Still better, if conditions are favorable, is the anchorage behind Hay Island, just east of Darien River and Long Neck Point. I have been there half a dozen times and always found it uncrowded and pleasantly reminiscent of the Maine coast."

John C. Devlin, writing in *The New York Times* recently, under a column headed, "Oh for a Quiet Cove," says, "Now you try the Connecticut shore and that old favorite, Zieglers Cove. Here there are great rafts of glistening floating apartments called 'boats' peopled by grog-laden types in fancy yachting caps. Their conduct and language are the despair of the local property owners brought up to believe that yachting is a sport indulged in by persons with breeding and manners."

What a difference a decade makes.

There is no place you can get down to Zieglers from shore. There are not, as a matter of fact, more than a few miles of public shore along the whole hundred-mile Connecticut coast.

The Connecticut mainland here, where it hasn't been brutally commercialized, is settled by a solid fortification of houses. Lining the beach like whitewashed stones along a gravel drive, they form a front from the New York State line out to Fishers Island.

We pressed *Nimble* in toward the light on Greens Ledge; we could now see the Norwalks in the lifting rain. They appeared as a series of indistinct darker shapes in the water, blending into sky and shore, but recognizable.

Presently, the rain lifted. *Nimble* turned the corner at the Greens Ledge Light, passed the mouth of Five Mile River and anchored off Sheffield (point 9, map 4), the largest of the Norwalks. There was enough light so we could enjoy the fresh-looking lawn around the lighthouse-turned-into-a-house ashore.

Just down the beach lay the ruins of a considerable mansion. As the rains lifted higher and higher, the light got clearer and clearer. Kim and I decided to go ashore in the dinghy and take a few shots of the ruins.

The thick cement and stone walls were fit for a fortress. The house is like a Mayan ruin in the still-ascertainable outlines of a formal garden. Grass slowly creeps in on it. The roof falls off into the living room. A stone window frame, a solid field of red tile on the floor and a huge stone fireplace in the living room were still intact.

Just off Sheffield is Tavern Island, owned once by the late Billy Rose. In its heyday, Tavern had exotic birds—peacock, etc.—and was landscaped within an inch of its life. Billy Rose was the man who gave us the Aquacade at the 1938 New York World's Fair.

Beyond Tavern, we could see the industrialized shore between Five Mile River and Westport (point 12, map 4) on the Saugatuck River. Five Mile River is a busy but fairly pleasant and informal place, one of the few good harbors without a yacht club of any kind. It has a couple of marinas and a restaurant that has a good reputation, Higgins Clam Bar.

We settled in for the night off Sheffield and had a small blow to contend with, and rain. *Nimble* bumped about a bit and coursed her regulation figures above the anchor. But by morning things were much better.

We had a glass-still Sound to look out upon. Not a breeze. A sense of peace filled the air, accentuated by the slow line of smoke coming from the chimney of the lighthouse ashore, smoke that moved up toward a fairly benign overcast.

We finally moved off, under power, at 11 A.M. on day four of the cruise, headed for Port Jefferson, 14 miles off. We took the eastern exit from the Norwalks, going past the mouth of the Norwalk River (point 10, map 4) and between Cockenoe (Ko-Keé-nee) Island and Goose Island.

A small sail-yacht that had gone into the nice horseshoe cove on Cockenoe, and her mast showed over the arm of the bay as we went past. If I were to pick a favorite anchorage in these islands, it would be Cockenoe. Here, you are out of sight of all the industry ashore and can feel more remote. Had I not been in a hurry to get an anchor in the night before, I would have moved up into Cockenoe's little bay.

Not so long ago, United Illuminated owned Cockenoe and proposed a nuclear power plant on it. United was surprised at the amount and vehemence of the opposition. They didn't know so many people boated. They didn't understand, either, that this shore, this water, these islands are a safety valve for the industrial pressure on the mainland from New York to New Haven that smogs the air, dirties the harbors, fills the wetlands, pollutes the streams, blocks the rivers. To destroy one of these rare precious islands amounts to holding your hand over the nose of a drowning man. The light company was persuaded to sell the island to the city of Westport.

We had a northeasterly; I watched the horizon because this is the wind that can bring in the big ones. But it was an OK wind, on our beam as we headed for Port Jeff. That's one nice thing about the Sound; there's always somewhere to sail to, regardless of the wind. If you're on the coast of Maine going down east, then you have a hell of a time with an easterly coming at you. There's nowhere to go but in the teeth of the wind. In Long Island Sound, going down east in nearly the same way (the Connecticut shore averages dead east just as the Maine coast does), you simply slant over to the other shore on a free reach.

The wind was moving us nicely past the bell buoy off Georges Rock, the farthest point east in the Norwalks. As we left the islands, the mast over Cockenoe grew small; Cockenoe faded into the Connecticut mainland. We were getting more wind, and the sky to the south and west started turning a dead, almost metallic color which I did not like. The wind, though, was hitting nicely abeam as we made almost due south.

And now the sun came out just a bit as the clouds broke. The wind freshened.

We sped blissfully along for over an hour until intercepted by a Coast Guard boat from the direction of Eatons Neck. The captain's voice came booming over the water—"Winds up to eighty miles an hour expected in three hours." We'd had no hint of this in the morning weather broadcast, but—come to think of it—I had not liked the hue of the clouds. Eighty miles an hour. That is, simply put, a hurricane.

This part of the Sound can get as rough as the ocean. In 1962 a sudden gale sank *Gwendolyn Steers*, a big tug, off Eatons Neck; none of her crew survived. I calculated that the weather coming in from the northeast afforded us a Hobbesian choice. We could make it back up Five Mile River in two hours, to the bottom of Northport Harbor in

two, or Mt. Misery Cove at Port Jeff in two. I chose Mt. Misery, not
only because of her high sand walls, which almost completely surround
the cover, but because it accorded with the cruise plan.

It wouldn't be a full hurricane, although the winds might briefly
reach hurricane force. Hurricanes don't just drop in unannounced. The
weather people, ever since the 1938 and 1945 hurricanes hit unexpect-
edly, track new hurricanes carefully for days; there had been none on
the way. Still, I watched the Danforth wind speed indicator with a
certain apprehension. The instrument is necessary on a multi-hull because the relative lightness and high speed makes judging true wind
speed difficult. Actually, what you feel aboard is only an apparent
wind, compounded of the wind itself and the wind of the boat speed.
In a beam wind, velocities may seem harder than they are, while following winds appear much weaker. With a simple calculation of wind
direction, wind speed and water speed, you can figure what the real
wind is, as opposed to apparent wind.

At any rate, I wasn't seeing any appreciable increase in the real
wind speed yet. We were coasting toward Port Jeff, with Smithtown
Bay off the port bow, and I had one eye out for the small harbors that
could serve for shelter if the winds seemed to come on in a hurry.

There are a number of small harbors in Smithtown Bay, between Eatons Neck and Port Jeff. The first, Asharoken Cove (point 5, map 4),
previously mentioned, is detailed by Wilensky in his book. It is a
dredged inlet for a power plant. The cove lies three miles down the
shore from Eatons Neck. It could serve.

Nissequogue (point 17, map 4) is eight miles down from Eatons
Neck, right after Sunken Meadow State Park. You can go in with eight
feet; there are a couple of marinas, etc. It is not a pretty spot and not
worth the trouble of getting in unless you need it.

Eleven miles east of Eatons Neck is Stony Brook (point 18, map 4)
for hulls drawing four feet or less. If there isn't too much surf, that is.
At high tide, you could probably get in with six feet, no trouble.
Stony Brook is fairly large once you're inside, and the village is very
pretty.

Now we boomed along on a very strong wind with Nissequogue and
then Stony Brook off our beam along Smithtown Bay; it seemed we'd
have no trouble making Port Jeff in time. Then on our weather band
we heard that the storm warning was off, and we relaxed.

The man for whom Smithtown Bay was named was a pioneer settler,
Bull Smith. He farmed and raised cattle in the 1600's. Smith's herd
irritated the Indians who had sold him the land. They weren't used
to seeing large mammals swarming through their countryside, dwarfing
and frightening the deer. Smith once drove a herd toward New York

and ran into a chief who owned the land along this shore. Smith asked the chief if he'd sell some. The Indian said, no, he wouldn't sell, but he would *give* Smith as much land as he could cover on the back of one of his bulls in one day.

Smith refused to take offense at the intended insult. Instead, he patiently broke one of his bulls to the saddle and appeared at the chief's several weeks later. When he announced he was ready to ride, the chief said all right. He would have been delighted, in fact, to see Smith break his neck. But Smith saddled up and rode off into the brush at a great rate and won more land than he needed, including the shoreline of what is now Smithtown Bay. We were now covering this shoreline nearly as rapidly as Smith had.

We moved in toward the blue-gray bulge of Crane Neck. The big twin stacks of the Port Jeff power station solidified against the sky. We were going to overnight at Mt. Misery Cove (point 20, map 4), but first—to pick up a couple of cruising friends, Bill and Judy Hazen—we would go all the way to the town of Port Jefferson (point 22, map 4), a settlement with very little charm but with a convenient grocery store. It was getting toward three o'clock so we hurried in under power.

The town docks were monstrously high in the low tide. The whole Port Jeff dock seemed set up for tuna boats rather than smaller craft. After rigging spring lines to keep ourselves from banging back and forth too much, we sent a quick expedition composed of Bea and Rickie to the grocery store, a handy three blocks off.

The town appeared as if it were somehow about to go under—a sort of 1930's depression atmosphere. There's a watchtower at the end of the city docks, which presumably prevents looting. The boats inside the piers were rigged bow and stern with lines through blocks; each line had, at its other end, a weight hanging into the water. It kept the boats in place during the tide changes, but the creaking of the pulleys when a wave washed through the marina was something like a flock of seagulls trying *Aida*.

Port Jefferson appeared to be a classic mill town; most people seemed definitely non-yachting. They had a keen curiosity about sailors, perhaps seeing us as exotic millionaire types, not as distraught skippers worrying about financing the hole-in-the-water-surrounded-by-wood-through-which-one-pours-money for another season.

Kim went up the mast to see if he could fix our broken masthead light. The forty-five-foot mast of *Nimble* is not so impressive from below, but once you are on it, it sways as in a hurricane. Kim is a competent rock climber and took this in stride. While he was up, Bill and Judy arrived and got their gear aboard.

We got our groceries on and headed for Mt. Misery's happy cove, a full two miles from Port Jefferson's piers. Enroute we passed the towering power plant and a freighter tied up there, rusty and huge, with water pouring out a hole in its side as if it had been mortally wounded.

It started to drizzle a little. The low pressure signs were still with us. We rigged a canvas for our cockpit. Ours was a serviceable $10 piece of tarpaulin, not the $400 candy-striped canvas rain shade that fancy yachts sport. We went chugging toward the opening of Mt. Misery Cove, ignoring the Geodetic Chart's designation "spoil area" and the lack of depth soundings. Dredging has provided a full fifteen feet of water in there, except over toward the western shore where it has shoaled.

Mt. Misery is the third of three "dug" coves on the itinerary—Sand Diggers on Lloyds Neck and Eatons Neck Cove were the other two. The commercial developers who had dug the sand to use for cement making had dredged the three anchorages for their barges to come in.

The sand walls at Mt. Misery greeted us as we slid through the entrance; the walls stretched up fifty to a hundred feet high. We anchored among the powerboats and ran the dinghy ashore. We took off our shoes and ran up the bank like kids.

Nimble, because of her three-hull structure, sometimes has an alarming way of coursing back and forth across her anchor like a restless greyhound on a tether. When we got back aboard, she was charging first over toward our neighbor on the right, then wheeling to the left. Here, a lady on a powerboat stood clutching a dachshund. She stepped back as if to get away from the blow and, as *Nimble* moved and swung off, patted the dog reassuringly.

The sun was now out again and holding its own. We lay around until the sun was obscured by the sand walls. The twilight was hastened by the approach of yet another cover of clouds, suggesting that bad weather was on for the night, at least.

We lit our newly repaired masthead light, turned off the cabin lights and watched the escarpments of the cove melt into blackness. End of day four.

Day five of the itinerary was wet. And the wind was nil.

We wanted to get to Stratford, fifteen miles across the Sound, a culturally enlightened Housatonic River port of call.

Rather than fight the light winds and a contrary floodtide pushing us back toward Port Jeff and in to New York, I turned the engine on after we weighed anchor. I am not one of those purists who will sit for hours fighting to make a buoy with piddling help from the wind and active opposition from the tide. I had enough of this in the days when I raced. We passed the entrance to Setauket town (point 20, map

4) and Conscience Bay (point 19, map 4), both to be left for another day.

The rain stopped. The wind came up nicely. The tide turned to ebb as we moved toward Middle Ground and Stratford Shoal, a big castle of a lighthouse. Behind to starboard lay the only port in the twenty-five miles between Port Jeff and Mattituck. It's Mt. Sinai (point 23, map 4), a good harbor (fifteen feet), but not as much fun as Mt. Misery Cove.

As we moved toward the Connecticut shore, I could see Penfield Light far to our left. Penfield Reef is one of the most substantial pieces of submarine real estate off the Connecticut shore. The reef lies between Southport (point 13, map 4) and Black Rock (point 14, map 4). Watch for it.

Southport is part of the town of Fairfield and has a nice harbor, but very little room for visitors. Its Pequot Yacht Club is one of the most famous on the Sound, though, and the town itself retains an authentic colonial aura.

Black Rock is not an outstanding port, but with a couple of yacht clubs that might well have moorings. Nearer us than Black Neck, the river to Bridgeport leads to a commercial, distasteful port. But, behind its double breakwater, Bridgeport's outer harbor is surrounded by parks, unaffected by the unpleasant upstream surroundings.

P. T. Barnum was once mayor of Bridgeport (there's a P. T. Barnum memorial museum there). Barnum, founder of Barnum and Baily Circus, was a superb showman and con artist. When one of his exhibits got too crowded, he hung a big sign over the back door, "This Way to the Egress." People flocked out to see this unfamiliar beast and found themselves on the street.

Bridgeport is a suggested terminus for a Port Jefferson-Bridgeport cross-the-Sound-bridge, a monstrosity such as to stagger even P. T. Barnum. Today the Port Jeff-Bridgeport ferry suffices to transport cars.

We headed for Stratford Point, east of Bridgeport. The tide, though it was helping us toward shore, was also washing us gently out toward the Atlantic. We sailed ahead on a corrected course.

Kim had taken to fishing with a pole off the stern with a deadly fishing lure, the Rebel. He hooked a fish and brought it in, a nice, small bluefish. Rickie wanted the rod. She hooked a big one right away that bent her pole in a big fat U. She was so astounded she let the fish pull out the line to the end. There it hung. Rickie couldn't reel it back in because the end had been tied in a loop and wouldn't take up on the spool. By the time we got this straightened out again, the big one had gone. But then Greg hooked and boated a second bluefish a few minutes later. Bill Hazen took out his fishing pole and made it three bluefish. We had enough for tomorrow's breakfast. That evening we were planning to sup richly on the picnic grounds of the Shakespeare Theatre. Wilk had been working on a menu in his mind.

The southerly which had been behind us all the way from Stratford Shoal was swinging west now and brought us toward the Housatonic channel on a broad reach. I picked the outside mark up without using the binoculars; it must have been a good mile and some off and only about twelve feet high. You get so tuned to a particular signal that, when the tiny image of the mark at sea dances across your retina, zap! Your mind reaches out and says, "Mark!"

We turned into the Housatonic on a stiff beam wind, making about eight or nine knots in the water against the current and about four over the bottom, as the river drained against us.

We went past the venerable Housatonic Boat Club and then past the Shakespeare Theatre (point 7, map 5), standing high and elegant in its Elizabethan way, banners atop and theatre-goers gathering beneath the walls for a matinee. We pulled into the Stratford Marina, got gas, water, ice and the rest.

During the cruise we had discovered leaks in the aft cabin deck, and the big blow the day before yesterday had bashed loose the front hatch cover. Our bedding needed laundering. We had to get groceries and alcohol for the stove, and everyone wanted to soak in a shower. We trooped up to the S.S. Relief, as it was called, and washed our bodies of a few layers of salt. Afterwards, we sat around in the cockpit, having a welcome lager and enjoying the surroundings. Greg announced he'd made his winter plans: "Buy a few acres in Maine, go up with an axe and a barrel of flour, hunt with my dog. Have a hell of a winter."

We finally emerged from post-sailing euphoria. Wilk went to town to get food and take laundry. Greg got out the caulking goo and proceeded to unscrew the offending bolts that were leaking into the aft cabin. I got out the typewriter and Bea and Rickie washed down the deck. Kim photographed up at the Shakespeare Theatre. Kim and Greg would leave us that evening via taxi to Bridgeport, catch the ferry to Port Jeff and take the Long Island Railroad home.

As time wore on, I realized I had made a mistake in giving Wilk a $20 bill. He loves to get rare meals together. By the exalted expression on his face when he reappeared, after two hours, I knew he had done it again.

I was right. We now had smoked fish and the makings for cucumber salad, fruit salad and tunafish macaroni salad. By the time Wilk had the macaroni cooked, we were late for the play. But we were removed enough from life ashore that the idea of eating instead of watching Shakespeare didn't seem of great moment. We carried our picnic baskets up to the tables in the park near the playhouse and sat eating three kinds of salad, watching the light through the giant trees on the lawn playing on the river. Boats coursed by with wakes shot through with the fire of the lowering sun.

Lighthouse on Sheffield, Norwalk Islands. (KIM MASSIE)

Nimble, *from the masthead, at Port Jefferson town dock.* (KIM MAS

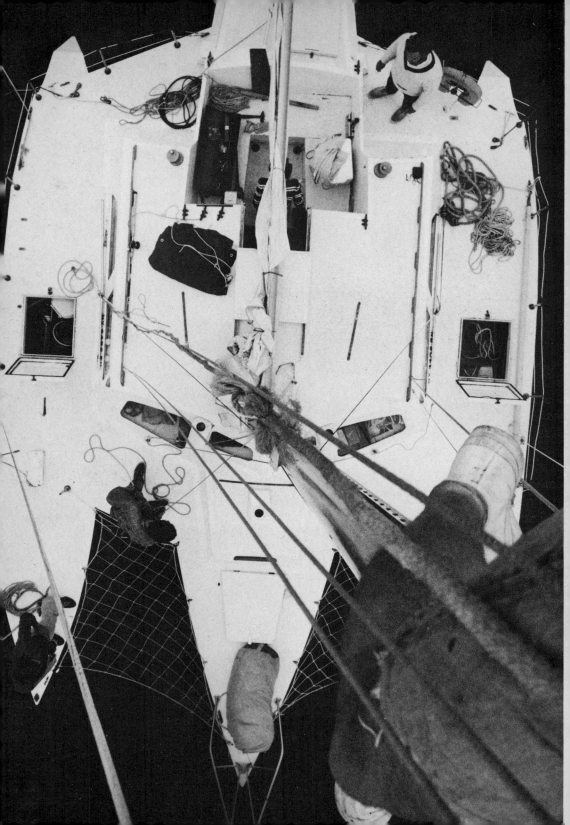

At anchor in Mt. Misery Cove, Port Jefferson. (GEORGE WILKINSON)

Sign at Stratford. (KIM MASSIE)

$\approx\approx\approx\approx\approx\approx\approx\approx\approx\approx\approx\approx$

THE MIDDLE SOUND—THIMBLE ISLANDS

$\approx\approx\approx\approx\approx\approx\approx\approx\approx\approx\approx\approx$

(DAY 6)

Now our goal was the best set of islands in Long Island Sound, the Thimbles, eighteen miles away. Abeam of our course, on the far Long Island shore was the twenty-five mile stretch of uniquely harborless, rocky, sandy shore from Mt. Sinai to Mattituck, a good shore to shun.

After Bea's breakfast of pan-fried bluefish, we set sail down the Housatonic. We turned the corner into the Sound early in the morning on the day six, headed east. A southeast breeze looked to give us a beat or, at best, a close-hauled tack, down to the Thimble Islands. I was anxious to get there expeditiously. We could have motored it in two or three hours, but we had no need to get there that fast. Even with the wind so close to our course, we could average three knots under sail—perhaps more, since we'd be sailing with the tide longer than against it.

The solution to making the best windward speed is a crux of sailing skill. I have devised a way of working the boat to best advantage simply by comparing boat speed to relative wind and direction. I then know how much speed I should pick up for every degree I go off the wind a bit.

This is a particularly important calculation on trimarans, which tend to get up more speed as they go off the wind compared to monohulls. It seldom pays to sail a catamaran or a trimaran very close to the wind. (Most mono-hulls are sailed, in my opinion, too close to the wind too, especially in light breezes.)

In order to calculate really efficiently, however, someone would have to build a "maximizer"—a neat little instrument that I have conjured up in my mind's eye. The instrument would make the calculation automatically and tell you instantly and continuously when you are really getting on to your goal faster or not with every change of heading.

The wind was steady, about eight knots; the Sound was rolling slightly from some storm on the Atlantic, invisible beyond the Sound ahead. *Nimble* settled down to her business and the crew settled down to relaxing, spreading out rail to rail, fore to aft. I calculated once that the thirty-foot trimaran has about as much useful sitting space aboard as a forty-eight-foot mono-hull, at the very least.

The Sound was giving us one of its great days. The sky was hazy but clear of clouds, and the sun was warming us; the wavelets were kicking in regular formation like a sea of Rockettes. Bill got out his surfcasting gear and was soon trailing a silvery Rebel; he sat relaxed against the lifelines that run around most of the deck. But not for long. He came up like a hooked fish himself when the rod doubled over and a bluefish surfaced aft, shaking the lure in its mouth.

Bill reeled. I brought the boat into the wind to lose speed. Pretty soon the blue, looking whitish in the water as it cut back and forth, came up to the *Nimble*'s side. I jumped from the tiller, took the line and gave it a mighty heave, pulling the shaking silver fish in an accelerating curve into the cockpit. Bill outdid himself. He boated two others, equally big. Dinner was here.

Now Rickie wanted to try. She had one within five minutes, but it was really big, maybe six or eight pounds. Wilk took over and reeled it in, only to have it shake loose at the surface beside the boat. Rickie got a second strike a minute later. Wilk took it again; Wilk lost it again. Rickie got a third on in another five minutes. Wilk lost it. There were no more fish.

We left the first two ports on the Connecticut shore behind: Milford and New Haven. Milford (point 9, map 5) is the most crowded of the Connecticut ports here, and that is saying something. On one of my early charters with *Nimble*, before I had a spare engine aboard, I had to make it into Milford under sail due to a defective engine, and that was like nothing else I've done since. Small sailcraft crisscrossed the mouth of the Wepaug River, not awfully wide, which serves as Milford's harbor. I wasn't so sure I could get in. I managed to dodge and shout my way through the small craft and managed to tack frequently enough to miss the moored craft. I searched through the sheaf of moving sails in front of us for a spare mooring or free dockside, but there was none. The only place we could sail to was the dock of the marine biological labs. As a federal facility they had to give us space because we were in an emergency. And we got the part we needed to fix the engine.

We had a talk with a couple of federal biologists before we left. The Milford lab works on the problem of the disappearing oyster.

The exact causes of oyster diminuation are something of a mystery. It is known that both dredging and currents derange oyster beds. Dredging in the Norwalk Islands, to deepen the channel has been halted by the oyster men, who pointed out that Norwalk would lose its million-dollar shellfish industry, were the dredging to continue. Luckily the oyster there has someone to speak for him. Even so, pollution is definitely threatening the oyster catch.

The original wild oyster in Long Island Sound nourished in such numbers as to form veritable shoals of shells, solid enough to menace navigation in the early days. These banks are no more. Wild oysters have been replaced by cultivated oysters, which are placed in the water to release eggs and start a life cycle. The female can produce 300 million or so eggs. Baby oysters, or spats, hatching in three weeks, are the size of a grain of sand. They attach themselves to old oyster shells provided by the oyster farmer. The oyster grows, layer by layer, attached for life with its own cement to something solid that raises it off the floor (it has no proboscis to project from the sand, as does the clam). The oyster pumps water into its shell through its gills with hairlike flappers. It's capable of circulating forty quarts an hour, straining out plankton—its only nourishment.

The oyster's natural enemy is the snail-shaped oyster drill that bores through its shell with a rasp-sharp tongue and has him for dinner. The oyster crab, on the other hand, is just a parasite; the tiny female stations herself in the oyster's gills and gets the pick of the food pumped by.

The oyster is the finest flavored of the clam-shaped shellfish. You can eat oysters *any* month. The rule that you can only eat them in the months containing an "r" is a myth. People used to avoid them during May, June, July and August because these are the hot months when, in the old days, the oyster, sans refrigeration, was likely to arrive spoiled.

If the Sound were cleaned of pollution, we would soon pick oysters off the beaches as handily as we pick up shiny stones. In the old days, they were underfoot by the bushel and grew to be a foot long; they had to be cut up to be eaten. The mental picture is so savory as to be almost unbearable.

Outside Milford, *Nimble* now left Charles Island (point 5, map 5, astern); the island is a rewarding anchorage, lots better than going up into the crowded river.

The next port east is New Haven, another place I normally steer clear of. It's a four- or five-mile ride up to protected water in the Quinnipiac River, commercial and dirty.

New Haven is an historic, if not altogether prepossessing, port. Back in 1839, a group of African slaves revolted in mid-ocean and seized the *Amistad,* a Spanish slave ship. The *Amistad* was steered into New Haven harbor, where the Negroes sought asylum. The U.S. authorities wanted to return them to Spain. New Haven citizens collected money and took the Negroes' case to court. Their revolt leader, an African named Cinque, learned enough English to testify in federal court how he had been kidnapped from his wife and three children. The case went all the way to the Supreme Court. John Quincy Adams argued for Cinque. The court ruled that Cinque and his fellows should be freed and returned to Africa.

During the Revolution (ours), a group of Yale students, led by a local captain, held off the British, General Garth and his troops until New Haven's West Bridge could be destroyed to keep Garth from entering New Haven that way. While Garth was engaged with the collegions, he was attacked on the flank by seventy-year-old Napthali Daggett, President Emeritus of Yale, who fired on the troops with a long rifle meant for squirrel hunting.

Daggett was promptly captured. He was asked if he would ever again dare fire on his Britannic Majesty's men. "Nothing is more likely," Daggett had replied crisply. The British beat him soundly and marched him back to New Haven in his bare feet.

New Haven Harbor does have a reasonably good anchorage at Morris Cove (point 10, map 5) and a good restaurant, Adams and Podoloff, at West Haven (point 11, map 5) and a theatre at Long Wharf (point 12, map 5). Yale, of course, is in town.

We left all this behind as we cut past East Haven, Short Beach and Branford. East Haven (point 14, map 5) is pretty shallow (three feet) and busy. You can dinghy up to the Trolley Museum, way up the creek of the East Haven River for a real trolley ride.

Short Beach, next door, has one small, pretty cove, protected from the west, worth noting—Farm River Cove. But it's small and relatively exposed.

Branford (point 15, map 5) is something else.

It has beautiful protection, good marinas, a couple of first-class boatyards, and guest space at the Branford Yacht Club, which has stakes that will hold you fore and aft opposite the clubhouse on the river. Branford is yachty. If it weren't for the Thimble Islands, Branford would be my pick between the Housatonic and Connecticut Rivers on this shore.

There are reefs galore going into Branford, so you must navigate carefully: I brought *Nimble* into Branford on the same ill-fated cruise that started with the engine going bad. We finally sailed into Branford to get the engine fixed. We got hold of one man in town to repair the engine. We took it back to the boat and left it on deck in the darkening evening. The next morning we took off under sail in favorable wind with the engine still lying lashed to the deck. We sailed out the harbor in a hurry, and just as we made it into the open harbor at the end of the river, we hit a twenty-five-knot wind and I saw a shroud go slack. I looked up at the mast; it came buckling down on me, landing in the cockpit between myself and a shipmate.

We started drifting into a nest of reefs known as Gull Rocks. We hurriedly stuck the engine in the well (we hadn't even tried it out yet), and, with a breathed prayer, pulled the starting cord. It roared and we were saved. We did look pretty sorry carting the fallen mast (it proved defective and was replaced without cost to us) back up to Branford, but we didn't care. We could have ended up in the dinghy, rowing for shore, with *Nimble* on the rocks.

The mast was replaced in a single day by the Johnson Branford Boat Yard, during a holiday, a feat for which I am still grateful.

On our present cruise, we were now headed for the Thimbles: a blissful few hours in a steady breeze, with *Nimble* drumming along like a torpedo; then the small blue humps of the Thimbles appeared in the sea haze.

We turned the corner to the channel toward the islands at the flasher off Negro Heads; it was like a return to Maine. The islands lay there in parallel lines, almost like hedgerows, typical of glacier-ground Maine coast islands.

A ketch, two sloops, and a yawl were homing in on the slot between High and Pot islands. I missed the slot at first and only found it when I saw how the ketch was headed. I had overlooked a hard-to-spot black can in the slot that marks it. We slipped past the can into the slot and came through the channel between bold granite sides of the islets. Smoke rose from fireplace cottages ashore. A series of gull flights came off a rookery; the gulls wheeled in ragged formation in the early evening light. It was delightful to be in island country, to motor within touching distance of a rock shore and thread lines of lobsterpots—nostalgia to a Maine sailor.

On the islands, kids were swimming, slicing around in sailing dinghies, outboarding, running on the rocks—paradise.

We anchored between Pot and High islands (point 17, map 5), the most protected spot. All the shores had a few weathered and unpretentious cottages. Everyone here was either wealthy or lucky. The islands are within cannon distance of New Haven. Prices ashore are astronomical.

Here came the mailboat from the mainland, or the milkboat—a ferry anyway—bringing commuters and a sunbrowned kid or two. What with the water at everyone's doorstep, there was a sort of Vietnamese fishing village feeling.

John Fisher, who writes the "Easy Chair" column for *Harper's* magazine, has a house on Leetes Island that has become, through filling in, part of Hoadley's Neck (point 19, map 5). Fisher describes the metropolis on Leetes as follows:

"For my purposes, the Leetes Island business district is just the right size. It provides the necessary necessities for bodily and spiritual comfort, no more. It consists of three wooden buildings, all painted the same dull shade of red. The largest is Bill Robinson's store, not much bigger than a freight car but roomy enough to stock the essentials, from bread and tobacco to *The New York Times*. On the other side of the parking lot is the liquor shop, run by Noreen Contois and her Great Dane . . . the third building is the railway station, about the size of a box stall with a dirt floor and a plank bench along the back wall. A one-car local stops there twice a day . . ."

On *Nimble*, in the middle of the Thimbles, we gathered around the glowing charcoal burner in the evening. Wilk treated us to Bluefish Wilkinson, lightly salted, with lemon butter, grilled lightly over charcoal. We sat back against the cabin and watched evening come down among the islands. The houses slowly darkened into the granite shore, and stars came out, promising warm decks in the morning.

Day seven, I was on deck early. The fog hung over the small bits of rock, trees and houses, but soon went inland under the urging of a climbing sun. Gulls started to wake with startled exclamations. A door or two opened on the islands. An outboard stuttered.

We took our time and had a swim. The water never seemed fresher than here where it ran through the granite in deep channels.

Finally we weighed anchor and headed out for the Connecticut River. We went past the gull rookery on Outer Island, where the birds were jockeying with each other with pulled-in necks. They each had a sunning place, like seals; they snapped at each other and waddled about, self-satisfied in their little circular stake-outs.

Nimble rustled between Outer Island and Horse Island, passing a well-kept small house with a large sea wall and a bulkheaded dock. A Thimble lobsterman was taking in the pots. Husky, thick-armed, he was standing in his little outboard taking up the trap lines, shucking out the undersize lobster, baiting the traps, then gunning the engine and throwing out the line of lobster traps as he took off. He let the marker float splash in last of all, leaving it bobbing in his wake. He seemed scarcely to need to slow down to pick up the next trap line.

We came around and asked if we could buy a couple.

He said, "Sure, take 'em and keep them." He had a big deep-eyed face. Loved to talk. Wouldn't take any money. Ed Pond of Branford. On a good week, he catches two or three bushels—a hundred lobster—a day. Lobsters like the Thimbles. "The islands give them good holding ground," said Ed. "They like to move around to the lee side of an island in a storm. Then they pot pretty good."

Hence the derivation of Pot Island.

We said thanks.

He said, "Sorry there weren't more, but they'll give you a good taste."

Amen to that. With a bucketfull of lobsters in fresh sea water on deck, we swung about and pointed *Nimble* down the coast. It was a brilliant day, with a southwester buzzing through the rigging.

In the early days, five- and six-foot lobsters were caught in the Sound. Today, they range somewhat smaller, but any lobster is an interesting vehicle. The North American catch amounts to about seventy million lobsters, a fair harvest from the sea. Some of these are the recently discovered lobsters who colonize the outer edges of the continental shelf, fifty miles from shore, huge ones—averaging six or seven pounds. But most of them are like ours, inshore lobsters, going on eight years old, weighing about two, two and a half, three pounds. Ninety per cent of all inshore mature lobsters get caught each season.

Luckily, the female lobster is up to the replenishing. She gets—through a ritual courtship dance—a sac of sperm from the male lobster. When she lays her eggs, *she* mixes the sperm with the eggs and fertilizes all seventy-five thousand of them. They float to the top, little skeeter-size infants who eat plankton, get eaten themselves (one per cent survive) and split out of their skins three or four times a year. They soon sink to the bottom and stay there the rest of their lives. They generally swim forward. When needing to swim fast, they buck backwards with jerky movements of the fat tail.

The adult lobster's molting slows down to once or twice a year; they grow 15 per cent with each molt. As the shell splits, the lobster, his claws preternaturally shrunken, extracts himself, with claws intact, from the old shell. The claws quickly swell up to a larger size than before. The new shell hardens and he's off again, hunting fish and bottom carrion with his sense-hairs on his feet, his substitute for smell.

The lobsterman who takes a lobster from the pot pegs the lobster's large gripping claw with a wooden wedge, or closes it with a rubber band. In either case, the lobster can't use that claw. A two-pound lobster with an active gripping claw is capable of snapping a small human bone, like a finger. Luckily, the lobster gets out of the way of man in the water faster than a man can move. But I once saw a lobster snatch hold of a man's calf on a dock. The man did the most interesting free-form dance for about twenty seconds until someone threw him down on the dock and stepped on the lobster, hard—the only way you can get the *Homarus Americanus* to let go.

Nimble, with her load of lobster, was now off Sachem Head, (point 21, map 5), just beyond the Thimbles. Sachem Head is one of the more picturesque points on the Connecticut shore. It is a big rocky point, split by a small, Maine-like harbor, where Sachem Head Yacht Club lies. We passed a couple of Lightnings from the club playing tag off Nun "20" in front; learning to be future Sound champions.

We were about to go into a new section of our itinerary, the Outer Sound.

Bill plotting courses en route to the Thimbles. (GEORGE WILKINSON)

Anchorage in the Thimble Islands. (GEORGE WILKINSON)

≈≈≈≈≈≈≈≈≈≈≈≈≈≈≈≈≈≈≈≈≈≈≈≈≈≈≈≈≈≈≈≈

CHAPTER SIX

THE OUTER SOUND–MATTITUCK AND THE CONNECTICUT RIVER

≈≈≈≈≈≈≈≈≈≈≈≈≈≈≈≈≈≈≈≈≈≈≈≈≈≈≈≈≈≈≈≈

(DAY 7)

At noon we passed the imaginary line into the Outer Sound, narrower than the Middle Sound: at the Connecticut River, the width of the Sound has come down to about six miles again. This is the section of the Sound that meets the sea as the sea washes in from Nantucket and Martha's Vineyard and around Block Island.

The Outer Sound offers fine rewards: beautiful, serene, rich Fishers Island; Mystic seaport; Gardiners and Peconic Bays before the forks of Long Island (over fifty harbors); and, not least, the long reaches of the Connecticut River, where we were heading.

The white octagonal lighthouse at Falkner Island slid by in the distance to starboard. To port, a whole family out in a Lightning was

45

headed into Guilford (point 23, map 5), just past Sachem Head. Wilk shot them with his long lens, and the mother aboard adjusted her sunhat. Guilford is a hard entrance to make because of the rocks; if you're of a mind to see pre-Revolutionary homes, this is the place to go, though. The town is lovely, unspoiled, and has a marvelous pre-Revolutionary feel to it, even now. There are a number of houses preserved from the 1600's and 1700's, including the Lyman Ward Beecher house. He was the father of Harriet Beecher Stowe, who wrote *Uncle Tom's Cabin* and became "the little lady who started the Civil War," as Lincoln put it.

To the west of Guilford is West River (point 22, map 5), with a high-tide shipyard, Browns.

We took down our sails just off Nun 14 outside Madison (not a port, just a town ashore) and tried out Wilk's underwater camera. And we played with the jellyfish. This was the first we'd seen of them, although they drift through all parts of the Sound. These were a pink jellyfish, known as the red Arctic jellyfish. In her excellent book, *The Outer Lands,* Dorothy Sterling tells us that this jellyfish has a sting that is mildly hurtful. We watched one and it seemed more cute than dangerous. It raised its mantle like a delicate Elizabethan lady raising her skirts to cross the street, and then dropped it again and whooshed ahead three or four inches. A series of long streamers went curling down into the water, sort of like long fingers of protoplasm. The mature jellyfish often shelters minnows in those arms, keeping them safe from larger fish who cannot swim in without getting fatally entangled.

Each arm has a bunch of tingling stinger cells that you don't want to mess with barehanded. But we picked one up on a paddle and put it in a bucket, the better to watch its little dance. The thing feeds as it pulsates, straining plankton through itself in its swimming motion.

There's a Portuguese man-o-war jellyfish (we saw none this trip) that carries a bulging sail atop itself (actually a gas-filled skin), far more dangerous than the red jellyfish. An eight-inch-long man-o-war might have stinging tentacles one hundred feet long trailing behind and beneath in the water. Swimmers have become quite ill after tangling with these coelenterate warships. Their tentacles, even dried flat on the beach, can give you a severe burn.

On *Nimble,* we were right across the Sound from Mattituck (point 20, map 5), the only harbor into which you can take anything bigger than a dinghy along forty miles of Long Island's north shore from Port Jeff to Orient Point.

The last time I got into Mattituck was at night, a memorable experience. I had just bought *Nimble* and was moving her out to Three Mile Harbor, where I had arranged to keep her. We had a great sail from Mamaroneck—a beam reach at speeds from six to twelve knots. We coasted in toward Port Jeff and I suggested we might make it to Mattituck by evening. I was soon to learn: Never pass Port Jeff to make Mattituck in the evening.

As the shore lights started to go on, I picked out what I thought was the four-second Mattituck flasher light, and we headed for it.

We got to the place; instead of the lights of Mattituck, we were amongst a bunch of barges. We had come to Jacobs Point, an offshore oil tanker depot. The flasher was going every five seconds instead of every four. We located Mattituck down the shore; it had a considerably dimmer flasher. At that point, two things happened. The tide turned and the wind turned. We started the engine and got a nowhere response. Something was strongly wrong with it.

We spent six hours sailing to Mattituck, three miles away. A heaping sea swell came in from The Race; we fought like Cape Horn sailors to keep the boat from losing ground against the shore, occasionally winning a few yards. The waves broke over our bows and the wind howled. It was sheer frustration—a cold, dark, wet hell—all because I had been careless.

There were three things I should have done. First, made careful plotting to Mattituck while there was still light and I knew where I was. Second, checked the characteristics of the shore lights in the *Light List,* a booklet that everyone should have aboard. The *Light List* would have told me that, yes, there is a strong flasher going in the barge area, but that beyond it, weaker, is the Mattituck flasher. Third, I should have timed the flasher carefully. I have since gotten a stopwatch for the purpose.

Mattituck Creek is rather narrow and winding, a dredged stream with commercial yacht docks lining it all the way back to the little basin at the end, a mile and a half or so up the river. There's a park with picnic tables at the town waterfront and plenty of marina service. In case you don't have plenty of power, there is a minus: a four-knot tide running against you when the tide is outgoing. Hundreds of fishermen—charter boats sixty feet long, outboards sixteen feet long—lie in Mattituck and fish the rich waters outside.

Back to our cruise.

On *Nimble,* this seventh day, we were underway toward the Connecticut. We came past a couple of Lightnings full of kids, moored together off the shore, just as if they had been on bikes around the neighborhood. A great way for kids to live.

2:00 P.M.: We passed Hammonassett Point, with Clinton Harbor (point 24, map 5) behind it. Clinton is a nice, recently well-dredged harbor, the pick of the ports between Stratford and the Connecticut River. Beyond Clinton, Stone Island Reef breakwater runs out about a mile or so from shore; it can trap you on an inshore tack if you don't watch for it.

The wind strengthened. Small craft warnings flew from the mast ashore on the point; the bowl of sky was fresh and clean. Outside the Clinton breakwater we picked up a forty-foot sloop trailing a dinghy, moved up to him and took his picture as we went by. We entered him in our book, *Bigger Boats We Have Passed*. The wind was blowing away now at a steady twenty-five, and we were logging seven plus, not bad for a thirty-footer with a full load.

We next passed Duck Island Roads (point 3, map 6), formed by two breakwaters in a V-shape, intended as a yacht and commercial craft haven. Duck Island Roads is recommended only if it is as far as you can get. I have spent a very unquiet night in it, rolling in an uncomfortable swell caused by a Long Island thunderstorm overhead. I would pass Duck Island Roads by, except in an emergency. If possible, I would go to the harbor of Westbrook (point 4, map 6), behind it. Recent dredging has made Westbrook into a reasonable place to stop if you have to, with marinas, grocery stores, etc.

We spotted the Orient Point-New London ferry: the second of the two main ferry lines across the sound. (There continues to be loud loose talk about bridging the Sound at this point. This talk never includes a reference to the possibility of increasing the ferry service, which seems to me a better solution.)

We now approached the Connecticut River, made a left past the big Saybrook breakwater light and motored to Old Saybrook (point 5, map 6), the first of the ports on the river. Terra Mar Marina here is something that one just must see.

It is a high, glass-fronted "boatel," the whole luxury bit at the waterside, Florida in the Sound. Here one of the greatest collection of powerboats in the Northeast with more comings and goings than the revolving door at Gimbel's during a sale. There are three pools in front of the marina, plus a slew of cabanas. One pool is for kids, one for singles, and one for marrieds. Every six feet there are outlets for the man who lives by electricity.

We tied up across from a powerboat named *Quixotic*. Life aboard it seemed quite normal for this marina. Dad was evidently at the office for the week, but his family was holding the fort. Cocoa and Brindle, the poodle and the basset, were romping on and off the stern (the yacht was stern to the dock), aided by a special dog-stool set on the dock which let them aboard at will. Mother was on the phone to a friend. We could see her gesturing away in a thirty-minute talk. After the call she set her hair on the afterdeck, facing the dock. Then it was dinnertime. The Mrs. left, resplendent in a pants suit, for the cocktail lounge in Terra Mar.

We took showers up in the marina, threw laundry in the laundromat, and Judy set out steaks on our Aqua Barbeque grill. Steaks were done to a T and corn steamed in the big boiler.

While we cleaned up after dinner, there was constant turning on and off of engines round about to charge batteries. And televisions crackled; some of the TV masts seemed to rake higher off powerboats than *Nimble*'s mainmast. It wasn't peace and purity a la coast of Maine, but interesting nevertheless.

Up the line from Cocoa and Brindle was a Lhasa Apso, with hair in its eyes, blinking adoringly at its young mistress, who was wrapped around a fishing chair reading *Vogue*. Inside a glass-enclosed cabin, further toward the marina office (where uniformed dock attendants are stationed), a man in a yachting cap was standing alone, looking out toward the sea, cocktail in hand, saying "Quack! Quack-quack! Quack-quack!"

Up at the nightclub in the base of the boatel—the heavy beat of rock music. The girls in the lounge were dressed to the teeth. The men wore their yacht club T-shirts under their jackets. On television over the bar, President Nixon was speaking to three caged astronauts (we had gone into cruise orbit the day they went into their moon orbit). There were no tables next to the dance floor to be had, we were told. Perhaps it was because Wilk had a Lhasa Apso haircut or because of my two-day beard, two-month sideburns and battered captain's hat. Anyway, it was fun to stand and watch. We finally got a table in the bar, had a beer and then tottered back to the *Nimble*.

A ninety-footer, the *Sojourn*, a sort of junior-Onassis-sized motorboat, slipped in to the outer dock in the evening light. Two uniformed boat ushers tied her up, erected a collapsible tea-cart, and headed off for the shops that were still open in the marina. They came trundling back with the cart a few minutes later with some brass snaps, a can of oil and Worcestershire for the Bloody Marys aboard.

Having had our look at grandeur, we were off for a quiet anchorage, Lord Cove.

We motored by the New Haven and New York railroad bridge to the channel leading into the mouth of Lord Cove behind Calves Island (point 6, map 6). Lord Cove is one of the ten or twelve fine gunkholes within the first forty-five miles of this navigable river. The Connecticut is a miniature Sound within itself, rewarding those who have time to work its shores and secrets.

We motored up the channel through the middle of the cove, which is unmarked, then puttered to the big inland lake, using our depth finder. The extent of Lords Cove is considerable. *Nimble* draws only two and a half feet, so we had no trouble crossing the cove to where Lord Creek comes in. As we approached the place where the creek widens, we knew we were guaranteed solitude. Such little creeks off the Connecticut River are nearly the surest places on the Sound to have to yourself.

You could spend a week on the Connecticut. It is a fine river; you can go all the way up to the head of navigation at Hartford, the state capital, forty-five miles from the sound. The town of Wethersfield, which is forty-two miles from the Sound, has an attractive, nearly landlocked harbor. This is probably as far as even a shallow draft powerboat ought to go, because there's not much in the way of gas north of Hartford. There are several places of interest closer.

First, there comes "new" Saybrook, with its sheltered Ferry Point Marina (point 7, map 6) and then comes what, by concurrence, is one of the most beautiful town anchorages on a Sound cruise: Essex, well over six miles above the mouth, and three miles from Calves Island outside Lord Creek. You can anchor off all by yourself behind Nott Island (point 8, map 6), across from the town and dinghy over to Essex (point 9, map 6), or go up into North Cove to what is a very pleasant, tasteful marina, Essex Island Marina, and walk to Essex from there. The town is probably one of the least commercial, certainly most congenial, places to walk around that you'll come upon in this itinerary—Martha's Vineyard and Nantucket not excepted. You can tie up at the Steamboat Dock, near where the *Oliver Cromwell,* the first ship of the Continental American Navy, was built in 1775, and have a look around the Griswold Inn, adjacent, which goes back to 1776. It has a fine restaurant and cocktail bar.

Another mile up, you leave Brockway Island (point 10, map 6) to the left, and to the right the entrance of Eight Mile River that shortly leads into Hamburg Cove, another of the fine gunkholes on the river. It has its own yacht club and grocery.

About one mile and a quarter above Hamburg Cove, on the same side of the river (east), is a not-easy-to-find, unmarked entrance to Selden Creek. It looks like a marsh entrance and is just above a high cliff at the river edge.

The creek widens and gets high-sided, with trees nearly bending over it. It's like going up a hidden stream of your childhood, with a secret behind every bend. Anchored fore and aft in the creek, you can go to bed listening to the birds, the sighing wind, the run of the water against the hull in the imperturbable quiet. It's as if you were in a dense forest, and no one could blame you for coming on deck to look ashore for a few Quinnipiac Indians.

Another chance to explore on the river is the dinghy trip into Whalebone Creek, a couple of miles north. Here, you can walk through the fabulous public grounds of Gilette's Castle, just above Whalebone Creek, and watch the little six-car Essex-to-Hadlyme ferry go across to the base of the castle.

I once had an experience that endeared the Hadlyme ferry to me. I was directing a small green Hudson Hornet somewhat over the speed limit along the Connecticut Turnpike outside Hartford. I had just pulled out into the middle lane (the highway wasn't divided then) to pass, going over a solid line to do so, when my passenger, who was the same Bill Hazen now aboard, said "There's a cop. He's coming after us."

I hastily swung off the highway at the first right. Out of sight of the highway I had another look at the highway map. There, down the Connecticut River, was a ferry! We drove down, got to the marked landing and waited. And here she came, all forty feet of her, looking like something out of another century, the six-car Hadlyme ferry. We crossed the river hoping that the police at the Hartford Bridge, who by now had instructions to keep an eye out for a Green Hornet, would soon think of other things.

Above the Hadlyme ferry, there is yet another place worth a visit: Salmon Cove. It's another creek and another cove, even more winding and secret than Selden.

We were saving all of these things for another time on *Nimble*. We got up to a breakfast of fresh oranges, bacon and pancakes, sharing Lord Cove with only one other yacht. We took off under power, coasting down nicely with the tide into the Sound.

As we slid out of the breakwater, a rough looking sky lay overhead, gray and ragged. It was day eight of the cruise, and we planned to cross to Shelter Island, eighteen miles away on Long Island.

The Sound outside was rolling and the wind came in from southeast, sweeping across the sunken land bridge that forms The Race, which has a fierce foul tide.

We shot for Plum Gut, the slot in the still visible parts of the great land bridge that the great glacier had formed. The Gut between Plum Island and Orient Point is a tough tide run. Luckily, we were hitting it at high slack, according to plan. *Nimble,* nevertheless, pitched and rolled in the beam sea. Rickie was getting whiter and whiter as we closed in on Plum Gut.

Plum Gut Light stood out like a medieval castle, besieged by blinking armored waves, reflecting the dull light of the heavens. Rags of sky were blowing by and overhead, a hint of sun waxed and waned to nothing time and again. *Nimble* rolled like a crazy ferryboat. Rickie turned from white to green.

The Gut tide was slack but even then the tossing pony manes of the rips boiled around us, sucked and made squashing noises against the hull, eddying so hard that our speed was cut way down. There is nothing like water turbulence to kill hull speed.

We broke past Orient Point ferry landing (point 18, map 6) and sailed into Gardiners Bay proper, heading for Coecles Harbor on Shelter Island (point 19, map 6). We had come through the land bridge now. There was nothing to port between us and the Atlantic, except Block Island, and that was too far off to do much good. We tried to stem the tide of green pallor across Rickie's face by applications of Dramamine and succeeded when she finally fell asleep halfway to Coecles Harbor. *Nimble* still wallowed shamelessly.

We finally got Gardiners Island between us and the Atlantic; then we were home free, coasting in to Coecles. We had been closely followed across Gardiners Bay by a Tahiti Ketch which had no business keeping up with us but did. As she drove by us in the harbor entrance, we discovered her secret. Her motor was putt-putting.

We were in the smooth, ample waters of Coecles. *Nimble* chugged into place for anchoring. We splashed the anchor down in the unspoiled cove behind Sungit Point, the best place to lie. We were glad to be in harbor.

Lobsterman hauling traps off Thimble Islands. (GEORGE WILKINSON)

A tack past the light at the entrance to the Connecticut River. (GEORGE WILKINSON)

~~~~~~

CHAPTER SEVEN

THE OUTER SOUND—SHELTER ISLAND AND THREE MILE HARBOR

~~~~~~

(DAYS 8 AND 9)

Shelter Island is a big Rorshach ink blot dividing Gardiners Bay from Peconic Bay. It has at least three good harbors on it, and a dozen more surround it on the shores of Shelter Island Sound—the channel around the island. You could spend two weeks circumnavigating Gardiners Bay, Shelter Island Sound and Peconic Bay. Aside from the main towns at Sag Harbor and Three Mile, there are nearly fifty small harbors here. This comprises a *third* of all the recognized harbors for the entire Sound.

On *Nimble* in late afternoon in Coecles Harbor, however, we seemed to be isolated from all this. Coecles is so large that the entrance becomes indistinct enough to give that relaxed, "this is our lake" feeling. There were only one or two homes visible ashore.

The Tahiti Ketch, which had come in with us, was lying ashore, not far off. I decided to row over and ask them if they had had their engine on the whole time they chased us.

I was welcomed aboard by an all-male, very gay crew and was so flabbergasted at the festive reception replete with drinks and before-dinner snacks that I completely forgot to ask about the engine. That's one of the fascinating things about cruising, the people you meet.

I rowed back to *Nimble* for dinner, and we settled down for serious eating with Bea handily coming up to snuff as a gourmet cook, out of cans; we hadn't been to a store for three days. (See her menu advice in an appendix to the book.)

Clouds along the horizon turned pink as the sun went down. Tomorrow was to be Bill and Judy's last day aboard and they packed their gear in preparation.

In the last light of evening, I saw a roundish object, a beer can not fully sunk, come in with the movement of the water. I had just been reading *The Frail Ocean* by Wesley Marx. "It may be difficult for us to accept that our progress may mean death to the ocean," Marx wrote in his opening chapter. He is right. Not only can we be faulted for fouling the oceans directly (Thor Heyerdahl, the *Kon Tiki* man, sailing in an Egyptian reed boat from Africa to the Americas, reported he saw acres of trash far out in the Atlantic), but we can also be faulted for failing to see what our treatment of the land can do to the sea. Biologist Paul Ehrlich has written, in *The Population Bomb,* that the continued use of pesticides ashore can kill off the sea organisms, beginning with plankton, *in this decade.*

Instead of killing life, man could cause more life to grow in the sea, by feeding it the right things. We may not know what stuff to put in the sea, but surely it is no more difficult than obtaining the composition of moon dust, and much more important to us. Marx again: "In the marine realm, opportunity and calamity are not far separated."

The sun came up bright in the morning of day nine. As the sun shot higher, the clouds scattered, and a deep blue sky held sway. The northeast wind was in our teeth as we ran out of Coecles entrance into Gardiners Bay. We were to circumnavigate Shelter Island, a seventeen-mile run in Shelter Island Sound, then head for Three Mile Harbor. We had a couple of intermediate stops in mind, so we took off while the breakfast dishes were still being bagged (always paper dishes on *Nimble*—technology's most useful gift to cruising). Onshore, a clam digger was scooping shells from the shallow water into a floating basket with an inner tube.

To our right, coming out of Three Mile Harbor, was the summer cruise of the Off Soundings Club, 250 strong. Off Soundings is none of your bar-and-beach yacht clubs; mail in your application and you join the two big yearly cruises. There's a race every day and then, at night— a different harbor every night for three days—they anchor, play banjos and guitars and row in to the host yacht club to hear who won the prizes that day.

We watched them come at us: big slick yachts, little jaunty ones, a single sail cat rig, a big Dutchman with leeboards, yawls and ketches, sloops and schooners.

They were headed for Dering, where we were also going.

We traveled with the leaders of the fleet up the channel between Orient Point and Shelter Island. We passed the anchorage at Long Beach (point 20, map 6), the town of Orient (point 21, map 6), Gull Pond (point 22, map 6) and then Greenport, the biggest commercial fishing port on Long Island. We ran into Dering (point 24, map 6) with a big schooner on our tail; she was traveling like blazes, pointing as if she were a six meter instead of a big two-masted hull. We dropped anchor with the vanguard of the fleet off the Shelter Island Yacht Club. Bill and Judy were rowed ashore. Small dinghies from the fleet piled in to a well-deserved lunch after a morning of racing in sun and rain. The women in the dinghies were deeply tanned, with wild, short-cut hair, while the men ran the gamut from lean junior copy writers to buoy-shaped corporation president types.

Bill, as a parting gesture, left us his Rebel and one of his poles. Wilk was now using the pole to fish up flounder and whatnot from the bottom. He soon had three flounder, one blowfish and one green crab. He had them all in one bucket—an aquarium. The green crab kept hitting out at the fish with a sort of peevish backhand, refusing to use its claws except to swat. The blowfish, with its top-positioned eyes like a pair of pilot's goggles, turned pale with rage and then back again to dark, mottling in agony at having been cast in the same bucket with a couple of mud-lying flounder. The flounder flexed their tails in quick upward motions and flitted around the bottom perimeter. Their agitation at last gave way to lassitude, and they let themselves be flipped around like leaves, one side white, one side grey.

We decided to try them all for lunch.

When it comes to food, one of the handiest cruising books is the extraordinary *Stalking the Blue-Eyed Scallop,* in which Euell Gibbons, who could best be described as a "survivalist," tells how to catch, strip, cook and eat waterborne fauna. Gibbons says that the blowfish is an offshoot of a tropical family, come north to delight us. The blowfish puffs itself up when caught—or if it doesn't, can be made to when tickled in the belly. It is now being recognized for the delicious, if ugly, morsel it is. Euell says blowfish will gang up on a crab. One will engage the crab frontally, while others bite off its legs from the flank, one by one. Then they turn it over and eat it out of its shell.

We cleaned the blowfish by turning it inside out, a la Gibbons, and pan sauteed him, a la Wilk. We took Gibbons' word that the green crab was edible and put him in the pan too. The French call him *crabe enrage*. He will go after a man in the water—the feistiest of the feisty crab family. Flounder are so commonly caught and eaten that Gibbons doesn't even bother to talk about them, but we sauteed them anyway. They were all delicious.

We sailed off anchor (motor off anchor in front of such a fleet, never!) with a real northeasterly weather coming on. The breeze freshened in flashes, giving us the staggers as we accelerated around Shelter Island.

We were passing the harbors on Shelter Island Sound like so many watch-ticks: Mill Creek (point 25, map 6), Town Creek and Jockey Creek (Southold) (point 26, map 6). And so past the narrows between Great Hog Neck and Shelter Island, we turned east with the shore of the island, leaving to starboard the gap into Little Peconic Bay. We also bypassed the north end of the Shinnecock Canal (point 34, map 6), leading to the south shore of Long Island.

To starboard a bit further on as we turned was Noyack Bay and the long finger of Jessup Neck, one of the most beautiful stretches of land on the itinerary.

Jessup Neck is a wild bird sanctuary. You can slide in there with about three feet at the base of the neck in Noyack Creek (point 35, map 6). It's a wonderful couple of hours' stroll out to the tip and back, especially on a weekday when there are liable to be few others.

We now headed into the strait between North Haven Neck and West Neck Harbor (point 38, map 6) on Shelter Island Sound, a scarce four hundred feet wide here.

West Neck Bay (point 37, map 6), a long way—almost two miles—up West Neck Creek out of West Neck Harbor, is the most remote and satisfying harbor in Shelter Island Sound. You can go all the way with six feet draft.

Sag Harbor (point 43, map 6) is not an easy port to get into (there is a nasty set of unmarked rocks right outside it, north of the light; I once left a bit of *Nimble*'s fiberglass skin there), but it's an interesting town —with its small and large colonial, Revolutionary and 1800's houses. The peaceful streets remain much the same as when whaling crews and captains strolled them. (Melville, in *Moby Dick,* has a sailor known as "Sag Harbor.") After Nantucket and New Bedford, Sag Harbor was the biggest whaling town. I rode down two blue whales once off British

Columbia. The flukes were nearly as wide as our outboard cruiser was long. We were so close I could clearly see the barnacles on their backs. I had absolutely no desire to put an iron shaft into one of those huge, barnacled islands of flesh.

We drove *Nimble* past Sag Harbor right at Mashomack Point (point 40, map 6), where there's a little creek on Shelter Island.

I've rowed up Mashomack Creek in a dinghy into the marshes there, all privately owned by a hunting club, but not patrolled vigorously. The creek makes a great ride back out in the dinghy on an outgoing tide, or, if you want to splash over and swim up it, as Bea and I once did, you'll get a grand free float back. The creek's water is guaranteed to be ten degrees warmer than Peconic Bay itself.

Nimble rounded Mashomack Point, but we were having no luck with the wind. It was going northeast against us, so we sailed with much tacking. Ahead of us now was Cedar Point (point 39, map 6), a lovely place for a swim. And that was just what we were intending to do.

We headed for the calm water of Cedar Point while being overtaken astern by a beautiful white yawl scratching out a white chalk wake, bearing up proudly under the pressure of the wind, fifty feet of gold-plated pride. She had the bearing of a certified first settler, though our trimaran had longer historical and genealogical antecedents by far.

Cedar Point is a public park, one of the few available to yachtsmen on the Peconic, a sandy hook of land, like a miniature Cape Cod; its arm would keep us from the sea swell in Gardiners Bay beyond. The end of Cedar Point is graced by a gorgeous Victorian lighthouse, abandoned, supplanted by a single automatic flashing light pole beside it.

We now slid into the beach at Cedar Point, putting one of the hulls on the beach. The sand falls off steeply due to tide action so we could dive off the stern into six feet of water.

We put on masks and snorkled around a bit, looking for "conch" shells. Not finding any, we lay around on various parts of the ample deck and sunned outselves. It was a quiet, contemplative time. The waves lapped at the shore and at *Nimble* equally, and the sun took itself slowly down over North Haven.

By the time we had had dinner, darkness was coming on. With it came a sifting of heavy droplets that went from mist to a veritable fog. In dead darkness we left Cedar Point for the four-mile leg to Three Mile Harbor. The Cedar Point flasher dimmed and disappeared behind us in the night's fog. We were out in Gardiners Bay without a light in sight.

I had enough gas for a couple of hours motoring, but I wanted to save that in case of emergency (like missing Three Mile and going off into the Atlantic via Montauk Point). Besides that, I wanted to be able to hear the water lapping against shores or rocks before they could spring at us out of the fog.

We sailed close-hauled for about an hour, as if inside a pitch barrel. There was nothing to hear or see other than an occasional flash of phosphorescence flung aside by the swash of the bows. It was now past time for a landfall. I was pinching *Nimble* to keep her speed down, wondering if I had allowed correctly for the tide that was sweeping us out toward Montauk, last stop before Spain. Were we being silently moved out to the ocean amidst warning flashes from the plankton? Wilk was probing the depths with a flashlight but the depths were as unpenetrable as the night above.

Finally we saw a glow ahead, a gauzy light. We had no idea what our visibility was. It could have been a half mile or fifty feet. We turned on the engine and went slowly toward the light. It seemed to race ahead of us. I wondered if we were tailing a freighter, headed for the Azores. But no, we were able now to distinguish two lights ashore and then more.

We got into shallow water, stopped the engine and hailed the houses. Someone stepped out on a porch. "Ask them where we are!" said Wilk. "Yes, ask them what country," said Bea.

We were at Sammys Beach, a quarter of a mile from the entrance to Three Mile.

After about a ten-minute coast along shore, we could spot the wet radiating light of Three Mile's breakwater, flashing on and off in the prescribed intervals. We puttered up the arms of the breakwaters into the channel up to Dick Sage's Maidstone Boat Yard (point 44, map 6), *Nimble*'s home yard. She nuzzled into her accustomed corner, rocking gently between the spiles. We secured her, springing her against the tides so that we could all have a vodka and tonic in good conscience. After a second one in even better conscience, we dropped off into a welcome sleep.

East Hampton (in which Three Mile Harbor lies) was once picked as the most beautiful town in the country by the *Saturday Evening Post*. The town was settled early, in the 1600's; its streets are lined with trees, or, rather, *drenched* in trees. There's a village green and graveyard beside the village pond; Lion Gardiner's tomb, a grand thing, presides over the plain headstones of the first farmers. The nicest of the East Hampton houses still have the salt-box, shingled look that suited farm people and fishermen.

Straight through the town and to the other side from Three Mile Harbor is the East Hampton beach, part of the long, long stretch along the south side of Long Island, pounded fine by the long waves that roll in from Europe. The beaches that front East Hampton (you can call a taxi and get to them for a couple of dollars from Three Mile) are as good as those anywhere in the world. On weekends, still, they are not crowded except for one or two spots.

Down from the East Hampton beaches are the Amagansett beaches, one of which, the Amagansett Coast Guard Beach, is famous for its stand-up crowd of singles doing their mingling thing. In fact, everyone is so set on meeting everyone else that *no one sits down*. This scene has caused the native baymen to call the place "Asparagus Beach."

We borrowed a car from Alan Bauer, a fellow Greenwich Village inhabitant who also keeps a boat at Maidstone Boat Yard. We were headed toward the public tennis courts for a few rounds of the game, to get away from the water for a while, to smell the roses and the trees and the grass and have an ice cream soda afterward in the proper East Hampton mode.

After our tennis, we went back to the boat yard, where Bea took a soap-and-hose bath on the unique boardwalks on top of the bulkhead. Maidstone's Dick Sage is favorably inclined to sailing hulls, and his yard is 90 per cent sail. The exception is that he has racks for storing small motor boats and a fork lift to put the boats in. It is one place where you can keep your small craft ashore and have it launched by fork lift in two minutes.

Maidstone Boat Yard is built boldly out into the water, facing on the channel; we watched the parade of yachts, the movement of the fishing boats, the play of the wind on the water and the run of the tide out the channel.

Three Mile has lots of marinas. Inside, on the channel north of Maidstone Boat Yard, is Maidstone Marina. Down the harbor there are others, including Gardiner's Marina, owned by Bob Gardiner, scion of the Gardiner family and hereditary owner of Gardiners Island. There is room to anchor a fleet of several hundred yachts behind Sammys Beach.

East Hampton is a baymen's town. Lyman Beecher was for many years the pastor of the East Hampton Village Church. On work days, if nothing else was in the wind, Beecher was down at one of the bays on the Sound side, like everyone else, extracting what he might from the sea. One day, the story goes, when he'd caught a surplus of eels on a handline, he found he was unable to carry them in the small sack he had brought. He took off his pants, tied up the legs, slipped the eels inside and walked back to his house in his skivvies.

Outside the town itself, there are freshwater ponds and broad plains of farms, both products of the glacier that heaped its pile of rock and gravel to form the backbone of Long Island. The gradual melting of the glacier spread the gravel out in long flat fields, the "outwash plains" characteristic of the country inside the Long Island beaches.

The freshwater ponds mark the sites of the last stubborn glacier blocks that stayed and melted long after the main glacier had retreated. The runoff from the huge blocks washed away the gravel and created "kettle holes," so called, from a hundred feet wide to a mile or so wide. They stand now filled with fresh water to give East Hampton people freshwater swimming away from the sea. The best living in East Hampton is on these ponds.

This living is enjoyed by Truman Capote of *In Cold Blood,* by novelist Jean Stafford, by Adolph Green and Betty Comden from Broadway and by Craig Claiborne, the *New York Times* food man, in his orchard on Gardiners Bay. Jackson Pollack lived here making his intricate flung-paint canvasses, until he was killed in an auto accident. William de Kooning still lives and works here, in a huge concrete and glass studio. There are more things in the East Hampton woods than a few germinating Levittowns. (Housing developments are beginning to creep in all around.) "Living in this part of the country," said one of the wives in town (one who deserted Park Avenue for here), "is heaven. The kids grow up with animals in a way that's very free. They're completely aware of birth and death, and have a solid connection to the land that one certainly doesn't get in the suburbs."

Ketch off Sag Harbor, Shelter Island Sound. (MORTEN LUND)

Hulls motoring out to the Three Mile Harbor Channel. (BARRY STOTT)

Evening, Sammys Beach anchorage Three Mile Harbor. (MORTEN LUND)

Bea does a dockside shampoo at Sage's Maidstone Boat Yard. Three Mile Harbor. (MORTEN LUND)

～～～～～～～～～～～～～～～～～～～～～～～

CHAPTER EIGHT

THE OUTER SOUND—ACABONAC HARBOR, GARDINERS ISLAND AND FISHERS ISLAND

～～～～～～～～～～～～～～～～～～～～～～～

(DAYS 10 AND 11)

Morning of day ten at Three Mile.

The sun rose over Dick Sage's Maidstone Boat Yard to find us ready for several more hours sleep, which we all took. The western breeze rippling acros sthe wide expanse of harbors, descending from the expensive summer cottages on the far side of Three Mile went unheeded until mid-morning, when we got up, sat around on deck and enjoyed the aroma of the breakfast bacon Bea was cooking below. There's nothing more enjoyable than breakfast in the cockpit with the prospect of a nice sail ahead.

We were going to make it into Acabonac, one of the famous creeks typical of Gardiners Bay and the Peconic. Acabonac is five miles off, and a great place to have a seafood dinner.

First we got a couple of East Hampton friends aboard, Larry and Dinah Witchell. Larry owns a house not a mile from the yard. As a consequence, he has a shellfish permit. That was number one: clams. Number two: stop at Tabor's Dock on the way out and pick up some lobster.

We got the Witchells aboard and shortly after noon backed out of the slip and turned through the gate to the bulkheads. It is worth noting that the Three Mile channel is narrow, and the underwater sandbanks to both sides are very shallow. On one side of the channel is a marshy peninsula just inside Sammys Beach. I've clumped around on this low, marshlike land and watched for razor clams and horseshoe crabs while Bea busily collected huge conch shells—the shells are a kind of whelk, not real Bahama conch, of course. Mostly they are the crowned shells of the knobbed whelk, sometimes nine or ten inches long. It is the largest of the mollusks of Long Island, a real bully that uses its shell like a hammer to crack open the shells of smaller mollusks.

Razor clam shells are like the blades of an old-fashioned straight razor: long, thin curved sheets. Occasionally you can see a live one, but you have to be very sharp to catch them. The foot of the razor clam protrudes through the open bottom of the shell and it can dig like fury. First it digs a bit, then the whole clam raises itself vertically and plop! It digs itself down faster than you can grab it. If you do happen to catch it by the shell, you have to really pull to get it up again because the digging foot hangs on by expanding like a rivet under the sand.

Horseshoe crabs are likely to be found any day in the small tidal canals cutting through the peninsula. The horseshoe is descended from the antediluvian giant sea scorpion and is related to modern scorpions and spiders on land. Happily, the horseshoe's long scorpionlike tail doesn't have a stinger. The tail just turns the horseshoe right side up if it gets flipped while ashore.

The horseshoe was the oldest animal species we were likely to see on the cruise, barring sharks. The horseshoe is 200 million years old in its present form, having outlived contemporary dinosaurs and survived the glaciers, a testimony to its hardihood and superior adaptation.

The horseshoe crab has eyes on its back (looking up from the shell); it breathes through gills on its stomach, and crushes the softshell clams it eats against the spines on the upper sides of its legs. The crabs frequently travel in pairs, with the smaller male hanging onto the stern of the female until the eggs are laid and the male fertilizes them. They scoot along on their legs like spiders and bury themselves in the sand in a wink if pounced upon (while buried they can still see you through the grains of sand).

If you throw one far ashore, it will unhesitatingly head for the water, provided it can see the sun. It has some sort of sun-compass going for it. In deep water, it can turn over and swim like a boat, shell down for speed.

The horseshoe crab was once so numerous that Long Islanders scooped them up off the beaches to be ground up for fertilizer. Now the horseshoe is relatively scarce; often they are killed wantonly by commercial clammers because they eat clams. The horseshoe crab could disappear just at the point when scientists confirm that one of the crab's fluids is a cure for cancer; they won't be able to find the last one.

We on *Nimble,* motoring past the marsh peninsula, came up to Tabor's, bought the lobster for our dinner and headed out the narrow sand throat to open water.

We motored along the breakwater, where ten or so people stood fishing. They seemed more interested in viewing the glories of Gardiners Bay outside than fishing. There was lots to see: the parade of boats coming across Orient Point through Plum Gut, the rush of the tides to and from the harbor and people swimming and sunning along the beaches on both sides of the harbor.

We moved out past the bell off the Three Mile breakwater, passing Lionhead Rock, a huge, sea-stained rock unusually high out of the water, looking as regal as its name.

Coasting southward, we turned into the narrow mouth of Acabonac (point 2, map 7), in a stiff tide, needing all our eighteen horses to keep steerage.

The tide runs strongly at any narrow place in Gardiners Bay, be it a creek entrance or a slot through a sand bank. Gardiners Island impedes the flow in and out of Peconic Bay. As in a Bernoulli tube, the speed of the water increases proportional to the impediment. I was once caught off Gardiners in a sailing kayak and had to be towed back to Acabonac by a fisherman to keep from being washed out to sea.

We had left the sails up as we motored in to Acabonac—now we cut the motor and went winging about on the mill-pond surface, just for the fun of it, like traveling through a canal in Holland. Acabonac Creek has summer places on it, but it is large enough so that it doesn't matter. The charts say three feet reported here, but I make the channel out to be better than that, probably five to six; it's at least that if not more inside, provided you stick around the channel entrance. We threw in the anchor a few feet from shore and went swimming, except for Larry, who went off with his clam rake to fetch some hors d'oeuvres.

Acabonac is a baymen's harbor. It had three or four fishing craft berthed a bit farther in from us; we could see local clammers working with baskets floating in inner tubes beside them. East Hampton takes some coloration from Acabonac. A "Bonaker" is a bayman from Acabonac and, by extension, any baymen in the area is a Bonaker. The East Hampton high school football team calls itself "The Bonakers."

By the time Larry came back, Dinah and Bea had the lobster pot out boiling; we had vodka and tonic and clams on the half shell, sensing the oncoming feast in the hot steamy smell of boiling lobster on the charcoal grill. The lobsters tasted every bit as good as they promised.

After dinner we took the Witchells ashore to a waiting car; we settled in to spend our last night on Long Island.

The morning of day eleven dawned beautifully. We figured our course to Eel Pond, sixteen miles away on Fishers Island. Here we were to pick up Sid Reichman, coming over on the ferry from New London; we up-anchored, zipped out of Acabonac on the outgoing tide and set sail west of Gardiners Island.

We had a great breeze and went hurtling up the shore of Gardiners Island, along Cherry Harbor (point 5, map 7).

In the middle of this bight is a windmill, and to the north of that a hill with a mansion on top, the historic Gardiner home. Below, cut into the beach, Bob Gardiner has dredged a harbor for his black speedboat on which he carries, legitimately, he has said, the Jolly Roger as his private flag.

Bea and I once spent an evening on *Nimble* in Three Mile with Gardiner, who is a nearly non-stop entertainer. He proudly insisted Gardiners have fought on both sides of every war and law, so that they always end up with part of the family on the winning side.

The original Gardiner, Lion Gardiner, did some good military work for King William and Queen Mary on the Connecticut shore and was, in 1639, rewarded by being given the right to buy from the Indians not only Gardiners Island but the eastern end of Long Island. The Gardiners, with all their land, weathered the Revolution by being friends to British and colonists alike. Eventually the original grant was incorporated as part of the political structure of the newly freed state of New York.

In the War of 1812, according to Bob, the British fleet arrived in the vicinity and was happily victualized by the Gardiners on their island. The fleet went on to the Potomac River and burned Washington "with Gardiner food in their bellies," Bob said. "See what kind of patriots we were?"

Gardiners Island, to this day, is a sort of small power off the coast. Bob told us that the original grant allowed the reigning Gardiner to appoint the court on the island. He said he'd toyed with the idea of setting up a big party for all his enemies, and then holding an *Alice in*

Wonderland trial at which he would preside and his enemies would all be duly tried, sentenced and in the morning, hung. He thought it would be perfectly legal. "But I could do it only once," he mused, "since naturally, after that, the right would be revoked."

Bob's big black rum-runner cruiser with twin 250-hp engines under the deck usually sits at the Gardiner Marina on Three Mile, unless Bob is on the island (he has a more luxurious home right in East Hampton). The pirate flag on the mast is registered in Lloyd's. Bob said it was legitimate, because one of his ancestors was a friend of Captain Kidd's. In fact, in 1699, Kidd left twenty-four chests of treasure on the island in his safekeeping. The Crown had given Kidd letters of marque, allowing him to privateer, but decided to revoke them and brought Kidd to trial on a trumped-up charge of killing a sailor on his own ship. Kidd's treasure became the property of the Crown. A messenger from the Crown duly arrived at Gardiners Island to claim the treasure, giving John Gardiner a receipt for it that is still in the family vault. If a receipt for Kidd's treasure doesn't entitle one to fly the Jolly Roger, then what would?

Bob has been building ashore on what remains of the original Gardiner grant there. He built a shopping center on the south shore, seventy-five miles from Gardiners Island (so far did the grant extend). The shopping center was leased to a corporation. During the negotiations the corporation wanted to know how good Gardiner's title was. Bob took the corporation people down to his vault in New York City and showed them the original deed from the Indians. It had the Chief's mark, the Chief's wife's mark and the marks of the Chief's children and an attached attest by a notary that these were indeed the said Chief, his wife and his children.

Bob Gardiner's mother, where history was concerned, had an acute, extended sense of propriety. Bill Rockefeller, the grandfather and genius of another rich clan, made his fortune selling cancer "cures." Bill's son, John D. Rockefeller, parlayed the money by sharp business practice. When Bob Gardiner, as a New York City lad, wanted to go play with John D.'s grandchildren Nelson, John, Winthrop, Laurence and David, Mrs. Gardiner said sternly, "No Gardiner will ever play with the grandchild of a gangster."

Speaking of gangsters, Gardiners Bay environs were prime grounds for smuggling bootleg whiskey during Prohibition. Smuggling was openly accepted by East Hampton's baymen; the freighters would come in to be met by the fishing boats, and the cargo transferred. The fishermen would run the whiskey back to town in broad daylight. Then came trouble. Organized criminal gangs from New York moved in. The story of how the baymen got rid of the racketeers is told in *The Great*

Bonaker Whiskey War, by onetime East Hampton resident-writer, Ralph Maloney, who is an expert on whiskey in his own way. Between bouts of writing, he bartended on the Upper East Side in Manhattan.

We on *Nimble* were clearing Gardiners an hour after our departure from Bonaker country. The wind had progressively weakened, and even holding *Nimble* way up into it, I could see that she was not going to clear the bank north of Gardiners. The bank goes way out to Gardiners Point (point 6, map 7), which is an island rather than a point, 1.4 miles north of the main part of Gardiners Island.

On Gardiners Point are the ruins of a castle. Cyrus Field, who built it, had some reason to be fond of the Atlantic; it was Field who caused the first Atlantic cable to be laid. Now his castle has been bombed to bits by Navy planes target-practicing; there are supposedly unexploded bombs on the island; no one can visit the ruins. Gardiners Point remains another example of the strangling of an island by government mishandling. It could have been an extraordinary point-of-interest stop for a day cruise from anywhere in the Outer Sound. The original Field fantasia might have been preserved, like San Simeon, Hearst's castle in California.

Facing the problem of clearing Gardiners Point, I decided to try to sneak through one of the slots in the bank between the castle and Gardiners Island being exposed by the falling tide. I sailed boldly for a slot in the bank only to be swept into the side of the bank by the current. There we stuck. We went over the side, every man and girl— all heaving while the tide went creaming by us as we stood in the slot as if hip-deep in a salmon stream. If that tide wasn't going nine knots, it wasn't going one. Finally, by grunting and full-throttling the engine, we got off. Somewhat shaken, we put back out with flapping sails to the same side we had come in on. We rounded the bell off Gardiners Point and proceeded past Great Gull Island, the remains of the ancient land bridge once extending clear across the Sound above water through Fishers Island to the mainland; it made the prehistoric Sound a lake rather than a salt Sound.

Nimble started bucking the Race tide, which, when outgoing, comes through from the Sound over the shallows of The Race *into* Gardiners Bay. With power on full, we churned through past Old Silas Rock (Silas Marner?). Hitting at slack tide is critical if you don't have a good six knots under power. I was in one race when we missed the tide; we were chasing a competitor through the gut. He made it. We remained anchored there for six hours.

As I headed *Nimble* for Fishers, a tanker came on to our right off the Atlantic. It was coming on fast. I decided to let her cross us. The move was a good one; the tanker ran incredibly fast and went churning past our bows at what seemed to be well over twenty knots. We watched her go down the shoreline. One sailboat had misjudged the tanker's speed and had inched dead into her path. The tanker swerved in a swift arc, a black Moby Dick haughtily deciding not to destroy a whaleboat. The sailboat went scot free.

Fair warning: Don't cross a tanker in the Sound without making sure you have the speed to do it. He may see you and he may not.

We headed for Silver Eel Pond (point 11, map 7), where Sid Reichman was coming on the Fishers Island ferry from New London (point 9, map 7). The only space shoreside is at the ferry dock, the Navy dock or a private dock. On a weekend, you can sneak down and tie at the Navy pier, but this was a Tuesday. I had timed it so we'd arrive with the ferry. (I carry the schedule because it is a lot easier to pick up a crew member at Fishers than to go up the river to New London to do it.) We came abeam of Race Point, the west end of Fishers, as the ferry went steaming in to Silver Eel Pond.

We waited for her to go in, discharge and then leave; then we sailed in and found Sid waiting on the ferry dock, eager to get aboard for his vacation.

It was an ideal day to make it to Bushy Point Beach (point 12, map 7), on the mainland just off the route to New London and Fire Island. Bushy Point is one of the very finest beaches on the coast, public, but rather unfrequented, because there's no road to it.

We went straight in toward the beach west of Pine Island (point 16, map 6). Pine Island is the handiest anchorage to New London, up the Thames River, just west of the Pine Island Harbor. To pick up people in New London from the ferry dock when they arrive by train from New York, anchor at Pine Island until train time. New London is the Sound's most convenient transportation center. The ferry dock and the bus and train stations in New London are just a block apart. Tie your boat to the north side of the ferry pier and wait for the train.

The Greyhound Bus Terminal opposite the railroad station has a parking lot, where for a price, you can leave a car for weeks. The Fishers Island ferry coordinates with the train and also the ferry across to Long Island at Orient Point.

New London is a sailor's town, as is obvious when you look around from the railroad station at the bars. It is also Eugene O'Neill's hometown; he courted a young lady named Beatrice Ashe on Ocean Beach, right across the mouth of the Thames from Pine Island. O'Neill made New London and Ocean Beach the setting of three of his plays, including *Long Day's Journey into Night*.

We put *Nimble*'s nose right up on Bushy Point Beach, throwing out a stern anchor on the way in (the waves were onshore). We were able to keep *Nimble* from pounding. Bea and I plunged into the surf. Then we all lay about on towels and watched the "sandhoppers": small, inch-long grasshopper-like beings without long hind legs. We had to watch closely to see how they were able to hop; they curl their strong tails between their hind legs and pop! Sandhoppers are related to shrimp, rather than grasshoppers, and can swim on their sides for a while. They're one of the few animals you see right in the surf, hopping around in the wet sand by the bushel, looking for plankton and small edible debris. Sometimes they bury themselves for the day in the sand, making little holes quite far from the wet sand. When they pop out for food hunts, they snatch plankton from receding waves.

Scientists have arbitrarily divided plankton into animals (zooplankton) and plants (phytoplankton). The name "plankton" is from the Greek for wanderer. Individually, they have a very limited mobility, usually no more than the ability to rise or sink by changing shape or by strokes of their extensions. They wander with the currents, and feed the entire marine world. Not a single living thing would survive in the ocean without plankton.

The plant plankton consist mostly of algae: small, single-celled plants that use photosynthesis to make food out of the dissolved minerals—nitrates and phosphorous for example—that abound in the seas. The two largest groups of phytoplankton are the diatoms and flagellates. The diatoms are one-celled plants which organize themselves into little boxes, "exoskeletons," to structure the material into efficient water-sucking and water-floating mechanisms. Flagellates keep themselves in the upper, sunlit waters by whipping their little arms around. Some flagellates, the dinoflagellates, become luminescent when the water near them is agitated, giving that peculiar phosphorescence to the water at night when it is stirred by an oar or a bow wave.

Some dinoflagellates are active light-seekers, having concentrations of light-sensitive cells that act as "eyes"; some also capture other plankton for food and so cross the line between plant and animal. Robert C. Cowen, in *Frontiers of the Sea,* says, "Even the experts aren't sure whether certain species are plant or animal or both."

The animal category, zooplankton, besides including the most active dinoflagellates which act like animals, also includes for-sure animals, "babies" from nearly every important group of animal and fish found in the sea. Most often the babies are in larval or egg form. Once born or hatched, they feed on other plankton.

The most numerous of the zooplankton are the copepods, which, while less numerous than the phytoplankton, are nevertheless present in staggering numbers. There are more of the single-celled copepods on earth than the total of all multicelled animals, including insects.

The total number of copepods can be grasped by a good example of their potential as food. The blue and the fin whales are the largest animals known to us. Larger than the largest dinosaurs, they weigh as much as thirty to forty elephants (think of a herd of elephants condensed into one swimming mass). It has been estimated that it takes one thousand pounds of plankton to make one pound of flesh, yet the blue and the fin whales grow to maturity feeding exclusively on inch-long "krill" copepods. In two years the whales grow to an adolescent weight of some sixty to eighty tons.

It has been suggested that such an enormous food supply as plankton might solve our world food problem. Why go hunting the whale when we could simply strain the water as he does? There are two practical answers. First, we haven't got as efficient a strainer as the whales have, and, two, we would have to strain, at a guess, one million tons of water for every ton of plankton captured, an enormous engineering problem.

From Bushy Point it is a short jump across to the main harbor at Fishers Island: West Harbor (point 15, map 7), where the town lies. Fishers is one of the must stops on any tour of this part of the Sound, an unobtrusively opulent island. We dived between North Hill Point and the big light on North Dumpling, past South Dumpling, admiring all the while the admirable view in Fishers Sound. The glacier left a lot of picturesque little bits sticking up out of the water here and there. We procceded into West Harbor to the Fishers Island Yacht Club and hung *Nimble* off its docks.

The Fishers Island fleet, at anchor, was surprisingly modest, with two or three real goldplaters. The island itself is full of goldplater people. There are five hundred year-round residents; triple that to get the summer population. You cannot buy or beg a house on Fishers. People here don't want to sell. We walked around the harbor and saw why. Fishers is a soft land, of green, of cut-grass smells, modest houses that have that bleached-shingle 1910 look (there are some grander homes, too, of course). Fishers is a tribute to nostalgia.

One of the cursed bridge plans for the Sound would have a bridge go from the mainland across Fishers, across to Great Gull, Plum Island and Orient Point. The people on Fishers may have clout enough to stop this horror all by themselves.

We wandered up the streets peripheral to the harbor and bought canned goods at a grocery store; we all had dinner at the only place open, a reasonably priced place with average food, Pequot Inn, overlooking the harbor.

After dinner we took an evening walk around the country lanes, which resemble the outer lanes at East Hampton—casual flowers, lots of seventy-year-old trees, bicycling kids, people walking, few cars.

The only place we found with any noise in town was the Harbor Bar & Inn, where there was a juke box, lots of kids, probably too young to really enjoy the peace of the island. It's not a teen-agers' island.

After a few beers at the bar there, we went to bed in *Nimble*.

Day twelve broke partly cloudy with swans in the harbor.

The swan group, led by a couple of males, was swimming through the fleet like a clutch of proud, miniature goldplaters themselves. We motored over toward them on *Nimble* and the leader came swimming at us, flexing his wings threateningly, while leader no. 2 herded the rest hastily off, single file, away from this large foreign three-bodied swan threatening the harem.

Nimble was bound for the miraculously restored Mystic Seaport. At Mystic, awaiting us, was the last example extant of an old sailing whaleship.

Cherry Harbor, Gardiners Island with wind-mill and Gardiner mansion. (BEA WILLIAMS)

Schooner close-hauled, Fishers Island Sound. (MORTEN LUND)

West Harbor anchorage, Fishers Island. (MORTEN LUND)

CHAPTER NINE

≈≈≈≈≈≈≈≈≈≈≈≈≈≈≈≈≈≈≈≈≈≈≈≈≈≈≈≈≈≈≈≈≈≈≈≈

THE OUTER SOUND—MYSTIC SEAPORT

≈≈≈≈≈≈≈≈≈≈≈≈≈≈≈≈≈≈≈≈≈≈≈≈≈≈≈≈≈≈≈≈≈≈≈≈

(DAY 12)

We bore in toward the mouth of Mystic River with a strong breeze. White flagging wavelets crested in the freshening wind like flocks of white leghorn chickens. Small craft warnings were broadcast over our weather station. Our course across Fishers Island Sound was buoyed to the teeth for good reason. To our right toward the sea we could see a fantastic reef formation. But Fishers Island Sound also has a more kindly characteristic; it has half as much tide current as The Race. Smart pilots make it through Fishers into the Sound, rather than go over The Race, whenever the tide is a factor.

As *Nimble* came streaming in toward the many-buoyed splendor of Noank, the town that is the gateway to the Mystic River, we passed

Mumford Cove (point 13, map 7) to port. It's one of the nicer gunk-holes of the Sound, where, with a good depth finder, you can go right straight on up the cove to a secluded anchorage. Off to the east in Mumford Cove is Venetian Harbor (point 14, map 7), one of those house-and-dock complexes that are familiar to anyone from Long Beach or Newport, California, but of which there are only a few examples in the East—north of Florida, anyway. Every house has its matching yacht.

We on *Nimble* headed for Ram Island, which divides the approach to Mystic River. Since the channel to the left (west) is better marked, we took that way in. The channel runs right alongside Noank, and we paid attention to our charts and scooted alongside with no trouble. We went *between* Whale Rock and shore, then swung to the right of the abandoned lighthouse on the point and made a hard left around the big Noank Light toward land. Here we passed one of the few old hulk-relics of the Sound, the *Alice Pendleton,* a 228-foot four-masted dere-lict lying on her side at the Noank Shipyard, which once turned out ships by the score, in the days of wood ships and iron men.

Just up the channel from the *Alice Pendleton,* at Noank, was a big dock to the restaurant, Skipper's Dock, the most renowned of water-side restaurants on the Sound. We had lunch in the big three-story place, rustic with really *good* food.

We came off Skipper's Dock, took advantage of our shoal draft and coasted across the Noank anchorage.

Mystic River abounds with sailing anachronisms, character boats, carefully tended. We came abeam of a gorgeous fifty-foot gaff schooner going the other way, and whisked past gaff-rigged sloops, blunt-nosed older designs. We went through the first swing bridge under sail (it was already open, as it is most of the time) and now we were in the river-narrow, edged with marinas, berths and slips. We passed a Coast Guard vessel. Every head aboard her swung as they saw us go piling ahead under sail. Around the bend, I knew, the second bridge was waiting. We dropped our sails. Here was the second bridge in front of us and a whole fleet of boats waiting to go through; the bridge opens at quarter past the hour. As we came gliding in, the Coast Guard men came gliding in behind us (they had turned to follow us) and seemed satisfied that we weren't going to ram the bridge.

The bridge broke in two parts and let the whole fleet through.

The draw is downstream from Mystic Seaport (point 16, map 7). We could see the square-rigged spars of some of the historic Mystic ships. In front and to our right was Mystic Wharf, not actually part of the seaport organization, but the place where, privately, the *Mystic Whaler,* a big old gaff-rigged schooner, is kept in readiness for trips through the Sound. She carries people on week-long or weekend trips, but is nearly as much of an historic hull as the officially preserved ships upstream.

There is a small bay right after Mystic Wharf. Then the channel cuts right across to the Mystic Seaport harbormaster's dock (Hobey's Dock). As we came churning up in our procession of boats, the young man at the harbormaster's shack asked if we had reservations—over an electric hailer. (It's usual to reserve when you want dockside space at Mystic Seaport because there are so many yachtsmen who want to come here during the season.) I said no, we did not.

I prefer to anchor upstream, in the basin, off the channel, just beyond the seaport. You can sneak your anchor in at the edge of the channel and no one bothers you, since the channel peters out right above the seaport. If you tie up at the wharves, you have two problems: first, the land tourists think you are an exhibit, and indeed you are. Second, since there is not only the hailer at Hobey's, but a second hailer further in at the *Charles W. Morgan* pier, it's noisy. The hails are given all day long along the Mystic Seaport waterfront. The upriver berth is quiet, by comparison.

We cruised by Hobey's and in front of us we could see the jut of land with the square-rigged spars of the *Morgan* and the *Joseph Conrad* directly behind. Past Hobey's in a small bay is another interesting Seaport ship, the *L.A. Dunton*, the last remaining Gloucester Fisherman, a gaff-rigged schooner with huge main boom sticking out over her stern. She carried more sail for her size than the square riggers. No one who has seen Spencer Tracy and Freddy Bartholomew in *Captains Courageous* at a tender age can ever be indifferent to a Gloucester Fisherman.

The fastest of the Gloucester Fishermen, according to Howard Chapelle's *The History of American Sailing Ships*, was *Elsie*, built in 1910 by Thomas F. MacManus of Boston. For many years she beat out the later "racing fishermen," built to race as well as fish. A Gloucester Fisherman, with all sails set, looks something like an over-canvassed sailing canoe—relatively low in the water; her huge gaff main overhangs the stern; three or four headsails burgeon over the bowsprit. She looks as if she'd capsize as soon as sail.

Off the bowsprit of *L.A. Dunton* was the village green, with a hundred people strolling, going into the little stores and the exhibits, enjoying the car-less atmosphere of a small Sound whaling port in the 1800's.

Nimble rounded the jut, passed the modern schooner *Brilliant* berthed at the end of it (donated by Briggs Cunningham, she is used for trips in the Mystic youth sea school program) and swung astern the *Joseph Conrad*, the three-master used as a school ship in Denmark until she was sold to Allan Villiers, the resourcefull square-rigger captain. Villiers saved her by paying a pittance, sailed her off with a few seasoned hands and a complement of kids. In the middle of the Atlantic, a gale whipped up and put the ship's sails aback. On a square rigger, particularly an old one, this is a dangerous situation; a fore-and-aft rigged vessel will automatically fall off but a square-rigger will make sternway and seas will start slamming her astern. The crew under Villiers took the pressure off by brailing in the spanker, the aftermost sail, and the ship swung off.

"Not bound for the depths this time," was Villiers' terse comment.

Past the *Joseph Conrad*, the main part of Mystic came into view: the shore-front, gray, clapboard and shingle houses and stores. It is in spirit, if not in actuality, the way Mystic was a hundred years ago.

The next pier up the shore belonged to the *Charles W. Morgan*. The old whaling ship made thirty-seven voyages in eighty years, some of them circumnavigating the globe. She was launched in 1841 and was still whaling in 1921. She was peacefully rotting away at Padanarum when the founder of Mystic, Carl Cutler (a Mystic resident who himself had been to sea in square riggers), discovered her. Phillip Mallory, one of Mystic's godfathers (Mallory's great-grandfather had been a sailmaker at Mystic), put up $7500 to have her towed to Mystic. She was re-rigged for another $8,000; today as we passed her they were still trying to keep the years away, replacing some of the 130-year-old wood along her sides.

We on *Nimble* continued upriver until we could throw down an anchor beyond the Cruising Club of America station; we got the dinghy down and rowed in (with laundry) to the *Morgan* pier.

The harbormaster kindly let us tie the dinghy to his dock. We piled up to the CCA building where they have a laundry and took turns waiting and washing while the rest went for the luxury of a hot shower in the yachtsman's facility next door. Then we were off through the town, through the crowds.

We wandered through the "shed of shapes" as I call it, the North Boat Shed where the old naptha launches sit side by side with deep-bellied little sailboats. In the days when yachts were scaled-down schooners, they took on the appearance of guppies. The shed also houses an early steam launch looking like a displaced miniature locomotive.

We walked down the docks to the *Bowdoin*, named for my alma mater. She was sailed by one of Bowdoin's most famous graduates, Captain Donald Macmillan; he continued taking Bowdoin boys on ecological sails to the Arctic when he was well into his eighties.

We boarded the *Charles W. Morgan.* There's something fascinating about a vessel that could cruise self-sufficient for three years, capture and process thirty to forty whales into two or three thousand barrels of oil and come back with a profit for her owners.

The impact of whaling on the New England economy was immense. The second and third largest towns in Massachusetts were New Bedford and Nantucket, whaling towns. Mystic, with its eighteen whalers, was not in the same league with New Bedford, which put out three hundred or more, nor even with Nantucket, which had eighty-eight in its heyday. A cash crop like whale oil, however, made the difference between a sleepy fishing village and a well-to-do commercial town. Mystic grew because it shared in the oil boom.

Herman Melville, in *Moby Dick,* wrote: ". . . we whalemen of America now outnumber all the rest of the banded whalemen in the world; sail a navy of upwards of seven hundred vessels; manned by eighteen thousand men; yearly consuming 400,000 of dollars; the ships' worth, at the time of sailing, $20,000,000; and every year importing into our harbors a well-reaped harvest of $7,000,000 . . ."

The eighteen thousand whalemen had to hate humdrum, household and hearth with passion enough to absent themselves for three years at a stretch, on a job that was alternately unpleasant, dirty, dangerous and boring. The accommodations were brutal. What do you see when you look down in the forecastle of a whaleship such as the *Morgan?* Narrow bunks ("You have to get out of them to turn over"), confined quarters, no ventilation other than the hatchway. The only thing they had of luxury was oil illumination, the finest. They burned whale oil for light as if they were merchant princes.

Provided one liked whale steak, one could also eat like a prince. Stubb, a character in *Moby Dick,* was a whale steak fancier, he ordered his steaks rare and oily, cut right off the whale by the ship's cook: "Well, then, cook, you see this whale steak of yours was so very bad that I have to put it out of sight as soon as possible; you see that, don't you? Well, for the future, when you cook another whale steak for my private table here, the capstan, I'll tell you what to do so as not to spoil it by overdoing. Hold the steak in one hand, and show a live coal to it with the other; that done, dish it; d'ye hear?"

R. B. Robertson, in *Of Whales and Men,* disagrees. He has a method for getting the oil out of the meat. "Hang your cut of fin rumpsteak upon a hook, preferably in a fairly warm spot exposed to the sun. Leave it there for three days. The horrid black mass you will see when you return at the end of that period may put you off whale meat for the rest of your days, but do not be deceived or discouraged. Hold your nose, cut away all the black crust and bury it deeply

far way from your house. In the center of the cut, you will find about
two pounds of fresh, juicy, oil-free fatless steak. Put this under a
scorching broiler and char it quickly on both sides. Then put it on the
table and cut from it the finest pound of medium rare steak you ever
ate."

The whale steak of an average blue whale would supply 100,000
men with steak for a meal.

The "baleen whale," the blue and the right whales among them,
were superefficient convertors of plankton—krill or brit—to prime meat.
In *The Whale Fishery of New England*, a pamphlet published in
New Bedford, the manner of the conversion is described like this:
"The Right Whale was so called because it was supposed to be the
right whale to capture. It differs from the sperm whale chiefly from
the fact that it has long strips of whalebone in its mouth which catch
the small fish for food, the whalebone serving in place of the teeth
of other species. A right whale usually has about five or six hundred
of these parallel strips, which weigh in all about one ton; they are over
ten feet long, are fixed to its upper jaw and hang down on each side
of the tongue. These strips are fringed with hair, which hangs down
from the sides of the mouth and through which the whale strains the
'brit' on which a right whale feeds. The 'brit' is a little reddish shrimp-
shaped jellyfish which occurs in such quantities in various parts of the
ocean that often the sea is red from them. With its mouth stretched
open resembling more than anything else, a venetian blind, a sulphur
bottom or right whale scoops at a speed of from four to six miles an
hour through the 'brit' just under the surface and thus sifts in its
search for food, a tract fifteen feet wide and often over a quarter of a
mile long. As the whale drives through the water much like a huge
black scow, the sea foams through the slatted bone, packing the jellyfish upon the hair seive. When it thinks it has a mouthful, it raises the
lower jaw, and, keeping the lips apart, forces the great spongy tongue
into the whalebone seive. It then closes its lips, swallows the catch and
repeats until satiated."

Until it was discovered that baleen or whalebone would build my
lady's corset, the American whalemen mostly spurned the right whale.
They could never go fast enough to catch the fin whales or the blue
whales. They were mostly after the "sparm" whale, slower, but the
most dangerous of them all. The sperm whale is a meat eater, going
after such victims as the giant squid deep into the sea. While the
baleen whales have no teeth and a big scoop of a jaw (he'd hit you
with his tail), the sperm whale has a slender, piercing lower jaw set
with teeth sharp enough to sever a leg. Used to attacking large moving
objects, it often sliced whaleboats in half, at a bite.

In North Boat Shed, there is a fully rigged whaleboat, with oars, harpoons, tub of line. It is a thing of beauty, about twenty-eight feet long, narrow, almost as delicately balanced as a crew shell. The line runs from the harpoon back to the stern post or loggerhead, where a turn or two served to brake the line and keep the whaleboat near the whale (unless the whale dived in which case the line was let out as fast as possible). From the sternpost the line went to the tub amidships where 1800 feet of line was coiled. The end was left free because the whale could, as Melville put it, "run the line out to the end in a single smoking minute . . . he would not stop there, for the doomed boat would infallibly be dragged down after him into the profundity of the sea; and in that case, no town crier would ever find her again.

"Thus the whale line folds the whole boat in its complicated coils, twisting and writhing around it in almost every direction. All the oarsmen were involved in its perilous contortion; so that to the timid eye of the landsman, they seem as Indian jugglers, with the deadliest snakes sportively festooning their limbs. Nor can any son of mortal woman, for the first time, seat himself amid those hempen intricacies and while straining his utmost at the oar bethink him that at any unknown instant, the harpoon may be darted and all those horrible contortions be put into play like ringed lightnings. . . ."

Sitting there, with the noose that could wrap around his neck idly slapping at his wrist, the whaleman was to give his all rowing in the chase. Once fast to a whale, the boat was likely to get dragged behind the whale (the "Nantucket sleigh ride") while the rope whizzed out. Each whale represented between two and four thousand dollars; each seaman's share might come to ten or twenty dollars; they were extremely loath to give that up. If you got caught in a coil, that was likely to tough luck. Conan Doyle (of Sherlock Holmes fame) once went off whaling and reported that in his whaleboat a man was suddenly caught by the line (even as was Melville's Ahab, at the end) and hauled over the side of the whaleboat in a flash; one of his friends in the boat lifted his knife to cut the line when another screamed, "Hold your hand, the whale'll be a good present for the widow!"

The excitement and glamor of it turned to butchery once the whale turned belly-up (the whale simply bleeds to death when he's landed enough). The dead whale was fastened to the side of the ship and his head severed by a crew working with sharp irons at the end of long poles. Then his blubber was sliced in strips. Sharks would attack below, and the harpooners, who were also the "skinners," would attack from above. A tackle from the highest yard let down to pull the blubber off. A whaler, such as the *Morgan*, would heel over, pulled down as if under a gale, as the tackle was winched tighter. Then, as the blubber strip pulled free, the ship would straighten, and a huge length of blubber would be hoisted aloft and stowed in the hold. This would continue until the whale was stripped. Sperm whales had their head "bailed out," the huge reservoir of pure sperm oil saved. The head and carcass were eventually set adrift.

Then the real fun began.

The blubber was minced in a scene that would make a slaughter house seem tidy and the chunks tossed into the huge bubbling kettles of the try works. In Melville's *Pequod*, the kettles were buried in the ship, mouths flush with the deck. On the *Morgan*, the kettles sit up on deck in the breeze, which may have been an advantage. The smell of boiling blubber was something so acrid and stupefying that first-time whaling seamen often got sick in the calmest water.

The try kettles boiled a big whale down to about eighty barrels of oil. To this day, whale oil makes the best candles. No wax fraction of your Texas oil well's production can come close to the fine, long-burning quality of the spermacetti candle.

We came off the *Morgan* and wandered around to the "rope walk," a long shed where the machinery for twisting individual strands of hemp into the arm-thick anchor ropes strong enough to hold a *Charles W. Morgan* in place against a surging sea have been preserved.

We scurried off to pick up our laundry, now dry and clean, and went into the Seamen's Inne, just a hundred feet behind the CCA facilities, where the whole crew dined in style. No whalesteak, but nearly everything else.

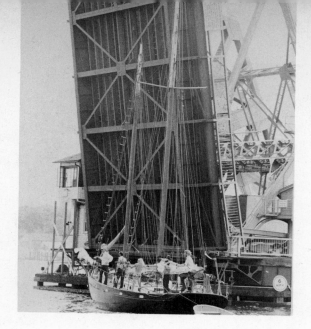

Draw over the Mystic River en route
Mystic Seaport. (MORTEN LUND)

Bowsprit of Joseph Conrad, *with* Nimble *at anchor, Mystic Seaport.* (GEORGE WILKINSON)

Rigging on mainmast, Charles W. Morgan, *Mystic Seaport.* (GEORGE WILKINSON)

Yawl off Noank, en route Fishers Island Sound. (MORTEN LUND)

CHAPTER TEN

BLOCK ISLAND SOUND—BLOCK ISLAND

(DAY 13)

We arose the next morning to tour the town: Bernie Morris and his wife Ellen were coming to join the crew. Wilk and Rickie were leaving to go West to Aspen.

On day thirteen, I planned to go twenty-odd miles to Block Island, into Rhode Island Sound and, for the first time, open sea.

Block Island sits right out there by itself, ten miles from the nearest shore. The glacier, which so lavishly dumped its moraine off the Connecticut coast to form Fishers Island, Gardiners Island and Long Island, dumped an extra lump twenty miles eastward where Block Island now is. After that the glacier didn't leave anything above water for another twenty miles, when it made the piles that are now the Elizabeth Islands, Martha's Vineyard and Nantucket.

In Mystic, we spent the morning walking through Americana: the old apothecary with its glass jugs of ancient hue, containing nostrums of dubious efficacy, the Charles Mallory rigging loft and ship chandlery (sails, buckets, boxes and bundles of undoubted efficacy) and the ship carver's shop (pop art). There was the smithy where a man banged out a red-hot harpoon on his pedigreed New Bedford anvil, and there were ships in bottles in the Stillman Museum and ships' logs in the G. W. Blunt-White Library. There we read that Albert Burrows of Mystic, 1851, had shipped as a cabin boy on the *Romulus* and complained, "For dinner each day, salt beef and pork assisted each day as follows: Sunday, "duff," flour water and grease with a few dried apples for the crew and raisins for the cabin, thrown in and boiled with the beef in a canvas bag. Monday, bean soup. Tuesday, boiled rice. Wednesday, pea soup. Thursday, "duff" again. Friday, no extras. Saturday, salt codfish.

"When there were potatoes or other vegetables on board, we had them occasionally, besides vinegar once a week and flapjacks every 1,000 barrels of oil. We had flapjacks accordingly, three times in the course of the voyage of three years."

We can see Albert now, coming off the *Romulus* at Mystic at the end of three years, tan, seventeen and *lean*. We see the owners of the *Romulus* coming down to meet the ship, joyous, prosperous and rotund.

Bernie, who had owned *Nimble* first, arrived with Ellen. We dinghied out to *Nimble*, wound up the engine, and ran down the Mystic River, past the bridges, and turned hard left past the gong off Ram Island. We were headed down east through Fishers Island Sound to Old Harbor on Block Island, twenty-five miles off.

We went along at a great rate, but were anticipating fog at sea ahead of us; the outline of the horizon was vague.

To starboard we were now clear of land, watching the breakers pile up on the shoals that extended clear across our bows from Fishers Island to Napatree Point to port. We headed boldly for the Watch Hill passage between Fishers and Napatree. The waves were tossing across the reef of little Wicoposset Island with spectacular force, sending spouts aloft every two or three seconds. The whole line of below-surface rock in the passage gave us a Fourth of July display that sent Sid to checking the charts to make *sure* we had headed between the right two rocks. There are a couple of good-sized wrecks in the passage, still visible.

Beyond us was Stonington in Little Naragansett Bay, guarded by Sandy Point and Napatree Point. (Sandy Point once hooked down and joined Napatree Point but it was washed free in the 1938 hurricane,

New England's biggest.) Inside Sandy Point down toward Napatree, you are in one of the more delightful places in the Sound. It's a large, protected body of water under Watch Hill (point 19, map 7), with the warm sand of Napatree between you and the wild waters of Watch Hill passage.

There is a lovely account of sailing these waters called *The Thousand Dollar Yacht*, by Anthony Bailey, whose home port is Stonington. Bailey records the reminiscences of the locals on the occasion of the hurricane. In fifteen minutes in 1938, the hurricane wind swept thirty-four houses off Napatree, drowned fifteen inhabitants and blew two surviving families clear across the bay in the upper stories of their houses. Four people—three men and a girl—caught out in the old fort at the end of Napatree Point, took shelter in a huge old gun emplacement, which filled with ten feet of water. They had to swim around in the emplacement with the hurricane booming overhead for six hours. They got out alive.

In the harbor by the Watch Hill Yacht Club, out of our sight, like as not, lay *Diogenes*, the big Avard Fuller ketch on which Captain Fuller, Bunny Rigg (editor of *Skipper*) and I once sailed in each other's company during an Annapolis to Newport ocean race.

Before the wind, *Nimble* was lifting under the relentless pressure of a spanking westerly. To our left was the long, long beach that runs fifteen miles out to Point Judith without a single harbor to break the shore. The surge was lifting us, rolling us with each wave. Valleys suddenly appeared under the bows, sinking us, and then the high, oncoming bulge of water would push us reluctantly heavenward.

Then the fog came on like a noose.

I've had my good fog days and bad fog days, but they are at best a bit unnerving. It was especially unwelcome today with Block Island out there out of sight before us, lots of craft in the water besides us and a minimum of navigation marks (one) enroute. We quickly laid a course, calculating on the tide run, and limbered up the radio direction-finder, aiming it for Block Island's radio beacon, which pierces fog as her lights do not.

We sailed in a silver circle of fog; it coursed with us and we with it. The wind held so we sailed, since this gave us a chance to hear. We were alone. No thrum of engine came out of the fog, no tinny call on a sailor's horn, no boom from a powerboat's fog sounder, no low beat of a trawler or tanker. Just silence. And the silver circle. We sailed and sailed into the blank future.

Bernie handled the radio direction-finder by the minute. I hadn't had time to calibrate it to the compass; there is always an rdf deviation, but I hoped it would not be excessive. The invisible radio waves looping from Block Island toward the boat, like traveling humps in an invisible skip rope, told us Block Island was out there. Straight on.

Unless I am going to anchor off and just enjoy the scenery, I prefer Old Harbor on the far side to the Great Salt Pond on the near. Though it is narrow and rather small, Old Harbor is right in the middle of the unique Victorian resort town. Even more important, it is right where you can rent a bike for exploring Block Island.

We heard the first deep sound: the Great Salt Pond horn, where it should be—off to starboard, and west of our bearing on the radio beacon at Great Salt Pond (point 21, map 7). Fog navigation, nothing to it.

Without a depth finder, what I was going to do would have been somewhat risky. We would pass close to the north end of the island where North Reef goes out nearly a mile with a five-foot depth at the end of it.

One of the most famous wrecks on the coast took place right here on North Reef. The German immigrant ship, *Palatine*, so one account goes, sometime in the early 1700's, had headed for the colonies, but the crew had mutinied and taken over the stores. They profiteered by selling them at exorbitant prices. Poorer passengers had died of starvation and were thrown over. As the ship approached shore, the mutineers got off in longboats and left the ship running dead west for the Sound; she struck North Reef. The Block Islanders, according to the custom of islanders immemorial, came out to salvage. While they found some people still alive, that didn't prevent them from "salvaging" their personal goods. When the wreck broke loose, they set fire to it and made off with the booty as the screams of those trapped in the floating pyre rang over the water.

Off North Reef, a flaming ghost ship now every so often sails in an accompaniment of shrieks and moans, according to the good, gray New England poet, Whittier:

> Behold! again, with shimmer and shine
> Over the rocks and the seething brine,
> The flaming wreck of the *Palatine!*

Whittier later admitted he used poetic license, that the islanders may just have gone out for legitimate salvage and taken survivors and bodies ashore. There is a place where the islanders are supposed to have given the *Palatine* dead a Christian burial.

In *Block Island Lore and Legend*, in tracing the history of the *Palatine* legend (which has become one of the major sea legends of the Atlantic), Ethel Colt Ritchie quotes an old islander:

"Of course, far back, there were 'wrackers' and pirates here . . . One dark and stormy night, the buzzards tied a lantern to a horse's tail and run it around and around a haystack to make it look like it was hung on a ship rigging riding in a rough sea. Any ship that saw that light would steer a like course and end up on the shore. One did. And on it was a Block Island lad who had run away to sea, but was on his way back to see his mother. The 'wrackers' were out and Bill's mother with them. The only man to reach shore was Bill and he sure was glad to see his mother until she leaned over him and said, 'Bill, you know the island rules.' And with that she up and hit him over the head with a 'pebble' and shoved him back into the undertow. Poor Bill never showed up again."

Not wanting to be salvage ourselves, we kept our depth finder going. The minute it showed shoaling, we headed straight north until it stopped. We had caught the very tip of North Reef on the depth finder; we knew now just how far north of the island we were.

We made our turn down the invisible shore of Block; we heard—we thought—the indicated whistle buoy off the east shore of Block as marked on the charts. We had a regular swell and the whistle was whoo-ing regularly, so it seemed. Ahead was a deeper, regular bellow of a horn I took to be the breakwater horn at Old Harbor (point 22, map 7). We went at the higher sound, so as to leave it to port, to stay well out from shore, but it seemed to go off before us. I got anxious about the thing. Our dead reckoning showed that we were supposed to have gotten to the whistle long ago; we really sweated it out. And finally we passed it to beam, blind, out of sight, and were homing for the deeper horn when we heard breakers and saw the white strip of water in the grayness, like a lapping rapids going across the bow. I'd done something wrong.

We sailed past a fisherman who informed us that there were shallows ahead, which, indeed we knew, and that we'd gone past the mouth of the harbor, which we didn't know.

It turned out that the "whistle" was really the horn at Old Harbor, a high-pitched mother it was; the horn ahead was the one on the southeast corner of the island beyond the harbor. We hadn't heard the black and white whistle at all. We turned around and followed the fisherman in. I should have known that no whistle worked like clockwork; what happens in fog sometimes, is that you don't think so well.

We came running into the breakwaters at Old Harbor. A greenish monster eye radiating into the fog showed us the outer breakwater and a more sedate red one inside showed us the inner breakwater. We motored toward the craft riding at anchor. Further in they lay in berths; it was a home in the fog. We were glad to be in.

It was now somewhere around five P.M., and we were hungry. Thus, we motored to the side of the wharf and asked if we could tie to. The harbormaster said that would be O.K. if we tied bow to, so he'd have room for his fishing boats on either side. We heaved a stern anchor out as far as we could, and let that hold us off; in addition, with the kind permission of our neighboring fisherman, we secured to his bow, as he wasn't going off until early morning. We decided to try one of the restaurants right near by, and trooped up to Ballard's and sat down for a well-earned, quite expensive meal that didn't live up to Wilensky's billing of "excellent cuisine," but tasted very good just the same.

I had time to ponder my navigational errors again. There is a solemn warning on page XVI of the *Coast Guard Light List* which reads "Fog signals on buoys are generally activated by the motion of the sea and therefore do not emit regular signal characteristics." Also, on page XII, "The mariner must not assume (a) that he is out of ordinary hearing distance because he does not hear the fog signal . . . or (b) that he is near to it because he hears the signal plainly."

I had been fooled because the two horns, one higher than the other, were heard at the same relative bearings as the high whistle and the first horn should have been heard. Further, I had thought that the horn on the southwest corner would be out of hearing, or at least fainter. It hadn't been.

There was another way I could have spotted my trouble. I had the radio direction-finder on, and it was indicating that it was right in line with the second fog signal, the deep horn. (I figured it was just that there was a deviation in the rdf.) If I had looked at the chart carefully, I would have seen DFS, or direction-finding signal, printed near the southeast horn. Looking this up in my U.S. Coast survey booklet (available at any chart store), I would have found that this meant that the southwest horn and the island's radio beacon were in one building and so synchronized that all I had to do was count the difference in time between hearing the radio signal and the horn signal to know just how far off it was (divide the number of seconds by 5.5 to get nautical miles).

If I had calibrated my rdf to the compass in the first place, I would have known that it wasn't deviating, but right on. Your errors of omission become helpers for your errors of commission. Sometimes I think cruising is for Christians and mathematicians only.

After dinner, we went into Ballard's dance and drink parlor. I haven't heard the like of the band since my high school friends' Dixieland Delights disbanded. It was pure hokum-jazz. Bea and I jitterbugged— that old-fashioned dance of the fifties where you actually touch hands, you know. The crowd was made up of fishermen and wives—billed, braid caps and print dresses. The bar was full of non-wived fishing types, one of whom listed heavily in our direction as we left and said, "Who ever taught you to jitterbug? Haven't seen that in years, hey?"

We dropped down onto the deck of *Nimble* and into the hatches. One, two, three and the lights were out.

In the morning of day fourteen I woke feeling that the ship was somewhat askew, as if it were down by the head.

It was, but not for long.

It came up with a hell of a sharp report.

I scrambled on deck to find that our fisherman of the night before had left, as he had said he would, and that our stern anchor had not held us off. The rising tide had jammed the pulpit rail under a beam in the wharf and as the tide rose, *Nimble* had slowly gone down by the head. The pulpit rail finally gave way and bent with a bang. Now as I looked at it, the very nose of the rail had a new, raffish, downward rake to it. Damn.

Block Island, dumped by the glacier so far at sea, has the insular mode about it—special, different, resisting change, indifferent to shore opinion. On Block Island, this mode is manifested in the way its inhabitants built the fantastic Victorian fronts to their hotels and the equally indifferent way they have let them run down. I suppose the cure of the resort was salt air. Or perhaps whiskey water. The island's fleet of fishermen—charter, private and commercial—seemed to have kept the island's reputation for hard drinking intact.

All this in spite of the WCTU statue right up the main street looking determined to erase the very island to expunge the curse of alcohol.

All of us—Bernie and Ellen, Sid, Bea and I—got on rented bikes to ride past her formidable figure. Bea and I biked to New Harbor in Great Salt Pond, the others to the old cemetery off to the west of the big pond.

Block Island, physically, has a really beguiling, moor-like, Scotch heather look; there are lots of things about the island that disturb me, though. There seems to be a junked car, a torn-down building or jerry-built house marring every stretch of scenery. Probably the island is still between economies; having given its raging youth over to the Victorian excesses of resort hotel life, it has not yet quite recovered from the ravages of the subsequent decline. It has still to assume the full sedateness of a summer resort, which is where it is now heading.

As with New York City—which can be very very nice if you know exactly how to go about handling it, but which can be rather unseemly otherwise—so with Block Island. It is delightful for those who know it.

Great Harbor, at the inner end of Great Salt Pond, has a dock area that is rather like the unkempt, unpretty commercial charter boat atmosphere of a Montauk or Sheepshead Bay waterfront, rather than that of a isolated island harborfront. Bea and I biked down to the end of the pier and looked out over the Great Salt Pond. There weren't more than a handful of boats in those watery acres, nearly two miles long and a mile wide. A great place to go and be alone if that's what you want. The crowd of yachts bordering the pier at New Harbor would hardly impinge at all on your vision if you anchored out toward the nothern shore.

We biked back toward Old Harbor and turned down along Crescent Beach. You can stop anywhere along the highway here and go over the dunes to the ocean. It is a nearly unbroken beach, three miles or so long, full of magnetite grains (iron) to create large dark drifting patches of sand against the lighter crystal quartz grains. The magnetite can be drawn from the other sand with a magnet. Once magnetite was used as premier blotting sand for quill pens. There was a scheme afoot once to mine the iron by chewing up the beach, but it came to nothing; at least this face of Block has the natural fineness nature has given it.

Block is largely glacier outwash plain, peppered with kettle holes; these depressions became the island's many beautiful and often secluded ponds.

Pipewort and arrowheads in these ponds stick their heads above water on rigid stems; water lilies float themselves; pondweeds live under water and take the oxygen out of the water with their leaves, as fish do with their gills; waterweeds float below the surface without being rooted to the bottom; small green, nearly invisible plants divide and redivide to form floating mats. Sphagnum moss, sedges and rushes join the surface mat.

The explosion of greenery turns the ponds, eventually, into bogs. The overhead mat forms an oxygen-proof cover; the fall-out below forms peat rather than bottom mud. The peat or "tug" bogs of Block Island became a valuable fuel source after most of the trees were cut. This island was heavily forested when the Italian, Verrazzano, touched here in 1524, calling the island "Claudia," a rather nice name for an island. The trees have come back in many places, but there is still a primeval, pre-forest, barren look to much of Block Island.

Adriaen Block, landing from his *Onrust* in 1614, gave the island its present name. The first Englishman on the island was John Oldham in 1636. The Indians, the Maniseean tribe of Narragansetts, killed him. Governor Endicott went in in 1658 and subdued the Indians. The Massachusetts Bay Colony gave the governor the island in recognition of his services. He sold it in turn to sixteen settlers who, with their seventy dependents, became Block Island's first families; they moved in on about three hundred Indians, who already had cornfields growing there. The Indians tolerated the whites, but not their diseases. The Indians soon died out.

The people who are slowly taking over the island today are second-home settlers here to seek refuge from the extraordinary hustle of city life. Land is now scarce and expensive.

"It is a casual kind of place," a summer resident's wife said. "You don't need a dress the whole time you're here. You just wear something clean at night if you are going to cocktails. And cocktails are always a drop-in kind of thing. You just meet somebody in the grocery store and ask them to come over later.

"It's a marvelous place for bringing up kids. What do we do all day? We go for walks, picnic on the beach, read, hike, bicycle, work in the vegetable garden, berry pick and hunt for wild flowers."

Before the wind, Nimble's en route Block Island. (GEORGE WILKINSON)

CHAPTER ELEVEN

~~~~~~

RHODE ISLAND SOUND—
POINT JUDITH AND NEWPORT

~~~~~~

(DAYS 14 AND 15)

At Block Island, this fourteenth day of our twenty-three day cruise, at noon, the fog was still out there on Rhode Island Sound, and the horns were still going. But now we saw the fog starting to lift. We backed *Nimble* out into the small turnaround space in the inner basin (point 1, map 8), and pointed out past the big red and green lights through the outer harbor north over the sea. We were headed across Rhode Island Sound to Galilee, the fishing village on Point Judith Pond.

The littlest state of all, Rhode Island, has a big coast. It begins in the west at Little Narragansett Bay and Watch Hill. Then it goes fifteen miles over to Point Judith; next east comes Narragansett Bay, twenty miles deep—a world in itself, like Peconic Bay. Next is the Sekonnet River, another twenty-mile inlet. In all, the Rhode Island coast encompasses some two hundred square miles of bays, 250 linear miles of shore and at least thirty-five good ports.

We had eleven miles to go to the breakwaters of Point Judith Harbor of Refuge. Another mile and a half through it into Point Judith Pond would put us at the docks of Galilee.

It was a raw, dark day, with a cold feel to it. *Nimble* hadn't gone more than a mile when we were right back in the fog again, with the wet mist coming in like trailing gray wash on a clothesline. We directed our attention to the rdf again and got a bearing—the radio beacon of Point Judith Light. The breeze was nosing us from abeam hard enough to give us three knots. We checked the tide current chart and it showed the tide flowing north on the flood on this side of Block (it ebbs *south*). A few boats could be distinguished by ear; they were powerboats out poking around for fish. This is one of the premier fishing grounds for charter and private fishing on the Atlantic Coast. Point Judith radio beacon, like others, shares its frequency in rotation with several stations; it came back on the air every few minutes to tell us we were all right.

Then we hit some relatively thin fog. A lobsterman was out here, circling around, picking up his traps.

"How far to Point Jude?" He guessed about five miles. "Got any lobster?" He said if we'd wait a minute, he'd give us all we wanted. So we did. We hung about until he emptied a couple more traps and then he came over and said, "Hand over your pail." We did and he filled it with shorts. We felt a little guilty, but we had had early breakfast and only scant lunch and the squirmy lobster looked so good that we decided to eat them, short or not. We thanked our man profusely, and he chugged off into the fog with a wave.

Bea tied down the lobster kettle to the alcohol stove, which she had set on deck. While the westerly drove us on and the sea swell rolled us, that lunch was cooking on deck well before we were near where the breakwaters were supposed to be.

So we ate.

And we ate. Lobster never tasted so good. We sat in the cockpit and devoured the little ones, "limb from limb," (as a Maine man would put it) and threw the carcasses over our shoulders. "Do you suppose they taste so good because they're illegal?" asked Bernie.

We were cooking and sailing, cooking and sailing into dead fog until the Point Judith Breakwater came at us out of the fog with white breakers foaming at its base, like the front of an enormous scow.

We came hastily into the wind and turned on the engine while the lobsters cooked and the crew wrestled the canvas down. We headed around the breakwater under power and found the western gap of it.

We followed a fishing boat in through the gap inside the huge angle formed by the two walls. As we made the turn, the sun came out more strongly and, shining through the fog, backlit the whole western breakwater. We could see a line of people on it: kids with poles, old men with pipes, girls, women, all walking from rock to rock piled inside the breakwater wall or standing silhouetted against the glowing fog while white and black gulls flew a patrol to meet the incoming fishermen.

It was still rolling inside: "An uneasy godforsaken anchorage for a small yacht," is what one yachtsman said of the Point Judith Harbor of Refuge. Then we were through the hole in the shore and into Point Judith Pond. It was a lot better in here than outside, calmer and friendlier.

The town of Galilee (point 2, map 8) emerged on the bank to our right. It's a jumble, but a nice jumble, chaotic with fishing masts, docks, wharves, pilings, tuna towers, whip outriggers—all these at crazy angles above the solid banks of the shore. (We could have gone up the Pond another five miles to Wakefield—point 3, map 8—the anchorage there is quieter but more conventional.)

We shoved *Nimble* into a dock at Galilee and climbed up to inspect the town—before we realized we still had a bucketful of unused, short lobster on deck. Bea decided to shell the cooked ones and refrigerate them; we deep-sixed the uncooked ones, since they wouldn't keep. We let the dozen small grateful lobsters into the tide, somewhat reluctantly, before we went up onto the huge piers again.

The waterfront of Galilee is all piers, with a ferry dock (Block Island, Providence, Newport), charter boats, fishing craft and a few yachts. Mid-town is an even half-dozen or so buildings scattered along a half mile of main street. It's a rough, unadorned town; an amalgam of commercial charter boat men, fishermen, civilians who go out on the charters and people who just drive in for a look. It's messy and unplanned. I like it. The first restaurant on the street was right across the docks from us, so we went over to see if they had some clams. They did, and beer. They also had scallops and oysters. So we had clams and beer, scallops and beer, and oysters and beer. We sat back with our bottles of "Ganset Lager" and felt great. The raw fog outside had chilled us; we were now warm.

We walked down the main street and looked at a few fishing tackle shops, a couple more restaurants, smelled the raw-sea-odor air streaming in from the Sound and walked back to the boat. A big night in Galilee. Or big enough for us, anyway.

Right in back of *Nimble*'s berth, a powerboat under construction was being finished off by a barber named Andy Ambrosia. We sat down on the gunnel at Ambrosia's invitation and found out that this was *Misty*. She was going to be a party boat, mostly tuna. More tuna are caught here outside Point Judith than anywhere else in the world. They bring 150 tuna back to Galilee every year and another 150 are boated outside the town and taken elsewhere. There are plenty of other smaller game fish as well.

Ambrosia said he takes 150 to 170 parties out every year during the eight-month season; then he goes back to cutting hair for four months. His new *Misty* was appropriately named; he said Point Judith has more fog than any place on the Atlantic coast south of Mt. Desert, Maine, and north of Cape Hatteras.

Misty was a work of art—a high-bowed, spacious hull with a dance-floor cockpit. Ambrosia figured to clear about $11,000 a year on eight months work. I asked him if he didn't get bored cruising the same old fishing grounds 170 days a year. He said, no, this was what he hoped to do as long as he could. I asked him if many people got seasick fishing and he said, only a few.

One of his friends standing nearby said, "Well, one of mine went right on the dinette the other day. The whole ocean out there and he had to do that."

I asked Ambrosia if he was going to put in radar and he said there were lots of things he wanted to put in first. One was Loran. He said that with Loran, he could spot his position to within a boat length, and come back to it the next day. This was important; if he ran into a school of fish, he wanted to be able to go back there and pick them up again.

Schooling fish, he said, often stay put or mill about slowly. They don't move more than a few miles off during the course of a twenty-four-hour span.

We learned that in the great 1938 hurricane, eighty tuna boats had been in here for the Atlantic Tuna Tournament and forty of them had been sunk. With that cheery word, we all went below to our welcome bunks.

The morning of day fifteen was cold and blowy; we aimed to get to Newport, a favorite landfall of mine—a place of architectural spectacle, the country's best collection of really wild homes of the very rich.

In preparation, I re-rigged the downhaul for the genny and working jig before breakfast (always something to do). While Bea was frying eggs below, Sid went ashore to pay our two-dollar fee for docking overnight. He came back to say that the harbormaster had said he didn't like the looks of the weather.

A couple of charter boat captains who'd been kibitzing the work on

Misty the night before were hanging around on the pier.

"You really going to go out there? Good luck!"

On the basis of the radio forecast, I had decided it would not even be worth striking the big genny, but now I got the working jib readied and we slipped out into the harbor behind the breakwater. With twelve miles to go to Newport, we motored out through the hole in the east breakwater, and it wasn't bad. The sea was giving us twelve-, fourteen-foot swells, and a stiff chop, as per the weather report. Two fishing boats that were out with us were rolling and bucking noticeably; perhaps that explained the reluctance of the experienced skippers inside to go out. Fishing boats are not made for big swells with chop on top. A sailboat, even a light displacement one like *Nimble*, is relatively comfortable under sail in this sea, while a forty-foot fishing boat is not.

Sou'west and going about six to eight knots, the wind pushed *Nimble* along at nearly the same pace. By ten A.M. we were wing and wing and the sea seemed to roll onward with us. Wind on one quarter, swells on the other, we passed Narragansett Pier (point 4, map 8) and sleighed toward Conanicut Island and Newport Neck in Narragansett Bay.

Although we were not going to go any further into Narragansett Bay than Newport this time, one could spend several weeks moseying around up past Conanicut Island: the routes are West Passage (west of Conanicut), East Passage (between Conanicut and Newport Neck) and Sakonnet River (east of Newport Neck). They are "salt rivers" leading down from the inland cities of Providence and Taunton to the sea (have a look on 353SC, the best chart for the whole region).

The best West Passage harbor is at Wickford, opposite the upper end of Conanicut Island. Here you can get your supplies at the best set of marine stores on Narragansett Bay and then go back out to the privacy of the state moorings behind the breakwaters of the outer harbor.

Apponaug Cove lies in the northwest corner and, finally, Old Warwick Cove in the northeast corner of the passage. For a rundown of the Apponaug marinas, you have to look either at the numbers on the SC chart and match the numbers with the explanations on the jacket cover of the chart (one of the handy added things every SC chart has), or you have to go to volume two of the *Boating Almanac* (a more compact format), which also details the facilities.

Above is the Providence River and the city of Providence, capital of Rhode Island. You would not want to go all the way up there unless you were sailing in to meet someone at Brown University, or wanted to do research on Roger Williams, the great and tolerant spirit who founded Providence that ". . . it might be for shelter for persons distressed for conscience." Providence is about twenty-miles up from the mouth of the Narragansett. That's a long way to go, even though Providence has a seafaring history, and even though it was once port for a hundred sailing vessels at a time and had one of its downtown buildings' walls poked in by the bowsprit of a mismanaged ship. That was long ago. Today, the closest Providence people get to the sea is when a hurricane hits—every other decade or so. Then the wind blows the water up the river and floods the town fiercely. In the 1938 hurricane, so many cars were caught in the downtown flood that the short-circuited horns sounded like an enormous, never-ending traffic jam.

East Passage to Providence:

First stop here is, of course, Newport (point 9, map 8) on Newport Neck (Acquidneck Island); next, just above on Conanicut Island opposite Acquidneck Island is Jamestown (point 10, map 8). There are moorings available from the Conanicut Yacht Club here, but the port is pretty much Navy.

Naval installations and vessels dominate the rest of the shores past Potter Cove (point 11, map 8), including Coasters Harbor, (point 12, map 8), Coddington Harbor (point 13, map 8) and Melville (point 14, map 8). You wouldn't want to stop, except in an emergency. But there is a fine anchorage, a second Potter Cove, on Prudence Island, north of Conanicut. Potter Cove is one of the most beautiful in New England, forming a nearly closed circle with a hook of sand on the outside to insure protection in all weather. There's nothing but farms ashore and a well or two, and little traffic.

Before East Passage is joined by West Passage from the west and Mt. Hope Bay on the east, there is Bristol Harbor, one of the best in the bay. This is where Pearson, one of the biggest Fiberglass yacht builders in the world, has its yards.

The third passage from Rhode Island Sound inland is up the Sakonnet River. It begins with a commercial harbor, Sakonnet Harbor (point 17, map 8), a secure, small dredged-out place with breakwaters, on the east side of the Sakonnet River, just opposite the southern end of Newport Neck. Going north, the next good harbor is Sachuest on Acquidneck Island, untenanted by commercial installations (point 18, map 8). Above this you are into Mt. Hope Bay, where you can enter the Kickamuit River to the left (a pretty good, if largish, anchorage) and see Lizzie Borden's hometown, Fall River, Massachusetts. You have now sailed right through the middle of Rhode Island.

On *Nimble* we were headed for Newport.

We were eating Ellen's lobster salad sandwiches as we scooted *Nimble* toward the now-visible surf at the bottom of the curling, vicious cliffs that face the sea on Newport Neck. A little farther in, we made out the roof line of The Breakers, Cornelius Vanderbilt's summer home.

The huge house is flanked by other, determinedly rich-looking establishments.

Newport was where the rich met to spend money in conspicuous, well-approved consumption, and *enfin*, to actually enjoy the sea breezes and the ocean of Newport. The hubbub has died down somewhat but the remains are still impressive. Occasionally there is a social affair in one of the homes where fitful gleams of the old forced-draft social fires still shimmer, reflected in dowagers' diamonds, glints of gold and sparkles from champagne-filled glasses.

Nimble came winging under Castle Hill, the promontory that towers over the narrows between Newport Neck and Conanicut Island. Skirting the hook of Fort Adams, we sailed into Brenton Cove on *Nimble*. "Newport is the most practical longshore harbor capable of holding a fleet of yachts between Stonington, Connecticut and Padanarum in Buzzard's Bay," write Duncan and Ware in *A Cruising Guide to the New England Coast*, and that is so.

Directly ahead of us on *Nimble* was the Ida Lewis Yacht Club, a set of buildings on a little rock connected by the catwalk to shore. The club is the host yacht club for the finish of the biannual classic, the Newport-Annapolis, and for the start of the blue water classic, the Bermuda Race.

It also represents the New York Yacht Club, the host club for the *America*'s Cup races held off Newport every three years or so.

My first time on the Ida Lewis Rock, the Annapolis-Newport fleet was tied here, and everyone was congratulating Irving Pratt. Pratt is one hell of a sailor; I enjoyed getting his views for *Sports Illustrated* but, in truth, I got as much of a kick out of talking with another yachtsman who was there, who had thrown his crew together a day before the race. It consisted of a girl he'd met at a party who wanted to race, an old school friend, and two office compatriots. They had sailed all the way with a cold galley, eating out of cans, drinking beer and having a ball. They finished well up in the middle of the fleet, but no one was rushing over to talk with them. They seemed somewhat out of place in that crowd of high-powered, fine-honed yachtsmen.

"Ida" Lewis herself would have been at home with the pick-up crew. She was a plain woman, and this rock was her lighthouse station. The lighthouse is gone, but her legend remains. Idawally Lewis was a lighthouse keeper's daughter, and eventually took over his duties. She *rowed* to her rescues. In one typical rescue, as reported in the *Providence Sunday Journal*, a couple of soldiers stationed at Fort Adams hired a boy to row them back from the town of Newport, on the far side of Brenton Cove. A squall came up, the boy was unable to handle the waves, and the boat turned over. Ida Lewis heard the cries and leapt out of a sick bed into her skiff, in stocking feet and jacketless. She pulled out to the swimming men (the boy had already drowned) in a hurry and hoisted them aboard. In the deadly swing of the cold, dangerous seas, she rowed them safely ashore.

An account of this exploit and a couple of others appeared in *Harper's Weekly* in July, 1969. The magazine cover showed Ida Lewis rescuing two Fort Adams soldiers. Ida Lewis became a fad: Ida Lewis hats and Ida Lewis ties and an Ida Lewis Waltz. She probably would have appreciated her postmortem tributes much more: naming the yacht club for her and the design of the yacht club's flag—a lighthouse on a red ground surrounded by eighteen white stars, one for every life she saved.

The "revival" of the *America*'s Cup came in 1958. After a long wrangle, the deed of gift of the Cup to the New York Yacht Club had been amended to allow the cup to be sailed for in Twelve Meter yachts rather than the unlimited or J-boat class that had got just too expensive. The Twelve Meter, at about sixty feet, cost what the J-boat at 120 feet used to cost. In 1958, the most exciting part of the season of the Twelves was the elimination races among the American boats. We sat in a tug off Brenton Reef in July, 1958, and watched the spanking new *Columbia* finally put away, once and for all, the gallant old *Vim* sailed by Emil Mosbacher. (Mosbacher was thereafter given better hulls, and consequently he won two later *America*'s Cup races.)

It seems anachronistic that there are still people who will put half a million to a million into a boat to win a slightly worn old mug, but there it is, considerably less expensive than the race to the moon, after all. Newport, an anachronism itself, is the place for it.

The modern display of yachts at Newport doesn't compare with the one which was put on at the turn of the century, with Morgan's *Corsair* up from his Hudson River estate side by side with John Jacob Astor's *Nourmahal,* Gordon Bennett's *Lysistrata*, Jay Gould's *Atalanta*, and so on. In those days, sixty feet was small: one writer described the scene like this: ". . . there is a continuous blaze of kaleidoscopic radiance from countless multitude of craft that lie so close that it seems as though the harbor had disappeared, then one sees the water side of Newport in its supreme glory."

Newport still has a supreme glory; her mansions. On *Nimble*, we pushed the dinghy into the water, got aboard, and rowed in to the float at Ida Lewis. From there on, we spent the rest of an afternoon walking around the fantasia of Newport Neck. There are big rich houses and little rich houses, houses hidden in trees, houses like huge rearing rocks rising from the greensward, houses like Scottish castles on the rolling moor. There are pink marble houses, graystone graybeard houses, turreted gabled houses, pillared porticoed houses.

It's a thing of the past to have ostentation with such *élan*, such un-abashedness—the landscaping is almost tropical in its lushness. The total impact of the houses and gardens is overwhelming.

Ward McAllister, the social arbiter of early Newport, was an in-spired phrasemaker ("The Four Hundred") and a practical man: many Newport squires were away making money to pay for all this grandeur and suitable male substitutes were needed for social occa-sions. McAllister helped induce the Navy to start a sub and torpedo station here, with an appropriate complement of officers and officer candidates, and thus solved the problem neatly. I don't suppose, how-ever the Navy will ever admit that its premier base in the Northeast was encouraged in the beginning as an escort service.

The Navy is still being pressed into service in later days. The Norman Whitehouses' coming-out party for their daughter, Alice, found the Navy, as requested, providing a clutch of destroyers; their searchlights beamed in to provide the illumination for the lawn part of the party.

Another much more famous Alice at Newport was Teddy Roose-velt's daughter. She came up from Oyster Bay for the big times. (She later married Nicholas Longworth, of whom Teddy Roosevelt said proudly, "We were both Porcellian at Harvard you know)." Alice was severely reprimanded in *Town Talk* (the Suzy Says of its day) be-cause Alice admitted, "I danced the hootchy-kootchy on Grace Van-derbilt's roof at Newport." She added, "You would have thought the world was coming to an end."

Town Talk commented, "From wearing costly lingerie, to indulging in fancy dresses for the edification of men was only a step. And then came a second step—indulging freely in stimulants."

As Cleveland Armory writes in his splendid book, *Who Killed Soci-ety*? "The actual . . . passing of the Old Order . . . some date with the death, in 1908, of *The* Mrs. Astor. Surely, they point out, since that time, Society has never had a leader with anything like her autocratic authority. Even in her last years, when her mind had failed, and she lived in solitary splendor in her Newport cottage of "Beechwood," she was a lady to conjure with. 'Still erect,' said the late Lloyd Morris, 'still bravely gowned and jeweled, she stood quite alone, greeting imag-inary guests long dead, exchanging pleasantries with ghosts of the ut-most social distinction. . . .' "

We reached *Nimble* again after our little tramp among the gorgeous historical stones of Newport with what one might call an edifice complex.

We phoned a taxi from the Ida Lewis pay phone, went in to town, bought steak and repaired to *Nimble*, poorer but happier. Bea got out the charcoal grill, made rare to medium steaks, and we consumed them in their fragrance as night came over Castle Hill.

Breakwater, Point Judith Harbor. (SID REICHMAN)

Galilee docks, Point Judith Pond. (SID REICHMAN)

The Breakers, Newport. (MORTEN LUND)

CHAPTER TWELVE

≈≈≈≈≈≈≈≈≈≈≈≈≈≈≈≈≈≈≈≈≈≈≈≈

RHODE ISLAND SOUND—WESTPORT, BUZZARDS BAY AND CUTTYHUNK

≈≈≈≈≈≈≈≈≈≈≈≈≈≈≈≈≈≈≈≈≈≈≈≈

(DAYS 16 AND 17)

We were now, on day sixteen, going to leave Newport country behind and tour one of the most famous sailing regions of the East, Buzzards Bay; this is the land of the steady breeze.

On *Nimble*, we got underway in front of Ida Lewis under power, wanting to get out of Narragansett before the tide really started flooding in. We aimed for Westport (point 21, map 8), eighteen miles away at the brink of Buzzards Bay.

The day was fair with a cloud-strewn sky. We sailed around the front side of Newport Neck, held in as close to the reefs in front of The Breakers as we dared, steering nearly due east across the mouth of the Sakonnet River, and so past the harbor at Sakonnet Point (point 17, map 8) by noontime. There was something of a roll, and I looked anxiously in at the old lighthouse on Sakonnet to see if there were breakers. There was an intermittent gleam of white, but nothing big.

Westport lies east of Sakonnet Point behind Horseneck Beach. It's not a good harbor if it's breaking heavily. Fortunately, the roll of the sea was moderate, so we weren't too much concerned about broaching. "Broach" describes the condition of a boat when it's been forced into a spin to either side. A *full* broach means you have not only spun sideways to the crest, but have been rolled over and capsized, a very unpleasant experience.

The good weather held. Off Westport Light, a mélange of reefs makes it advisable to dead-reckon from mark to mark and take the buoyed route in. Nothing is easier than getting lost in a piece of water. By getting lost, I mean to lose track of your exact position. Perhaps a good navigator—one familiar with the methods of the "Bible," Chapman's *Piloting Seamanship and Small Boat Handling*—would feel it a challenge to avoid the reefs outside Westport by taking the direct course to Westport Light. I'd rather go mark to mark than make the effort; I save my seamanship for occasional unbuoyed approaches to harbors.

However, in the case of "no buoys" I usually navigate myself. As Chapman says, "It is the duty of the skipper to fix the position of the ship with such a degree of precision and at such frequent intervals as is required by the proximity to hazards to safe navigation. This is an absolute requirement of the person in charge of the vessel, whether he is personally doing the piloting or not. He can assign the function but he cannot delegate the responsibility."

If you're unsure of your navigating abilities, I suggest you enroll for the Power Squadron Course nearest you. There *is* very likely a course close at hand; their instruction is invaluable.

Incidentally, I consider a pelorus, or angle-finder, mounted on a portable compass, necessary for finding correct bearings. Sighting over your ship's compass is inexact. However, a simple hand-held sighting compass will do most of the time. I prefer the Silva, obtainable through Silva Corp., La Porte, Indiana 46350 ($14.95), because you can crank declination and deviation in and take quick bearings without bothering the helmsman.

Crossing into Massachusetts, we arrived at the outer end of the buoyed approach to Westport. We turned at the black and white bell off the beacon on Two Mile Rock and made straight for Half Mile Rock further in, then negotiated the turn around the light and powered up between the beach and the peninsula on which the light stood. From there we coasted in past Nun Twelve, took the left hand channel and threw in an anchor inside an imaginary line between Can 11 and Nun

12. Here, we had been advised by Duncan (who has good sailing direction for coming in there), we were opposite what is called Cockeast Boathouse, with Cockeast Pond behind it. The tides run strongly in the mouth of Westport River, but the holding was good; I was content to rely on my Danforth anchor, which has held in incomparably worse situations, to keep us where we were.

We were actually in the village of Acoaxet (A-coax'et). The actual harbor of Westport (point 23, map 8) is a mile up the channel, just this side of a couple of swing bridges at Westport Point. Westport harbor has less current than Acoaxet, but more people on boats.

The mouth of Westport River, where Acoaxet lies, is the confluence of the two branches of Westport River, the East Branch (point 24, map 8) goes up under the bridges and contains a windy channel six or seven miles long, going to the town of Westport, Mass. The West Branch (point 22, map 8) . . . well, get out Geodetic Chart 237 (we were still out of Wilensky's country—and Westport doesn't show on the MacMillan *Atlas* nor any of the SC charts) and find out for yourself. These two branches—with long shallows, interesting reefs and tortuous channels—constitute some of the best dinghying on the East Coast.

We didn't explore the branches. We took the dinghy over to the back side of Horseneck Beach, walked to the front and spent the rest of the day improving our tans. It's one of the East's great beaches, swinging out in a great white crescent to Gooseberry Neck and leading out past Hen and Chickens Reef to the sea. Beyond, out of sight (you can't see more than four miles from a beach normally), across the mouth of Buzzards Bay, lie the Elizabeth Islands, which were going to be our first offshore islands of the cruise.

Northward and eastward of the Elizabeth Islands, extending a watery wedge into the land and detaching Cape Cod from the mainland, is the body of Buzzards Bay, thirty miles long by ten miles wide. It narrows to five miles, finally to four hundred yards, the distance that separates Hog Neck from Hog Island. Here begins the canal to Cape Cod Bay, north of Cape Cod.

The further up the bay you go, the choppier the water; Buzzards, the whole of it, is known for choppy water. It's a great place for keel boats.

The first big-time sail race I ever observed was in Buzzards when, in 1955, the newly designated Olympic 5.5-meter keel boats raced for the honor of representing the U.S. at the 1956 Olympics in Melbourne, Australia. The dark horse was a boat called *Quixotic*, designed by Ray Hunt and skippered by Marblehead's Ted Hood, with John MacNamara and John Collins as crew. The *Quixotic*, by good sailing and a little bit of luck, was leading before the last race by such a score that the only way she could lose was to come in last while Andy Schoettle's hull, the second place boat, finished first. *Quixotic* was standing well up in the fleet during the last race when her mainsail suddenly slid halfway down the mast. MacNamara shinnied up the mast and tried to catch the main halyard fastening (which was what had let go) with the end of a boat hook in order to bring it down and reset the sail. He couldn't reach it. Andy Shoettle finished first. "I hung there knowing I was one yard from Melbourne," MacNamara said after the race, "and I couldn't make it."

Hood went on to bigger things. He became the leading sailmaker for the Twelve Meter yachts, designed his own cruising yachts, won the Bermuda. MacNamara won several national championships. John Collins later cruised with me to Maine and then went west to live in Grosse Pointe, Michigan, by the water.

Next port east from Westport is Padanarum (point 5, map 9). This name is how yachtsmen know it; on the map it is actually South Dartmouth on Appogansett Harbor, administratively part of the city of New Bedford. Padanarum is the name of the breakwater, and an ancient name for "the fertile crescent" between the Tigris and Euphrates Rivers.

Padanarum has a magnificent protected harbor; it is a well-known jumping-off spot for cruising the Cape and its offshore islands. It was the place where I picked up my first charter, *Neuron*. The circumstances were amusing.

The boat had been chartered for the preceding two days by one of my roommates in Greenwich Village. When *Neuron* limped in half a day late, the crew that got off was, to say the least, dispirited. Sullen might better describe them.

I found out later that they had taken off late their first evening, headed into a storm, and pitched about with every Jack and Jill seasick all night. They landed the next moring at Block Island, slept off the ill effects, and went ashore for drinking and forgetting. Back on the boat that night, they motored all the way back to Padanarum in rough water. The girls, who had come aboard with parasols and high heels, bearing a newly baked cake, had hung an ambitious menu on the galley wall. From that moment on, either sick or recovering or trying to forget, they had just barely managed to make up a few peanut butter sandwiches.

There was peanut butter on the bulkheads, implements and dishes strewn about the whole galley. The menu was still neatly tacked up over the sink.

The New Bedford Yacht Club dominates the water front at Padanarum. It was moved here after the 1938, 1944 and 1954 hurricanes consecutively wiped away its buildings on Popes Island, up in

New Bedford Harbor, the original site.

Padanarum is a good eight or nine miles up Buzzards from Westport; another four or five on up the bay is New Bedford itself (point 6, map 9) the greatest whaling port in the history of the world. New Bedford had some 330 whaling ships in her prime years, more than the rest of the American whaling fleet combined.

In her heyday, she was something. As Melville described her in Moby Dick, ". . . in New Bedford, actual cannibals stand chatting at street corners; savages outright; many of whom yet carry on their bones unholy flesh. It makes a stranger stare.

"But, besides the Feeans, the Tongatabooars, Erromangoans, Pannangians and Brighians, and besides the wild specimens of the whaling-craft which unheeded reel about in the streets, you will see other sights still more curious, certainly more comical. There weekly arrive in this town scores of green Vermonters and New Hampshire men, all athirst for gain and glory in the fishery. They are mostly young, of stalwart frames; fellows who have felled forests, and now seek to drop the axe and snatch the whale lance . . . Now when a country dandy like this takes it into his head to make a distinguished reputation and joins the great whale fishery, you should see the comical things he does upon reaching the seaport. In bespeaking his sea-outfit, he orders bell-buttons to his waistcoats; straps to his canvas trousers. Ah, poor Hayseed, how bitterly will burst those straps in the first howling gale when thou art driven, straps, buttons and all, down the throat of the tempest."

New Bedford whaling captains' stories are still told. One captain once picked up, per the owner's request, a quantity of the finest cigars and Madeira wine from the Philippines, before his ship got icebound in the Arctic and finally destroyed. The owner, getting the report of the disaster, asked how much of his cigars and wine had been saved. "All of it," said the captain. "Where is it?" asked the owner, slightly cheered.

"Well you see, while we were in the ice, I drank the wine and Mr. Jones, the mate, he smoked the cigars, and they certainly done us both a lot of good," said the captain.

New Bedford is now a fishery, her harbor holding several hundred draggers and trawlers and her downtown full of fishsmells. The change to fishing began when she sold many of her whalers to the government to go in the "Stone Fleet," sunk full of rock in southern harbors during the Civil War to blockade the Confederacy. By 1904, New Bedford's whaling fleet was down to twenty-odd ships. Soon after, it was reduced to one, the *Wanderer*, the last sailing whale ship to set out from New Bedford. *Wanderer* got as far as Cuttyhunk. Anchored in a storm, she went up on the Cuttyhunk rocks and smashed to bits.

Across New Bedford Harbor in Fairhaven, Joshua Slocum spent three years fitting out *Spray* for her astounding world circumnavigation. The first single-handed cruise around the world began and ended here.

Just above New Bedford is the Acushnet River. (*Acushnet* was the ship on which Melville shipped in a voyage that eventually produced *Typee* and *Moby Dick*.) There is a "Melville Tour" of Fair Haven and New Bedford. New Bedford's whaling museum has a half-scale whaler in it; and the New Bedford public library has a Melville Whaling Room, which holds a wealth of research on whaling in the old days.

Above New Bedford is the Cape Cod Canal (point 8, map 9). The near end of the canal is called Hog Island Channel. According to John Parkinson, Jr., (co-author with photographer Norman Fortier of *The Bay and the Sound*), the approach ". . . can be a nightmare, resembling the violent wave conditions on the Gulf Stream leg of the Bermuda Race." Parkinson strongly suggests it best to avoid most of the turbulence by holding to east shore as one approaches the canal of Buzzard's Bay.

The upper end of the canal is about twenty miles from Provincetown, inside the hook of the Cape.

It was at Provincetown that, in the summer of 1602, Captain Bartholomew Gosnold of England landed, armed with the volume of navigation instructions of his neighbor Richard Hakluyt (under the title *Principal Navigations*,) which contained routes for just such a voyage. Gosnold had come south from a landfall in Maine and had become "imbayed with a mightie headland." "Coming to anker" off what is now Provincetown, he went ashore eighteen years before the Pilgrims touched land at nearby Plymouth.

Gosnold's crew fished and "pestered our ship so with Cod Fish that we threw numbers of them overboard again." The captain quite naturally named the "mightie headland" Cape Cod before he sailed around it to the Elizabeth Islands.

North of New Bedford again is the harbor of Sippican, better known as Marion. Named for Francis Marion, the famous "Swamp Fox" of the Revolution, Marion has the best harbor in Buzzards. The Beverly Yacht Club is one of the best run, best known on the East Coast, a cradle of contemporary sailing geniuses. Fessenden S. Blanchard, in *Block Island to Nantucket,* notes that the motto of the Beverly Yacht Club is *Litmus ama Altum alii teneant*, meaning "I love the shores, let others have the deep."

Southernmost harbor on the east or Cape Cod shore of Buzzards is Quissett (point 19, map 9), only a mile or so from Woods Hole (point 17, map 9). Here the Elizabeth Islands meet the mainland of the Cape; Quisset really belongs more to a cruise of the Elizabeths than of Buzzards Bay.

Quisset's entrance is narrow and winding, but the outer harbor is safe and quiet. There's a rose garden ashore on the Webster Estate open to yachtsmen, plus a few houses and a marina. On the inside harbor is Quisset Harbor House, a yachtsman's restaurant with a good reputation and a wonderful view.

Nimble was to leave all these intriguing places behind for another cruise; we were headed for the islands, first of all for Cuttyhunk, ten miles away, on the far side of the mouth of Buzzards.

On day seventeen of our cruise, we came smoking out of the harbor at Acoaxet and headed across the mouth of Buzzards Bay with the wind blowing a good twelve knots, as befits Buzzards Bay. *Nimble* shot for Cuttyhunk, rapping through the chop like a motorboat.

Coming out of Rhode Island Sound, astern of us, was a faint, but fast-coming, ship that looked strangely familiar. She was—if you had looked at as many pictures of full ships as I have—very familiar. The *Eagle*, the Coast Guard's full-rigged training ship, was coming out of history and down the Sound. Thousands of her square-rigged predecessors had followed this route, bound for safe passage out Vineyard and Nantucket Sounds and around the Cape to Boston, or turning South, to the West Indies for rum and riches.

The *Eagle* soon caught us and passed. We ran for about thirty minutes alongside Hen and Chickens Reef. Then we saw Gong "3" as we had hoped, made a left turn to take the wind on the starboard quarter, and headed for Cuttyhunk Pond.

We were joined by a nice big yawl coming in from Block, then caught a Controversy sloop with a family aboard and passed them, all of us converging on Cuttyhunk in the haze. Finally we saw the island, a low, darker presence that solidified into a shore to starboard. Then Penikese, the small companion island to Cuttyhunk, appeared slightly to the latter's port and showed us we were only a couple of miles off.

In 1873, the great naturalist Louis Agassiz established the Anderson School of Natural History, forerunner of Woods Hole Oceanographic Institute on Penikese. The state took Penikese over in 1907 for a leper colony and then abandoned it. That's what it is now: an abandoned leper colony, another state-spoiled island. Little Gull Island, next to it, is in a "Prohibited" circle of water, as a wildlife refuge.

We rounded into Cuttyhunk Outer Harbor, following the line of buoys to our right. We were in a regular train of boats, all headed for the breakwater at the far end of the outer harbor. We started running upon the sloop in front of us; we were unfortunately just then being hemmed in from the left by a converging yacht, a small cabin cruiser not so sure of what all those buoys meant, evidently; we were forced to cut behind the sloop to the end of the breakwater.

Inside the narrow channel between the breakwaters, both wind and current were against us, so we fired up our Evinrude 18. It moved us steadily upstream between the walls. Kids and baby sitters were playing on the sandbars at the sides of the channel; whirls of water bounced between the sides in the strong current. Sailboats attempting the tide and current here with relatively small power have been known to get turned right around and shot downstream.

Cuttyhunk Pond (point 10, map 9) now opened up, displaying its large interior harbor with huge, filled-to-the-brim marina (there was a Tuna Tournament in progress).

The pond is dredged to a depth of eight or ten feet at its near end, but a good half of it, at the far side, is shallow. In the dredged part, we were into the most crowded circumstances since the anchorage at Sand Hole in Huntington Bay. We circled carefully, avoiding the boats in front and behind and finally made out in the game of musical anchorages by shouldering into an open spot.

After a bit of lunch, we rowed serially into the back side of the wharf where there is a seaplane float and went scrunching up the tar road to town.

Cuttyhunk town begins with a wide-open ginmill at the bottom of the hill—Scuttlebutt, a typical drink-em-up fisherman's bar. At the top of the hill, the town is positively somnolent. Small, nearly unchanged over generations, Cuttyhunk town seems to be happy about being that way. The only restaurant is Bosworth's, down a nearly hidden side street; the only store is the five-and-dime Cuttyhunk Store. Cruising men have come to Cuttyhunk for twenty years; here they still find it, unchanged.

Cuttyhunk's two streets peter out into dirt paths. There is only a house or two on the whole five-mile-long island; no plot lines for Cuttyhunk East or Cuttyhunk West have ever been laid out, nor will ever be. Cuttyhunk is still, as one writer put it, "An experience, completely surrounded by water."

The reasons for this excellent state of things run all the way back to Peleg Slocum who, in the last of the 1600's, managed to buy up the island. The Slocum descendants lived on the island, selling pieces of it sparingly to fellow fishermen for two hundred years.

Cuttyhunk was administratively part of the town of Gosnold, which also incorporated the Elizabeth Islands. The inhabitants of Gosnold when it was chartered in 1864 numbered some one hundred souls.

There aren't many more permanent residents in old Gosnold Town as you read this, in spite of summer influxes into Cuttyhunk (the only island in the Elizabeths to permit people further inland than the beach). According to the 1969 printing of *The Story of Cuttyhunk*, by Louise T. Haskell, the number of permanent residents on all sixteen islands in the former township of Gosnold is 125. Nearly fifty of these live on Cuttyhunk.

The year Gosnold was made a town, certain gentlemen from the City of New York, becoming dissatisfied with the Club to which they belonged, the West Island Club at Sakonnet Point, came to Cuttyhunk in a body and bought what turned out to be most of the land on Cuttyhunk Island. This was the salvation of the island. They ringed the island with fish stands, where a gentleman and a guide or "chummer" (he tossed in bait to lure the fish on) could surfcast to his heart's content without worry of interruption or cross-casting from competitors. The original purchases by the club were so extensive that it had to give back land to the town to make room for a church and a school.

When the fishing yacht took over the function of the old-fashioned fishing stand, the energies of the club declined. Its interests were brought out by the late William Wood, then president of the American Woolen Company. Wood wanted to perpetuate the idea of a gentleman's fishing club. He started negotiation with the remaining property owners on the island in order to have the island wholly his. He also started building a wide road flanked by grand walls to lead to the highest point on Cuttyhunk, the site for his proposed baronial castle. The fishermen, many of whose deeds ran back to the original Slocum, wouldn't sell. Wood was miffed. He never built his castle, which was all right by the Cuttyhunkers.

On the other hand, the Wood family, which still maintains a summer hole on the island, won't sell any land to speculators.

We walked up Wood's walled road to the top of the hill and looked out over the island—waves of sassafrass, bayberry and salt grass down to the azure sea. East toward Vineyard Sound, we could make out the skyward jut of Gay Head on Martha's Vineyard, and, north of that, the string of Elizabeth Islands. The view is one of the fairest in the world, comparing to the outlook over Penobscot Bay, Maine, and the classic island seascapes of the Aegean.

We made a few purchases at the Cuttyhunk Store and bought a few groceries and delivered it all by dinghy to the yacht and then walked up the hill again to Bosworth House. At the second or third left off the main road, a modest sign proclaims the road to the inn, famous—justly so—for its seafood. We had New England clam chowder, which really was New England clam chowder, and swordfish fresh from, I suspect, the tournament that day; it was excellent.

After dinner we descended to the harbor again and rowed out to *Nimble*. Under Cuttyhunk Pond lies old marsh, turned into a blue muck by the pressure of the land above it. Some muck has already turned to lignite, the black-earth stuff that becomes oil under pressure. There is enough once-living matter buried under Buzzards Bay to make up three and one half million barrels of crude oil. It will take eons to pile enough earth to build pressures to make the lignite into oil. But, by the time Buzzards lignite has turned to oil, man will have turned to other fuels, fuels that are less destructive of the air in which they burn.

Entrance to Cuttyhunk Pond, Cuttyhunk. (MORTEN LUND)

Coast Guard training ship Eagle,
off Newport. (MORTEN LUND)

CHAPTER THIRTEEN

~~~~~~

VINEYARD SOUND—GOSNOLD POND AND MENEMSHA POND

~~~~~~

(DAY 18)

Suppose you want to step onto that soil along the North Atlantic Coast where the first habitation was built by white men. Where do you go—Plymouth? No, you go to Cuttyhunk, around to Gosnolds Pond on the island's western end. On a small island in the pond, Gosnolds Island, you will be standing on the right spot.

Bartholomew Gosnold sailed his *Concord* around the hook of Provincetown and around two points of the Cape sticking out toward Europe, points which have since eroded away; he skirted Nauset Island, which now lies buried in the sea with its lighthouse. Gosnold went around Monomoy Point, which pointed due south, as it still does, and then Vineyard Sound opened before him. Reaching the westernmost island in the chain that bordered the sound to the north, *Concord* came to anchor off the west end of Cuttyhunk, which Gosnold called "Elizabeth Isle" for his Queen.

The island looked good to the English. Gabriel Archer, one of the chroniclers on Gosnold's voyage, wrote that "touching the fertility of the soil by our own experience made, we found it excellent; for sowing some English pule; it sprouted out in a fortnight almost half a foot. In this island is a stage or pond of fresh water, in circuit two miles, on the one side not distant from the sea thirty yards, in the center whereof is a rocky inlet, containing near an acre of ground full of wood, on which we began our fort and place of abode, disposing itself so fit for the same."

Early in the eighteenth day of our voyage, we were to cruise to Gosnolds Pond. We breakfasted together in the cabin on Bea's bacon and eggs, then got underway out the Cuttyhunk breakwaters; the wind was still standing in from the north but the rain was holding off. Our best shot at Gosnold Pond, west of us, would be to go south through Canapitsit Channel into Vineyard Sound, rather then north into Buzzards Bay, according to our Eldridge tide current chart and tables.

I planned it so that we went through Canapitsit right at the end of the flood; we would ride slack water through the channel, and then ride the beginning of the ebb to Gosnold Pond to the west. Then we could explore Gosnold Pond.

Canapitsit Channel slices through a beach and has a couple of big rocks in it. When the tide runs hard against the wind here, you get "square" waves which tend to lift you up quickly and dump you hard—bad if you happen to get too near a big rock. It is well to take it at high tide.

Thanks to our study of tide tables, we would be able to sail to Gosnold Pond, rather than motor. In cruising, your cunning penalizes no one; it only gives you a good cruise.

I do not abjure racing. It's tremendous training and sharpens your wit in ways that are useful in all sailing. For readers who are inclined to race, or spectate races with glee, there's a witty book on racing protests that were judged and appealed to the national appeals committee of the NAYRU, the "Supreme Court" of racing rules. The book is James Lipscomb's *So You Think You Know the Rules of Yacht Racing*.

While on the subject of rules, incidentally, be reminded that the rules of the road (the non-racing rules) are considerably different than the racing rules. The rules of the road can be summarized in four sentences: (1) The nearly invariable rule of starboard tack right of way in racing does not hold. In cruising, you only have starboard tack right of way over another sailboat when you are as close to the wind as he is; otherwise, the vessel closest to the wind has right of way, regardless of tack.

The next two rules are: (2) under power you keep to the right; in other words, pass all directly oncoming boats port-to-port (their port side to your port side, as in a car). (3) The overtaking boat, regardless of sail or power, keeps clear; this applies in great force in a narrow channel.

For instance, if we had run down our blue and white sloop of yesterday from behind, he would have had legal recovery for damages, even though we were sailing and he was under power.

The last rule is: (4) under power, converging boats to your right have right of way, and you have right of way over converging boats to your left, unless they are under sail and you under power, in which case sail has right of way.

There are a few good rules of thumb which are invaluable supplements.

First, never get into a position where a decision on the part of the other skipper can hurt you. That means, "stay clear!" Don't insist on the right of way.

Second, let the other boat *know* your intentions by clearly pointing your bow in the direction you are planning to take well in advance of necessity. *Show* the directly oncoming boat you *are* going to pass port-to-port. Show a converging boat that you plan to go safely astern. Don't make him nervous.

Lastly, watch *any* converging boat. If the angle his boat makes with your course remains the same, that is, if the converging boat continues to remain on the same spot at your rail, then you are on collision courses. Bear off behind him or turn parallel to his course until the situation clears up.

Luckily, happily, this day we were not in anyone's way or vice versa. Canapitsit Channel is not the most popular route out of Cuttyhunk Harbor; it is as described, a hair hazardous. We coasted up to the channel and rolled through gently without any trouble, breaking out into the wide vistas of Vineyard Sound. Sparkling, playful, riffling waters lay on both sides.

We turned west toward Cuttyhunk Pond and sailed to it in an hour. Our course lay down The Graveyard, as mariners called the waters off the western Elizabeths, because they were unable to predict the vicious tides. (Eldridge finally did it.) The flood here runs *north* and pushes you onto the shore.

Sow and Pigs Reef, at the west end of Cuttyhunk, is the underwater remains of a glacial moraine that points right straight back toward Block Island where it emerges from the sea again, as Block Island. Sow and

Pigs looked so nasty that we went nearly all the way out to the marker buoy at the end of it before turning shoreward toward the break in the strand of Cuttyhunk that is the entrance to Gosnold Pond (point 9, map 9).

We sailed *Nimble* into the little bight by the pond. Gosnold's monument showed up clearly, standing on its island in the middle of the pond. We threw in the anchor and dinghied and swam into the shore. Gosnold Pond, once fresh, was broken into by the sea some time ago. Now, at the beginning of the ebb, the stream was running out.

We trod up the shallow stream on a nearly solid bed of seaweed. These weeds provided the excellent holding grounds for the delicious mussel. (I hold them dear simply steamed and salted with melted butter.) I could feel the mussel shell colonies with my toes, shell to shell on the bottom, a walkway of mussels.

The water inside the pond was very much warmer than the water outside. Sid snorkled around the pond in his rubber top; Bea and I rowed out to Gosnolds Island. Here was a stone tower memoralizing Bartholomew Gosnold's attempt to colonize. In Gosnold's time this was fresh water: a whole lake of drinking water and for use as a moat besides, giving security from attack as well as plentiful warm water for bathing in season.

"The nine-and-twentieth we labored in getting of sassafrass," wrote Gabriel Archer, "rubbishing our little fort for our islet, new-keeling our shallop and making a punt or flat-bottomed boat to pass to and fro for our fort over the fresh water; the powder of sassafrass in twelve hours cured one of our company that had taken a great surfeit, by eating the bellies of dogfish, a very delicious meat."

"Rubbishing" meant bushing out the ground so the pioneers could build a fortified cabin. And "keeling the shallop" meant putting a new keel on their small ship's yacht. As for sassafrass, this plant was in high demand as a medicine. Sassafrass was supposed to cure syphilis and lesser evils. It grew relatively scantily in Europe; here it was abundant. The arrival in London of Gosnold's ship bearing the first shipment of sassafrass from the New World depressed the London sassafrass market for a month.

The day after they gathered sassafrass, Gosnold and some of his men sailed their *Concord* over to Hill's Hap (Penikese); there they appropriated a canoe from some Indians who had run off as the *Concord* approached

A couple of days later, the Indians ambushed two of Godnold's colonists outside the fort. The Indians wounded one colonist with an arrow; the other saved the day by attacking and cutting the Indians' bowstrings with his sword. The "belligerent" Indians so frightened the colonists, they voted to sail back to England on the *Concord*. That was the end of the settlement on Gosnold's Island.

Shakespeare's patron, the Earl of Southhampton, was a patron of a later American expedition to this area, so Southhampton was obviously interested in reports from the New World. *The Tempest* has many phrases strikingly similar to the published reports of Gosnold's adventures. *The Tempest* was supposed to have been written about 1613, eleven years after Gosnold returned. Very likely, Shakespeare heard stories of the New World from the mouths of the very men who had built the fort on Gosnold's Island, right under our feet.

We took the dinghy over to the channel into the pond and dug deep into the sand with our fingers to get the larger mussles out; big mussels lie deep in the sand, with penny-and quarter-sized mussels on top.

A mussel holds to a rock, or a shell, or weeds, by throwing out "byssus threads." These are strong filaments. They make a nest of mussels into an equivalent of a snarl of fishline. Mussels often have to be ripped loose from their beds; then small rocks, dead shells and debris have to be torn off before the mussels are put in a bucket.

We had a bucketful of big mussels for dinner in no time, plus several hopping mad hermit crabs and a fiddler crab; they all scurried around in the bottom of the dinghy, avoiding capture. We had a sandwich lunch and pulled off the mooring to sail down Vineyard Sound, toward Menemsha, to the little fishing port past Gay Head on the Vineyard.

The breeze freshened, giving us eight knots plus one and a half on the tide. Gay Head poked higher by the minute off the starboard bow. A rush of foam tunneled down between the hulls and jetted astern. The ship's company sat to leeward, feet against the life rails and backs to the cabin. We had a lovely two-hour ride with nothing to do except let the hulls slice cleanly through the water.

Off our beam, out of sight, was Nomans Land, an island nearly as big as Cuttyhunk, completely out of bounds to yachtsmen, a military bombing target. (You wonder just how much utility can be gained from setting aside such a rare, extraordinary piece of landscape. Aren't there some other places that would do?) Archer, writing from the *Concord*, said of Nomans Land, "We went ashore and found it full of wood, vines, gooseberry bushes, whortleberries, raspberries, eglantines, etc. Here we had cranes, stearnes, shoulders, geese and divers other birds which there at that time upon cliffs being sandy with some rocky stones did breed and had young."

Today bombs.

Actually, "Martha's Vineyard" was the name first given Nomans for its grape vines. (Archer: ". . . we could not go for treading on them.")

When Gosnold approached Gay Head, he first named what is now the Vineyard "Dover Cliffs."

But Marthas was the name that—transposed to the larger island—survived. Interestingly enough, Martha was the name of Gosnold's rich mother-in-law—Martha Gosnold was the daughter of a hugely successful merchant ship owner, Andrew Judd. Martha's Vineyard may be the world's only island named for a mother-in-law.

Nomans ("No-muns," the Vineyarders call it) finally took its name from Tuequenoman, the Algonquin chief of the tribe claiming the island as its hunting and fishing territory.

Gay Head now came at us like a cliff made out of a child's modeling clay, with the colors mixed in winding strata. The black, lignite-like layer of old forest and swamp lies hidden near the bottom. Above that are clays stained red by ferrous compounds and yellow and white by other mineral compounds. Daniel Webster once called it an "irridescent Niagara."

Legend has it that the black streaks in the cliff are embers from the great fires of the giant Maushop, a mythical Indian who used to broil entire whales over a fire of whole tree trunks up in the natural depression behind Gay Head. This area is now called "Devil's Den" or "Maushop's Den." Blood from the whales is said to have caused the red striations of the Gay Head cliffs.

The Dolphin Guide to Cape Cod, Martha's Vineyard and Nantucket by Fran Blake states the story of Maushop thus: "In legendary days, nothing but waters stretched empty and endless to the sea. This was in the time of Maushop, the good giant. So wide of girth and tall was he, no wigwam could be his home. He lived and roamed out under the stars and moon. In the chill and frost of the winter nights, he would often wake and find that the cold had crept within the bearskins that were wrapped around him. Then it was that he would arise and warm himself by jumping across and up and down Cape Cod . . . then it was that he twisted and turned, fidgeted and burrowed high and low; thus dunes were formed. Awaking one morning from such a restless night, he discovered his moccasins buried deep and brimful of sand. Impatiently he unearthed them. Impatiently he tossed their contents out upon the waters. Sand from his left shoe made Nantucket and from his right Martha's Vineyard came into being."

This is a pretty good primitive explanation for the action of the glaciers shoveling moraine into the sea to create these lands. (Myths exist to explain *something*.)

Nimble now crossed the ragged dangerous reefs pointing from Gay Head toward Cuttyhunk: Devil's Bridge, another name referring to the Maushop legend. The white man's view of Maushop was that he was the fiend. To the Indians, this reef was Maushop's Bridge, which he built to get to Cuttyhunk. (For all we know there may have once been a glacier-built land bridge here, since washed away.)

In some layers of Gay Head cliffs, prehistoric camel bones and those of wild horses have been dug out. Near the top is a chalk-white layer of true clay, malleable when wetted. The Gay Head Indians, who live behind the hill, use it in their exceptional pottery.

Gay Head stands as the most complete geological record in New England of the Atlantic Coast's upheavals and sinkings, and of prehistoric flora and fauna. The black lignite layer at the bottom, for instance, is a hundred million years old and contains well over a hundred identifiable species of plants, some compressed to mineral state.

We sailed past the accumulated history that is Gay Head and came into Menemsha Bight, where the "clay ships" coming from Boston for their cannon-mold clay used to anchor. We spotted the *Mystic Whaler* at anchor off the harbor breakwater. She had a full complement of singles—girls and guys. There was a rare incongruity in the bikinis sighted over the scrollwork of the stern of the old schooner.

We turned down between the Menemsha breakwaters and made our way into the harbor, which appeared through a slot in the breakwater wall to port.

We puttered in the narrow entrance under power. The harbor inside was exceedingly small and cramped. On our left lay a marina, looking out toward the Vineyard Sound, taking up the entire seawall. Dead ahead, an authentic-looking wharf was lined with commercial fishermen, bow-to stern, nets hung to dry, crews shoveling fish unceremoniously onto the dock. From that direction, Menemsha looked and smelled like the fishing harbor it is. To the right, Menemsha Harbor was built up with picturesque little shanties—some legitimate fishermen's and some affected by artists and summer people. To complete the picture, an old schooner was anchored outside the shacks in Menemsha Creek—almost too picture-postcardy to be true.

We motored in to the gas dock and were told, as we had surmised from a first quick look, that there were only two moorings in the harbor for guest yachtsmen and that only three yachts could nest on each. We could easily see that there were already three on each. As we watched, a fourth tried to hang on to the nest and was hailed by the harbormaster and told to go away.

We slipped ashore and bought a few postcards. Bea and I went down the boardwalks of the wharf and up the hill beyond it just to have a look around. There are a couple of small restaurants down behind the hill and a general store with better groceries than anything available in the harbor itself.

We had delicious fried clams at one place; then we tried telephoning Barry Stott, a photographer from Vail, Colorado, who was coming aboard in Vineyard Haven, down the shore.

Barry's phone was busy. It was late, and we were hot. We found out from the grocer that Menemsha was dry. And no beer. We sat on the General Store porch feeling dried out and thirsty when a gentleman came out of the store and said, "I'm a yachtsman myself, and I know how you feel after being at sea all day. Wait. I'll bring back something."

Sure enough, he came back with a solid glass of gin and ice cubes and two cold beers. We drank the brews first and then sipped the gin between phone calls. Barry's phone continued to be busy. By the time we raised him, the gin was gone. So was the light, nearly.

Bea and I went gaily back to our ship, and the crew cast off. We went churning out of the harbor at the end of flood tide and headed for Menemsha Pond (point 11, map 9), up the Menemsha Creek about a mile, a tricky run at any tide. The channel has a three-foot spot at low and is windy as hell. We got up to the pond with only one "touch" on the bottom of the channel.

When we broke out into the big expanse of Menemsha Pond, the water lay silvery and calm, slowly tinging with red; the lowering sun shot the clouds overhead with pink. We had an end of the pond to ourselves, except for a couple of yachts nesting off to one side.

Here, off the bayberry-beseiged shores of Menemsha Pond, we were to have our steamed mussel feast. We boiled the mussels until they opened and buttered them just like small sweetmeats. As we sat in the cockpit the lights came on around the pond; our neighbors' ports glowed against the dark surface and the bowl of night overhead was a dark blue.

Mystic Whaler *at anchor off Menem-sha, Martha's Vineyard.* (SID REICHMAN)

Schooner at entrance to Menemsha. (SID REICHMAN)

Menemsha dockside, Menemsha Harbor. (MORTEN LUND)

CHAPTER FOURTEEN

≋≋≋≋≋≋≋≋≋≋≋≋≋≋≋≋≋≋≋≋≋≋≋

VINEYARD SOUND—UP-ISLAND, VINEYARD HAVEN AND NAUSHON

≋≋≋≋≋≋≋≋≋≋≋≋≋≋≋≋≋≋≋≋≋≋≋

(DAY 19)

I woke and got up on deck in time to watch the fog lift off the pond. The herring gulls were streaming from their rookery on the uninhabited west bank of Menemsha Creek.

The herring gull, the common gull species, was nearly wiped out, like the passenger pigeon, during the 1800's. Women wore gull feather hats; gulls' eggs were sold on the market. Some of the nation's first conservation laws put an end to the gull hunt. The few gulls remaining who had retreated to Maine soon quadrupled their numbers and occupied the shores as far south as the lower Jersey shore.

The gull isn't exactly an outstanding songbird; still, he flies with a nice wheeling motion, and completes the seascape. And, he is one of the

117

greatest scavengers invented; he'll eat anything.

He is, finally, a living example of what a little conservation can do.

Southward, in the opposite direction from the gull rookery, lie two bodies of water connected to Menemsha Pond: Nashaquitsa and Stone Wall Ponds. Because the crew was asleep, I started day nineteen by motoring (to save time) in the dinghy a couple of miles across Menemsha Pond to the narrow pass—Pechalkers Creek—which opens on the inner pond, "Quitsa" or Nashaquitsa (point 12, map 9) and landed on the far side.

I stood right in the heart of "up-island." This is a particularly pleasing and historic part of Martha's Vineyard.

I got out of the dinghy on the near side of the bridge at the end of Nashaquitsa, walked up the earth path to a highway and looked down to where Stonewall Pond terminates, just fifty yards from surf on Stonewall Beach. It once joined the sea, completely dividing the island.

This land (Gosnold's chronicler saw and wondered at "the beautie and delicacie of this sweet soile") has been largely bought up by people who, as at Cuttyhunk, do not want to sell, not now or ever. Unless things go radically wrong in Martha's Vineyard, the island isn't going to change for the worse.

I walked down the highway, Middle Road, a mile or so to the "four corners."

Here was the Chilmark Library, a renovated farmhouse built in 1790. On the southeast corner, there is a grove of tupelo trees, brought as seedlings in flowerpots from India by whalers who had been apprised of this tree's wonderful properties: the wood did not swell or shrink under absorption. The trees and their wood made prodigiously successful bungs for whale oil barrels, as well as excellent mallets (beetles). Chilmark Center has been called Beetlebung Corner for a hundred years now.

Past Chilmark is West Tisbury, where the John Manter house sits. This is where Joshua Slocum lived in 1898, just after his famous single-handed voyage around the world. Slocum called his house "Fag End."

Outside Tisbury lies Tisbury Great Pond; its torturous coves wind like ten gnarled fingers toward Takemmy Trail, which goes right to Edgartown. A hundred years ago, a recluse poetess, Nancy Luce, lived on one of these coves. She was one of the strangest authors in American literature's history:

> Every time my head is wounded
> I never get over it.
> I wish I had never been in this world.
> I undergo so much with my head.

And murdered alive as I am.
They come from Vineyard Haven and Edgartown
And I feel sick all my whole time
I am murdered so much.

Luce wrote *lots* of poems on the hens she had, particularly Ada
Queetie and Beauty Linna. (*Harper's Magazine* called Luce "Laureate
of the Hens.") Her home became a regular stop on the island tour.
Visitors would sometimes tease the old lady. Luce hated noise. It made
her head ring. Some practical jokers once set a band to playing near
her house, and it took her a month to get over it. "They cruel'd me in
my sickness," she wrote.

Modern Vineyard people, with Nancy Luce, are here because they're
tired of being murdered by the noise of the world.

East of Beetlebung Corner, up on the east banks of Squibnocket
Pond on the old Simon Mayhew sheep farm, is a monument of piled
boulders. Archaeologists are agreed that no Indians would attempt
such a colossal piece of stone-piling. The top flat boulder is six feet by
six feet and weighs over a ton. The islanders call it the "Hog House."
Archaeologists have identified it as a "cromlech," or Norse burial monument. Squibnocket was joined to the sea until 1818. A shoal craft
vessel such as a Viking ship, could easily have used it as a harbor.
Norse sagas record that the Vikings who colonized the Americas in
1000 A.D. lived on the shores of a pond and "went out" to an island
(it could be Nomans) where they kept cattle.

Nomans was used as a Vineyard fishing station because it was nearer
good fishing than the Vineyard, and this counted in the days of sail.
Fishermen lived in a shanty town; wives and kids, ensconced for the
season, awaited their men's return each day.

One apocryphal Nomans story is about the doctor who was called
upon to attend a failing fisherman on Nomans. The doctor took one
look at the sea tossing and heaving, and refused to leave Squibnocket's
shores.

According to *Tales and Trails of Martha's Vineyard*, by Joseph C.
Allen, ". . . they jest laid hold of the doctor and hove him in the boat.
'Lay still,' say they, 'and we'll probably get through. Thrash aroun'
and we'll all go down.' "

West of Squibnocket, the road leads to Gay Head. Gay Head was
never sold by the Indians because it was the home of Maushop. In
Maushop's Den, on top of Gay Head, the Indians held their festival
dances.

The Martha's Vineyard Indians were the first whalers on the American continent. The English colonists were amazed that the Indians ac-

tually *pursued* the whale; in the English experience, you only towed dead ones ashore.

The Gay Head Indian harpooner, Amos Smalley, died in 1961. Smalley harpooned one of the few true white sperm whales ever brought in. When the Hollywood *Moby Dick* was released, its entrepreneurs invited Smalley to the world premier in New Bedford. "They kept telling me," Amos said, 'You're the only living man who's ever harpooned a white sperm whale.' But that isn't what counts and it never did. What matters is, white or black, that whale ran more than eighty barrels of oil."

The Martha's Vineyard Indians are mysteriously descended from the Maine Algonquin Abanaki. They are not the Connecticut or Massachusetts Algonquin. The Vineyard Indians came down the coast "on an ice cake," according to their legends. (Perhaps this is a reference to the Ice Age).

Within twenty-five years of the first white settlement, one Caleb Cheesy-Cateanuck, a Gay Head Indian, having mastered his Latin and Greek, graduated from Harvard College in the class of 1665. The remnants of the Gay Head Indians today farm and fish like the whites; near Gay Head Light is a museum of Indian clay and pottery making craft along with relics of whaling craft.

Maushop's pet, the great white whale that hibernated in Witch Pond, is still there, according to legend. Maushop is not. Legend says that when strangers came to his fishing grounds, he disappeared behind Zach's Cliffs. Only the smoke from his peace pipe returns, rolling in from the sea like a spirit.

I motored back to Menemsha Pond and hoisted the dink aboard *Nimble* in time to sit down to breakfast with everyone else; they were in the process of leisurely enjoying Bea's scrambled eggs and bacon. After breakfast, we up-anchored.

We swung past the harbor of Menemsha, where present-day fishermen go out to sea with harpoons as their Indian and white ancestors did. But they look for tuna, instead of whale. Tuna hunters sit above the cross trees of the rigging of their large craft, with scanning eyes trained for a tuna dorsal, instead of the plume of a whale spout.

We headed across Vineyard Sound to Tarpaulin Cove. This is one of the best beaches of the cruise, and the place where we'd planned a rendezvous with Barry Stott, coming over from Vineyard Haven in his powerboat.

The sky was gray overhead. We beat toward Nashawena along the Graveyard with the genny belted in tight. Quicks Hole (point 13, map 9) is at the far end of Nashawena Island, the westernmost boundary of the Forbes empire (the Forbes family owns all the Elizabeths east of

Cuttyhunk: Nashawena, Pasque and Naushon, west to east, respectively).

Quicks Hole—roughly half a mile wide and open at both ends, the far side opening into Buzzards Bay—is by far the easiest of the Elizabeth Island holes to navigate. It's named for a fellow privateer of Captain Kidd, one Captain Cornelius Quick. You can anchor in Quicks up close to the Nashawena Beach (a lovely beach, incidentally) in a westerly behind North Point and be pretty snug. There is a big freshwater pond behind the beach with water lilies in it.

Just off Quick's entrance, we tacked to bring Pasque on our port. Lee-bowing the current, we sailed the Pasque shore until Robinsons Hole (point 14, map 9) opened up between Pasque and Naushon; Robinsons is nearly as narrow a passage as Canapitsit. There is a small cove between Nuns 4 and 6 in Robinsons where it is possible to overnight with fore and aft anchoring to keep the yacht out of the channel through to Buzzards Bay.

Nimble coasted along Naushon. Our wind had deserted. The holes in the clouds were lengthening and getting bigger, but good-weather wind had not yet appeared. The current which goes north on the flood carried us close to French Watering Place, just in back of the Naushon beach. It supplied fresh water for French privateers that operated here during pre-Revolutionary times, trying for a few English ships (we were English then, so to speak) as trophies in the French and Indian War.

Nimble was past French Watering Place with the first whispers of a new southwester and a bluer sky coming on. We picked out the bright crescent rim of the sand beach at Tarpaulin Cove, behind Tarpaulin Cove Light. Tarpaulin Cove is smack in the middle of Naushon, like a bite taken out of its side—one of the pleasantest places to cast an anchor in this world.

Naushon Island is untouched land; it has had few people to contend with. It preserves some of the old wildness of our ancestral coast—principally because it has been a private estate since 1682; three families have owned it. The first was Boston's Winthrop family; next was the Bowdoin family (founders of Bowdoin College) and finally, in 1856, the Forbes family of Milton, Mass., bought the islands.

We nosed *Nimble* up to Tarpaulin Beach (point 16, map 9). As we came in, the temperature started rising perceptibly; it felt like approaching a reflector oven. Anchoring in about three feet of water, we hopped in to shore and went walking about with our bare toes digging in the sand. The sand at Tarpaulin is extra-sensuous—fine—almost velvet-like underfoot, holding heat like a bank of embers, inviting us to lie down and store up warmth.

We were all on the beach when a small yellow hull—waves spurting out from the bows—hove in sight: Barry Stott was about to arrive. Barry anchored off *Nimble*'s beam and brought ashore Marnie Wilks, a California girl, perpetually relaxed.

A herd of experimental Forbes cattle gave Stott something to photograph. Ellen and Bea, away from the beach, scrambled on a high rock under nearby oaks as the herd came ambling down. The cattle were like large musk oxen, some kind of Indian variety. The bulls looked a bit touchy. We moved slowly around them, trying to shoot them grazing in the salt grass with the boats in the background.

Enough excitement before lunch.

Tarpaulin Cove has been the site of two engagements: first, between the pirate ship *Good Speed*, captained by Thomas Pound, and the *Mary*, captained by Samuel Pease of Boston. In 1689, Pound, based in Tarpaulin, preyed on passing commercial ships. Pease had been sent to take the pirate and finally did after a bloody battle off Tarpaulin Beach. Pease died of his wounds. The pirates, sent to Boston in chains, were never tried. They had powerful protectors. Pound went back to England and lived as a country gentleman on his ill-gotten gains.

The second, a more peaceful engagement, was the first recorded American yacht race, between *Sylph* of Boston and *Wave* of New York. *Sylph* was owned by Robert Bennett Forbes, of the family shortly to own this island. *Wave* was skippered by John C. Stevens, commodore of the New York Yacht Club. The race began off Vineyard Haven and ended in Tarpaulin. A hundred years later, in 1935, the Forbes family organized the centenary race (that's how long they've been around).

We were occupied happily with the beach. Bea went crabbing around toward the lighthouse, got two or three small-sized ones and came back pondering how to have them for dinner.

We could have stayed and cooked dinner on the beach, because fires *are* allowed at the rock under the lighthouse end of the beach. There is also a certain amount of freedom about moving up off the beach under the great oaks that are the last stand of virgin timber on the coast of Massachusetts.

"Clan Forbes would open more of this romantic empire to the public had the public not proved itself untrustworthy. Not only are there frequent attempts to poach deer, but several times each summer, a bell at Hadley Harbor tolls, calling the clan to fight fires which picnickers have started and failed even to report. Downed timber from storms makes the fire danger especially acute." So wrote Baum in *By the Wind*.

We tacked out of the beach harbor and headed for Woods Hole and Hadley Harbor, where the Elizabeths meet the rest of Massachusetts.

If the wind had been fair, we could have sneaked over to the Vineyard shore to Lake Tashmoo (point 16, map 9), a big pond with a three-foot, low-tide connection to the sea. After its winding narrow entrance, you can go down a mile and a half, all in deep water, to James Cagney's place. *Mary Ann*, his nice white schooner, is tied up to his private jetty here. There are not more than a couple of yachts at anchor, locally owned, way down at the far end. Bob Love, past president of the Cruising Club of America, has a farm at the head of Tashmoo, and the Cruising Club has rendezvoused here. Big yachts used to be able to get in and out before the channel silted in.

We headed in for an evening at Hadley Harbor, a lovely, if busy, anchorage, reached via Woods Hole. The Coast Guard current charts devote their only special insert to the way the tides run in Woods Hole. Basically, they are caused by the following: (1) there is a six-foot difference in high and low in Buzzards, yet only a three-foot difference in Vineyard Sound. (2) The tide turns in Vineyard Sound three and a half to four hours later than in Buzzards Bay. (3) The current in Buzzards Bay is weaker than in the Sound. This means if you have to sail against the tide, you do better to cross into the Sound at Woods Hole.

There are two entrances to Woods Hole from Vineyard Sound; the westernmost is the easiest. Since we were coming from the west, we took it. (Woods Hole is buoyed *from* Vineyard Sound *to* Buzzards Bay. This works fine the way we were going in. But it can be confusing if you are coming *from* Buzzards Bay, since all marks are reversed.)

Little Harbor is the first of the harbors on the Woods Hole shore itself. This is where the Coast Guard station is. It's not a bad place to moor, but not nearly as good as Eel Pond, off Great Harbor, which is the next bay in. On a former approach to Eel Harbor, I had been advised to blow my hand horn for the draw bridge to go up (the draw has a good reputation for quick response but won't open when the ferries are coming in). Inside, Eel is a regular mill pond, a backwater full of salty-looking places ashore; there are not rocks to contend with inside, and there is a marina, if you need one.

Ferries run out of Great Harbor for Martha's Vineyard and Nantucket, and usually on time, although on some congested summer weekends they run a couple of hours late. Finding a place to leave your car is tough. One weekend, going out to Nantucket, I had to leave mine a full mile away from the ferry dock to find room to park.

I've spent hours in the aquarium of the Fish and Wildlife Service at Woods Hole and talking to people from the Oceanographic Institute, which runs several research vessels. There is a great restaurant and bar called Landfall on the waterfront.

We were now rapidly passing Woods Hole to starboard. We had

come in, as planned, just two hours after slack ebb at Pollack Rip. This gave us a slightly favorable tide inwards. When entering from this side, the tide floods *out* of Woods Hole and ebbs *in*.

Woods Hole Harbor was striking: its twenty or so marks were dotted with lobster red and shiny black, and the slick tongues of water rolling this way and that showed us the currents were not quite at rest.

The tides run strongest and wildest between Penzance Peninsula and Nonamesset Island. There are two passages through to Hadley; the shortest (from the Sound) is Broadway, leading into The Straight. In good tide, you have to watch for Nun 2 and Can 3 in Broadway. Both may be swept under by the five-knot tide. However, there are enough beacons fixed on the rocks so you shouldn't lose your bearings. Just be sure you have a good look at the charts before you go in; this is no place to stray out of the channel.

Once we were in The Straight, we had a clear shot at the black and red mid-channel marker dead at the end of The Straight. Next, two small marks, a can and a nun far up under the shore of Nonamessett Island, pointed the way into Hadley.

A nice little schooner astern of us tacked in, exchanging hails. We were soon between Uncatena and Nonamessett. Here we made a left turn to pass Bull, with its little dink landing, then put on the engine to make a sharp right turn to go between Bull and Goats Neck, part of Naushon. A final left around the point of Goats Neck put us down into Hadleys Inner Harbor, which contained a full twenty-four yachts, mostly sail, riding at anchor.

It's a hair unsettling to negotiate such an intricate entrance and find yourself in such a crowd but, nonetheless, Hadleys is beautiful. Ashore, a big Newport-like home, set on a ridge, marks the center of the Forbes kingdom. We nuzzled our way into a likely space between the other boats and carefully let down our anchor.

Here came a fantastic sailboat, wine-red sails, schooner rig, right up into the harbor through the boats. She was tacking—obviously not using an engine, and very likely having none—gliding in. In the final few yards her sails dropped like a shot, and she came smartly to the mooring and tied on.

Then a dink, a very marvel of nautical craftsmanship riding high and light in the water, was rowed ashore in quick, decisive sweeps by a member of the crew. Soon thereafter, a naptha launch, or the closest thing I've seen to one, came out from shore, riding slim and elegant out to the schooner to take its crew and land them by the Forbes Boat House. A most patrician entrance.

Barry, who had been busy shooting this breathtaking event from his "Yellow Terror," now came alongside with Marnie for Bea's dinner. It was a delicious roundsteak with fresh buttered peas and salad. We dispatched it all with right good will, as the old books put it; a red sun went down behind the mast of the schooner where its red sail had hung.

Menemsha Pond and Nashaquitsa Pond, Martha's Vineyard. (BARRY STOTT)

Cattle on Naushon, Tarpaulin Cove. (BARRY STOTT)

Bea with crab net, Tarpaulin Cove, Naushon. (BARRY STOTT)

Evening, Hadley Harbor, Naushon. (BARRY STOTT)

CHAPTER FIFTEEN

VINEYARD SOUND—VINEYARD HAVEN AND OAK BLUFFS

(DAY 20)

Barry Stott had motored back to his family's summer place on the shore of West Chop at Vineyard Haven the night before, but he had promised us a jeep tour of the Vineyard plus a guided talk on "Cottage City"—Oak Bluffs—among other points of interest when we came over to the Vineyard.

So we were off early on day twenty, heading for Vineyard Haven, seven miles away, bravely setting sail from under the Forbes' bonsai trees ashore (W. Cameron Forbes was an ambassador to Japan). We went out *with* the flood tide.

Outside Hadleys, we passed the two small entrance buoys and went sluicing down to the red and black mid-channel marker. The sky was deep blue, almost leaden, and the reflection of the sun behind the cumulus clouds lit contrary streams of water that oiled out of the deep like subterranean springs, billowing in spreading patterns whose opposing forces were distinctly felt. *Nimble* trembled and bobbed before the water gods.

As we progressed, I could not see black Can 3; it was under there somewhere in the tow of the current. I could see the two beacons on Middle Ledge, and they served to mark the spot where we had to turn right to go into Vineyard Sound via Broadway. We swung the corner and skidded sidewise on the current. In spite of a good breeze, we were being set sideways toward Red Ledge very fast. We had cut close to Middle Ledge so we were going to make it out all right, though. A boat behind us came through, and we marvelled at her sidewise progress; it seemed to be as fast as her forward speed, but her crew had gauged it too and she came sluicing out behind us. We sailed out one-two into Vineyard Sound, a couple of successful white-water sailors.

(We had the working jib up, happily. It was dusty and going to get dustier. Joshua Slocum, on his epochal single-handed cruise around the world, when a Malay pirate felucca set out after him in half a gale, had the judgment to shorten sail. A full gale materialized, and Slocum had the satisfaction of seeing the pirate's mast go overboard.)

A century ago, Daniel Webster reported that Vineyard Sound was the "busiest sea lane in the world with the possible exception of the English Channel." Webster actually counted well over a hundred commercial sailing craft passing through on the day he himself sailed on Vineyard Sound.

Vineyard Sound was as tricky then as now; and out beyond it were the dread Nantucket shoals. In some fifty years during the Age of Sail, some 1500 ships were lost, often with the entire crew, off Nantucket and the Vineyard.

The Vineyard pilots were therefore welcome heroes. They would race each other to incoming vessels and steer them through the perilous waters of the Elizabeths and the Vineyard. West Chop, where we were headed, was one of the "pilot stations" where they used to keep lookout and take their turns in meeting incoming sail.

Some of the pilots were no more honest than they had to be. One of them, known as "Whisko-by-the-by," would lie in wait for boats that had been missed by recognized pilots, he'd jump off his own boat and drag himself aboard the incoming ship, screaming "Up your helm. Rocks to starboard!" And then, when the helm had been swung, he would introduce himself ("Whisko-by-the-by") to the captain who, convinced he'd been saved a nasty accident, would reward "Whisko-by-the-by" suitably.

Slightly, but not far, down the rungs of the ladder of Vineyard heroes was the smuggler. He could be a pilot willing to risk something for money. West Indiamen loaded to the bow chocks with good Cuban cigars, Madeira and rum, came breezing through the Sound by the score. If you could catch one with your "bum boat" (a sailing barge full of goodies—fresh vegetables, pipe tobacco, etc.) you could effect some great deals. The only problem was keeping the booty from the U.S. Customs officers. One Vineyard smuggler used to bury his in a load of specially prepared hay and poison ivy. After one search there, the customs officers left the barn alone.

Wreckers were another thing: every Vineyarder was a natural wrecker; that is, he salvaged. What a northeaster brought in was anybody's luck. "You can leave your pocket book down on shore, and it will be perfectly safe as long as the wind don't blow nothe-east," an old captain said.

The passenger liner, *The City of Columbus*, in January, 1884, struck Devil's Bridge off Gay Head and settled down. The Gay Head Indians rowed out in the freezing seas to pull passengers out of the rigging. Much else was also eventually salvaged. There are linens and silver and inner doors (Martha's Vineyard was always short on lumber), now gracing some of the Vineyard's better homes, that came from *The City of Columbus*.

Nimble was now closing on the wide, yawning bay of Vineyard Haven, a big V-shaped body of water between East Chop and West Chop. On the verge of being wetted down, we thankfully eased into the wind-shadow of West Chop.

Out of the wind it was a warm day. We shed our foul weather gear as we slid into the blue welcome of the Vineyard Haven Harbor (point 22, map 9). Barry's six-five frame stood ashore in front of his family's summer place. We let a stern anchor go sixty feet off as a brake, slowed to a nice stop just a few feet from the beach, then heaved our forward anchor up on the beach, a neat landing.

Before Cape Cod Canal opened in 1914, Vineyard Haven was the jumping-off spot for the trip around Cape Cod to Boston; it was also an arrival port for vessels coming from Boston and Down East. A semaphore connection was set up in 1802, there were signal stations every few miles right into Boston to keep the Boston merchants informed of arrivals and departures of vessels at Holmes Hole, as Vineyard Haven was then called. Two hundred ships at a time lay moored there.

The great gale of 1898 drove some fifty vessels ashore or turned them over at Holmes Hole. That kept the semaphore busy for several days.

Vineyard Haven's present status as a resort town started with Oak Bluffs, east of Vineyard Haven. Oak Bluffs abuts the old Methodist camp meeting ground at Wesleyan Grove. A series of extensive land development schemes came out of the old camp meetings. The first was Oak Bluffs; the second was Vineyard Highlands on East Chop.

In 1871, Bellevue Heights was laid out between Highlands and Holmes Hole. Land which had sold for $20 an acre in the winter of 1871 was selling for $250 by next spring.

West Chop speculation boomed, too. In 1871 entrepreneurs Smith and Norton purchased a land tract for $4,000 and sold it to West Point Grove Co. for $10,000 a few weeks later.

For a while all was prosperous and exciting. A correspondent of the *Vineyard Gazette*, quoted in the present Gazette editor's *Martha's Vineyard: Summer Resort After 100 Years* tells the story:

" . . . Wesleyan Grove—Vineyard Highlands—Bellevue Heights—a territory bounded on the north by Lagoon Pond and about twenty-seven cords of painted stakes, on the south by Sengekontacket Bridge, on the east by Vineyard Sound, and on the west by a general exuberance of nature, the whole constituting one of the most remarkable districts to be found on the coast, or anywhere else. Here for three quarters of a year, the domination of desolation—the stillness of almost utter abandonment—prevails, and the few scattered laborers hurry along the avenues looking askance, as though the long lines of deserted tenements were so many platoons of ghosts; while during the other quarter all the hum and hubbub of a permanent metropolis may be heard in the land: crowds surge to and fro, intent on business or pleasure, horse cars pass and repass, newsboys yell, ladies go shopping, and everything bespeaks the city. Here the real estater comes to fleece his fellows, portraying with agonizing earnestness the merits of corner lots and water lots, Highland and Bluff; and here, on the testimony of your own prominent townsmen, in the shade of these pleasant groves and by these rippling waters, the Vineyard girls have long accustomed themselves to find their life companions, and the damsels of today and looking hitherward with longing eyes, looking at their destiny."

In 1873 came the bust. Empty lots went for pennies. In 1874, a lot in Bellevue went for sixty-six cents, another in the Highlands went for sixty-four.

But the speculators—in the long run—were right. It is next to impossible to get land in either Chop today. In West Chop, even wherewithal, say $50,000 on the average for a roomy cottage, is not a guarantee. You have to have the blessing of the private corporation that has the land on West Chop in trust. If you rent for a couple of years, and they like you there, you are allowed to buy the next home that comes up. It helps if you play good tennis.

Our first excursion from *Nimble* was over to the tennis courts in the "village" (West Chop has its own post office right next to the tennis courts.) Here was the world in white; sixty-nine-year-olds and nine-year-olds playing with equal expertise, savagery and politeness. Tennis had replaced conversation.

We drove on to Vineyard Haven town.

Barry drives a very fast jeep; he has "enginitis," the compulsion to bounce rapidly in accompaniment to the roar of exhaust vents. We rushed through present-day Vineyard Haven: a collection of chic shops and stately houses. Inside the latter are heirlooms in corners and cupboards: lacquer cabinets from China, Algaroba wood cribs from Ecuador, shells from the South Sea Islands—all testifying to the travels of the 1800's, when whaling was the order of the day.

There is a story in Tisbury town about a retired whaling captain who continued a grudge against a certain Tisbury harpooner who had once missed a particularly big whale. The harpooner, on his side, didn't like the captain's dog and loudly threatened to shoot it. "Go ahead and shoot," said the captain drily. "If you can't hit a whale, you can't hit a dog."

So many Vineyard men went whaling that a regular mail drop was established on Galapagos Island (where the whalers enroute to the Pacific or returning would stop to catch fresh turtle meat and get the latest copies of *The Vineyard Gazette*).

In Tisbury town graveyards you can still read of the price of fame and fortune at sea; " . . . struck overboard in the Mulgrave Islands . . . died at Port Au Prince . . . lost near the coast of New Zealand . . ." Once in a while, among the welter of violent ends there is a little humor, as well:

> Here lies our beloved Charlotte
> Born a virgin, died a harlot.
> For sixteen years she kept her virginity,
> Which is a very good record for this vicinity.

With Barry at the wheel, we drove around the bottom of The Lagoon (point 23, map 9). The Lagoon entrance has six feet coming in at low tide. During daylight, the drawbridge will raise if you blast three times. You can go in and lay at anchor in Vineyard Haven Lagoon in a hurricane with nearly perfect safety. The channel goes down almost two miles straight inland (watch for Robinsons Rock by black Can "D").

On the east side of The Lagoon, just past the entrance, is the state lobster hatchery, where they have solved the problem of hatching and raising lobsters. New lobsters are like tiny pellets. At four months, one is as long as a little finger.

A hundred lobster in the same tank will cannibalize each other so fast that in a few hours there will be only a couple of dozen survivors and no corpses. They eat each other shell and all. The hatchery keeps the water in the tanks moving so fast that the lobsters are kept busy swimming. The hatchery gets the lobsters through the first few weeks of life when their normal survival rate is one in a million.

We were now getting the mid-island tour through smaller clusters of houses inland, woods, fields, trees and the secluded summer houses of the 40,000 summer inhabitants of Paradise (in winter Paradise has about 6000). The half-dozen hard-surface roads on the island barely force passage through the lush trees, bending overhead as if to hide such a crass innovation as a road. Small, shady dirt roads, branching off, get closer to the heart of things: the bayberry bush, the salt grass, the gray-shingled unpretentious house owned either by a spinster teacher or a millionaire family—not possible to tell which. That's the way the Vineyard wants it. Instead of being a vice, propriety is a virtue, here, by being unenforced.

We drove country lanes that seemed to run on slightly depressed heather until we were on South Beach. The day was fair, but I didn't see a single soul on our several-mile stretch of beach, except for Barry, Marnie and the crew of the *Nimble*. We all sank into the sand and had a nice long recovery from jeeping, content to listen to the mild, sleepy measured thump, thump of the sea.

After an hour, we drove north into Oak Bluffs. It was the first true American summer vacation spot; people who came used a light cover of religion to give respectability to what was otherwise just the disreputable occupation of enjoying oneself.

The derivation of the New England use of the word "camp" to signify "summer home" traces to Oak Bluffs.

The new enjoyment was arrived at by way of Evangelical Methodism, where Salvation is effected through unbridled persuasion and open confession. The method reached the Vineyard in 1809, in Edgartown, with the arrival of the Rev. Erastus Otis, who shouted his evangelical arguments with such force that conversions came by the score, even in the face of disapprobation by the conservative Methodist, not to mention Presbyterians and Unitarians.

"Why sir," wrote one distressed, conservative Vineyard minister, "this place has been the stronghold of fanatical preachers. And not seldom patients have been transferred from the hands of the clergyman to those of the private physician. What think you of meetings every night in the week for six weeks, yes, for three months in succession, prolonged at times even into midnight, until the very floor by its apparent lifeless trophies, bears melancholy witness to the tremendous effects wrought upon the average nervous system by the machinery of superstition?"

The first outdoor or "camp" meeting on the Vineyard was held in 1829 on West Chop, not half a mile from the Stott home. There, the exhortations of "Reformation John" Adams brought forty sinners into the fold. In 1835, on East Chop, a second group, the Edgartown Methodists, met under an enormous grove of oaks, the largest in New England at the time, near Squash Meadow Pond. A preacher's shed and pulpit were constructed out of driftwood; nine tents were cut out of old sails and pitched in front of the platform, with a partition in each separating the sexes. By the time the 1835 meeting was over, "Wesleyan Grove" had been founded, a thousand people had attended and sixty-five new souls had been claimed for God.

"An awful sense of the presence of God pervades the encampment and the slain of the Lord lie upon every side . . ." wrote one of the early Wesleyan Grove witnesses upon surveying the twisted bodies of the sin-wracked trying to struggle to salvation (a sort of catharsis familiar today to the LSD circles of mystics).

By 1859, Wesleyan Grove was the largest camp meeting in the world, but by that time the spirituality seemed less pronounced. A Boston newspaperman wrote in 1859, ". . . although the day was the Sabbath, the scene, for a few hours, reminded me of the Fourth of July, minus fireworks and boisterousness. Everybody appeared happy, joyful, smiling; thousands of young and beautiful females, elegantly dressed, promenaded along green paths with young men, whilst an immense crowd listened attentively to eloquent and deeply impressive addresses. Many thousand persons visited the camp ground merely to enjoy a day's pleasure, and seemed to take not the slightest interest in the religious services; but not one individual interfered in any manner to interrupt or disturb true worshipers . . . I speak of the *tout ensemble* as an extraordinary show. I never before saw a finer display of beautiful women, better regularity or thousands conducting themselves as at this camp ground."

By 1870, Twenty steamers a day came to Oak Bluffs landing, carrying campers.

Thousands of sperm oil lanterns flickering outside the tents and cottages (more now of the latter) made Oak Bluffs and Wesleyan Grove a "city of lights." An annual celebration was inaugurated that persists to this day—a display of lights and lanterns, balloons, streamers and fireworks—Illumination Night.

Oak Bluffs still has strong reminders of its tent origin; a lot of the smaller cottages looked very much like peaked tents, open to the outside, rather transparent. The scrollwork on the porches or piazzas reminded one of circus tents' ornamentation: rounded scallops, dizzy designs indicating light-heartedness.

Henry Beetle Hough, in *Martha's Vineyard, Summer Resort After One Hundred Years*, described the tent and cottage city on East Chop: "Here was the encampment near the sea offering no real barrier of expense, no restraint that could not be reconciled, no reminder of responsibility, no stale Age from the past . . . So safe and respectable were the surroundings that the best families permitted their daughters to go "bluffing" and it was seldom that any harm came from the practice. Mere presence at the grove was sufficient for young people as for old, further introduction was unnecessary.

"Cottages were so near, moreover, that it was almost possible to proceed from one to another by hopping the gaps between piazza railings. Seated on these ornamented porches, the cottagers could hardly be said to be separated at all: they were part of one large concourse, a series in continual repetition of delightful family groups—delightful because this was the life, the freedom, the change in which they took an ineffable pleasure."

Having seen the homes with the best of the carpenter's scrollwork, we now drove off to Oak Bluffs Harbor, small and crowded, with a few guest moorings. It had the best grocery we encountered on the cruise, an S.S. Pierce with a full liquor store inside. Happily for yachtsmen (since Vineyard Haven is dry) the grocery had its own dock.

Further east down the Oak Bluffs shore is Harthaven, a long, peaceful pond connected to the sea; there are a couple of docks there and some anchorage room. It would serve as a place to keep your boat if you find you want to visit Oak Bluffs by sea and do not want to anchor in the crowd at Oak Bluffs Harbor itself.

Now the *Nimble* crew was going to retreat from land history and go off to maritime history: we had a plan to meet the *Shenandoah*, mightiest sailing ship in the islands, as she came into Vineyard Haven. The *Shenandoah* is the whim of a very wealthy fellow who could have picked any ship in the world to build (what a terrible freedom!). The yacht he did build was a 130-foot, faithful copy of the fast packet schooners that carried the mail to England in the days of sail.

We scooted *Nimble* out from Vineyard Haven with an extra crew, Barry's brother-in-law. Barry and Marnie tagged us in the *Yellow Terror*, to take pictures of the packet and trimaran together.

Shenandoah came at us, right on schedule. She was big enough so we could see her as soon as she left Edgartown, down the coast. There was no mistaking the ship on size alone: a square-topsail schooner, the reincarnation of those fast American schooners whose exploits made them the most widely admired of all American sailing craft.

As we swung around to go with her, she seemed to be logging a good nine miles an hour. *Nimble* was doing nearly that well, so we got a good long look as she slowly pulled under our lee and then moved ahead, throwing the swell to the sides with a smooth, regal motion, hardly nodding her bow. *Nimble*, running all out, held on for nearly twenty minutes before *Shenandoah* moved out and led us into Vineyard Haven.

We were invited aboard by her creator and captain, Bob Douglas. She was a delight in wood and workmanship, down to the oil lanterns, inlaid wood furniture and gimbaled wood tables below. She takes some thirty voyagers out of the Vineyard every Monday for a week, just to keep Bob's tax situation in hand. Passengers or none, he just likes to sail her; he is the only man I've talked to who could roll out the old words, like "main t'gallant," as if he used them every day. Bob handles *Shenandoah* with about ten men and occasional help from passengers. Had he built himself a full square rigger, he explained, he would have had to have dozens more in his crew.

At Stott's for dinner: patio steaks on the grill outside, where we could see the *Shenandoah*'s spars over the harbor. Once a hundred masts like hers raked skyward of an evening in Holmes Hole.

Shenandoah, *off Vineyard Haven*. (BARRY STOTT)

Shenandoah *mainmast, Vineyard Haven*. (BARRY STOTT)

CHAPTER SIXTEEN

VINEYARD SOUND— WAQUOIT AND EDGARTOWN

(DAYS 21 AND 22)

Directly opposite Vineyard Haven on the coast of Cape Cod is Falmouth Harbor (point 28, map 9), the first of fifteen or so harbors on the south shore of Cape Cod out to Stage Harbor and Monomoy Island. One of the loveliest of these harbors is Waquoit (point 31, map 9), a gentle beauty. It is no trouble at all to skip across Vineyard Sound to Waquoit, enroute to Edgartown. That's exactly what we planned to do.

The Cape ports represent a considerable safety factor, allowing a skipper to sail up under a protected shore, in a nor'easter say, and find himself shelter there rather than driving downwind to a lee shore harbor on the Vineyard.

The Cape shore is sandy—it never stands still. Nauset Beach shrinks; Monomoy Island, below, grows. A few years ago, Bass River was navigable by cruising yachts while Stage Harbor was silted in. Recently it was the reverse.

Regardless of the date of your information, if you are heading for one of the south shore Cape harbors, you will do well to phone ahead to the harbormaster or marina. *The Boating Almanac*, Volume 1, for the current year (G.W. Bromley, 325 Spring Street, New York, N.Y.) will give you the phone numbers.

We had breakfast on shore this morning in the Stott's home, which is typical for this shore.

As Bea described it (in a letter home):

"Really a nice house. Right on the water with about two hundred feet of beachfront, between two low stone walls running into the surf. Cape Cod style, but very old, all wood and painted inside. Gray shingled on the outside. It is set way back and is reached from the road along a path through huge maples and oaks with lots of greenery and bush. There is a large porch overlooking the seaside greenery, up behind the sand beach, an outdoor shower (it was fun to shower under open blue sky and sun with trees rustling to either side) and lots of windows on all sides of the house. The ceiling beams are low, with white wood walls and a fireplace and lots of sailing prints, yacht club pennants, etc. There is a large sprawling kitchen and a nice grassy backyard . . ."

We boarded *Nimble* off the beach, left all this comfort behind and with Barry and Marnie aboard, headed east across Vineyard Sound. Day twenty-one was a beauty.

We had the flood tide with us. The only way the tides in Vineyard and Nantucket sounds make any sense is if you think of these two sounds as one single great harbor with its entrance between the Elizabeths and Menemsha. Picture the tides entering this throat on the flood, having to go east to fill up the harbor; picture the harbor waters having to ebb west in order to empty. Then you have the idea.

We coasted out into the Sound and sailed dead for Waquoit with the southerly, leaving the Falmouth shore to port as we closed on the Cape.

Falmouth is a swinging town with lots of bars and restaurants. It has a good, if somewhat narrow, harbor. The town is a beauty with an especially good looking village green. The trees there were planted by Captain Elijah Swift, who in 1820 sent out Falmouth's first whale ship. Soon Swift was a considerable fleet owner whose crews had the usual run of rough living on whale hunts. The following is an excerpt of an extant diary from a Swift whaling ship:

"Sunday, Janury 9—Sixty fore days out of Falmouth Mass & not won single whale have we tuk yit.

"Monday, Janury 10—Vilents broke out in the galley today. The men says they would not eat the potatoe barging because there was too many cockroaches & other incests in it, and they maid Peter White, our neegrow cook, eat it insted. So ends this day, still no whales in site.

"Tuesday, Janury 11—Peter White the cook complaned of panes in the abdoming and died this day 3 o'clock p.m. The Capting had ordered the men questchinned trying to find out who is gilty of making him eat the potatoe barging, but all hands pleed innosensts. So ends, not a whale in these onwholly waters.

"Wensday, Janury 12—Fewnril sarvises wes held at 11 a.m. for Peter White. All hands cept the lookout called on deck to witness our last fairwell to our pore shipmate. He was laid in a box the Capting begun to reed sourfully from the scripter after giveing worning that any man that udders a disrespective word is going to get seesed up in the riggin. Suddenly the lookout calls thar she blows. The 1st whale we seen in the whole of this miserable viage. The Capting went on reeding over the departid & the lookout calls thar she blows and breeches and belches. The Capting drops his book and orders the men—Heave that damned carkiss overboard and lower way. But we was too late. So ends, our won whale, the only whale we seen yit—gorn."

On *Nimble,* we coasted past Eel Pond entrance and toward the jetties that mark the Waquoit entrance from the Sound. Inside, a string of private buoys marked a five-foot-deep channel to the far end of the bay. Waquoit was a real pond, with kids in Cape Cod Beetle Cats chasing each other as if it were the most landlocked lake in front of a Maine summer camp for kids. We anchored off the wooded shore at the far end of the pond and watched the kids go sailing home to the yacht club dock abeam of our anchorage. We had dinner, saw the sun go down and retired to the lap of waves against the hull.

Next morning, day twenty-two, we were out on the Sound early, anxious to get the ten miles to Edgartown put away quickly. Off our port quarter, to our regret, as we belted down the genny and looked back, we were leaving the long stretch of the Cape out to Monomoy, a stretch we would gladly have explored, had our time been more than the twenty-three days we were able to give ourselves. (We had planned to leave the boat at Nantucket and sail it back in a number of weekends to Three Mile, just to make the most of the twenty-three days.)

The nearest of the harbors along the Cape is a triple bay, or an island surrounded by three bays. The island is Osterville Grand Isle and the bays—clockwise from the west—are Cotuit Bay (point 2, map 10), North Bay-Prince Cove (point 3, map 10) and West Bay. In between West Bay and North Bay lies Osterville, where the famous

Crosby catboats were built.

The first Crosby catboat, *Little Eva*, launched in 1850, took a lot of kidding. There were no single-sail work boats on the coast then. But a single sail, in spite of the detractors, proved to be a good work boat rig. She was quick on her feet as a cat, so that is what they called her. ("Catboat" became the generic name for any single-sailed craft bigger than a sailing dinghy.) *Little Eva* was so shallow (one foot, three inches) that she would skim over south shore sand bars like a ghost ship. The Crosby Cat was wide as a dish (six feet for fourteen of length) so it would carry a good cargo.

East from Osterville, the best two harbors are Stage Harbor (point 12, map 10) and Chatham Harbor (point 11, map 10).

Stage Harbor, just inside Monomoy, is now relatively easy to get to. A new channel has been cut through Harding Beach and it's a straight shot in. Once behind the beach, you have the choice of the outer harbor just behind the beach, or the inside harbor behind Morris Island. From the latter, you can enjoy all the best advantages of being a Cape summer visitor—fishing, summer theatre, shopping at Chatham, swimming (the water in Stage Harbor is nice and warm, not like the ocean water outside) and exploring. You can sail or dinghy into two ponds further in from Morris Island. You can rent bikes and pedal through Chatham. You can rent a boat over the dunes in Chatham Harbor and explore the nine or ten miles of the intriguing harbor of Chatham, behind Nauset Beach, without having to take the tough ten-plus mile route around Monomoy Island to get there.

Nauset Beach was called "The Great Beach" by Henry Thoreau, down from Walden Pond for a visit. The Great Beach faces the Atlantic all the way up to the hook of Provincetown; it has been made a National Seashore—just in time to save it from private exploitation.

The waters out past Monomoy to Pollack Rip and Nantucket Shoals have been the scene of over two thousand recorded shipwrecks, so there is little inducement to cruise these waters unless you cherish adversity. John Hay, in *The Great Beach*, wrote, "In a great storm occurring in October of 1841, the town of Truro lost 57 men, being already burdened with a large population of widows, and on the day after the storm, nearly a hundred bodies were recovered along the Cape Cod shore."

These wild waters even deflected the course of history. In November, 1620, the Pilgrims' *Mayflower* sighted the Cape, their first land since Holland. According to the eyewitness account, the Pilgrims ". . . tacked about and resolved to stand to the southward (the wind and weather being fair) to find some place about the Hudson's River for their habitation. But after they had sailed that course about half the day, they fell amongst dangerous shoals and roaring breakers and they were so far entangled therewith that as they conceived themselves in great danger, they resolved to head up again for the Cape, and thought themselves happy to get out of those dangers before night overtook them, as by God's providence they did. And the next day they got into the Cape harbor; where they rid in safety."

Thanks to Pollock Rip, the Pilgrims came to Plymouth instead of New York.

We were leaving the Cape astern, running full tilt for Edgartown. As we came abeam of Cape Poge, a fast Boston Whaler came bounding out like a big whippet, her pilot high on his seat, steering with bare feet. He circled us, waving, and was off down the Vineyard coast, west toward Vineyard Haven.

Then, from Edgartown in the slot between Cape Poge and the main body of the island, came a procession of big yachts, some of them unlimbering, candy-colored, peppermint-striped spinnakers. The annual New York Yacht Club cruise was coming out of Edgartown Harbor. We tacked leisurely through the oncoming fleet, spectating some of the most beautiful yachts made by man. The big yachts cleared us and went off astern like a trailing cloud.

We were now well into the entrance to Edgartown, surrounded by a fleet of small one designs, sleek little meter-boat hulls milling around us like fleet schooling fish.

We tried to hold a course without flinching as the small hulls flashed across the bows and flickered at our sides and stern. At the same time, we were keeping an eye out for the Chappaquiddick ferry that runs back and forth across the entrance to Edgartown's inner harbor like a yo-yo. We came about right in the entrance, just short of a monster yacht tied up at the town dock. A woman on the bridge of the monster, cocktail glass in one hand, had begun making frantic motions with her free hand. The captain, in braid, stepped up to the rail, slapped both hands on it and leaned over to make sure we didn't touch.

We crossed through the meter boat fleet again on our leg to the anchorage behind the Chappaquiddick Beach, where the Edgartown fleet lay in random rows at moorings. Settling down between a large mahogany sloop and a seaplane among a very rich crop of yachts, we were soon bobbing about on our anchor, watching the Chappaquiddick ferry run to Edgartown and the meter boats infiltrating the anchorage, mooring here and there with a swift dropping of sails and immediate hails for the yacht club tender.

From where we had come to anchor, Edgartown Harbor proceeds southward between the Vineyard and Chappaquiddick Island. The two shores aren't more than a few hundred feet apart at first. As the pas-

sage bends around the corner, it widens into Katama Bay. Here there
is a second anchorage, away from the madding yachts, if you want that.
There is always a good current in Katama Bay and in the channel to it;
Katama is open to the sea (although the break is too shallow to be
navigated) to the south, and the tides run through at three knots or
so. But there is plenty of room to swing in at Katama; up where we
were in the anchorage, we seemed to be far enough out of the main
current so that there was no problem with dragging.

Katama and Edgartown were explored thoroughly early in the history of the coast. Thomas Hunt, sailing Capt. John Smith's ship up from
the first English colony, Jamestown, arrived here in 1614. He incau-
tiously took some Indians prisoner at Edgartown, intending to sell them
as slaves. The next group of whites that came to Edgartown, under
Thomas Dermer, were therefore set upon by the Indians and slain, all
but one. (At this point, of course, the *Mayflower* had not yet even left
Holland.)

According to the *Martha's Vineyard Guide*, put out by the Dukes
County Historical Society in Edgartown, Hunt sailed for Europe and
tried to sell his Indians in Spain. The Spaniards, who had had a good
century's experience with Indians, declined. He proceeded to London
where one of the slaves, Epenow, learned English rapidly and told
stories of gold nuggets lying around like pebbles in Edgartown. These
tales encouraged Shakespeare's patron, the Earl of Southampton, and
Sir Ferdinando Gorges, to fit out a ship. With Epenow aboard, the
ship sailed to Edgartown. When it hit the harbor, Epenow gave his cap-
tors the slip, and the explorers had no luck finding the gold. They
sailed back to England, having been had by an Indian. Later, Epenow
was to astound the Pilgrims at Plymouth by greeting them in English.

Happily for Indians and for the islands, the first permanent island
settlement in the New World was made in 1642 on the Vineyard at
Edgartown by Thomas Mayhew, a humane and eminently fair man. His
treatment of the Indians worked so well that when King Phillip's war
broke out ashore, and the mainland Indians were massacring colonists,
the Indians on the Vineyard were given extra rifles by Mayhew and
trusted to keep the shore Indians off the island.

Edgartown was so named by the British Colonial Governor of New
York, Lovelace, for the son of the Duke of York, heir presumptive.
The town grew very slowly for fifty years; there were only thirty-six
houses there by 1694. Five generations later, there were hundreds of
homes, and Edgartown was known as a shipping and whaling port
throughout the world. Her captains daily set out for the Indies, the
Pacific, Hawaii, Japan, the Indian Ocean and the Arctic.

By 1835, of fifteen hundred people in Edgartown, three hundred (half the male adults) were making a living at sea. Eighty of Edgartown's sailors became whaling captains, masters who went about making first landings in Polynesia, Micronesia and Australia. Captain Nathaniel Jernegan of Edgartown was the first white captain to set foot in Japan after Perry opened it to the West.

Edgartown's present preoccupation with summer resort business was presaged in 1830 by an early summer visitor, Nathaniel Hawthorne, who had come down from New Hampshire to spend a few months and do a bit of writing. In his collection of short stories, *Twice Told Tales*, Hawthorne records in *"Chippings from a Chisel"* that an Edgartown tombstone was engraved with the following iconoclastic legend:

> By the force of vegetation
> I was raised to life and action.
> When life and action shall cease
> I shall return to the same source.

Daniel Webster arrived twenty years later; summer guest business was beginning to bloom with the usual attendant diminuation of independence of spirit. Webster, who was swarthy, arrived in a coach with Negro servants. The innkeeper told Webster that he did not take in colored. The innkeeper meant Webster. But Webster thought the innkeeper meant the servants so he calmly signed the register.

The first appearance (of many) of the New York Yacht Club cruise came in 1858. The squadron was thirty-eight strong and included in its number *America*, which had not so long before come back from England with the prize destined to be known as the *America*'s Cup. The younger sailors of the fleet, nattily dressed, ventured into this strange seaside town. They soon arranged introductions to the best families; things went very quickly. They hired the town hall for the night ($2.50) and set up a dance. The girls of the town came and the Squadron stayed on an extra day.

We hailed the Edgartown Yacht Club launch and got a ride to the Yacht Club landing at Dock Street. We set out on foot and made a tour that, first of all, took us by the present site of the *Vineyard Gazette*, a couple of blocks off. Since 1920, it has been run by Henry and Elizabeth Hough, and is one of the most literate newspapers in the country. Hough's *Martha's Vineyard*: *Summer Resort After 100 Years* is a model of historical writing.

Up away from the harbor, we found the winding salty streets of the whaling port with captains' houses angled from each other so as to get the best view of the sea—white clapboard siding, flower boxes of red geraniums and pink petunias, huge old trees, white picket fences, lush gardens, the pagoda tree brought by a whaling captain from Japan, the harbor views from the hill (the town goes somewhat uphill), the Dukes County Historical Society buildings and the "Moby Dick House" of Captain Valentine Pease on whose *Acushnet* Herman Melville shipped out in 1641. (Melville skipped ship for the more kindly atmosphere of a mid-Pacific cannibal island and got back to the United States by joining the Navy.)

We were here on a Saturday. As we walked back to the harbor front, the streets were afloat with people. Down toward the waterfront, the restaurants crowd the shops, the shops abut hotels, the hotels jostle the inns. There are clam bars, seafood counters, bar bars and restaurants quite like pizza parlours. There are also welcome restaurants like Seafood Shanty and Harborside, which would rate a couple of stars on anybody's list. The cars were nearly static in town, squeezed by people —mammas, pappas, kids, yachtsmen and tourists, spilling from curb to curb.

This is all to say that Edgartown is commercial. It is lively. We enjoyed it. Bea and I had a great cocktail hour in the Harborside, overlooking the harbor, and dinner: lobster served cold and deep-dish apple pie.

Harbor-watching from the Harborside with the sea all around made for a nice accompaniment to our coffee. A skin diver was at work, swimming through the floats, trying to locate a lost mooring on the bottom. The harbor is clean; it is always full of small craft traffic. There is always a breeze.

Edgartown is renowned for its great—sometimes too great—winds. The southwester blows for days. It is a solid wind and a great racing wind. The annual Edgartown Regatta is the third most important regatta on the East Coast (after Larchmont and Marblehead). At regatta time, the town is really filled "not even a wild rabbit can make its way through the traffic," groused one resident), but the lovely day-after-day wind, the girls (oh to be twenty-one and in Edgartown during race week), and the caliber of the racing makes Edgartown's the most satisfying race week on the coast.

After dinner Bea and I took the short-line ferry over to Chappaquiddick Beach and walked until we were abeam of *Nimble* in the anchorage. If we had had the time, we would have rented a bike in Edgartown and explored Chappaquiddick, which, next to Forbes' islands in the Elizabeths, is the least-touched land in Dukes County.

We spent the hour before dusk watching the small boats come in, drop sail and get picked up by friends and head in for merry times in Edgartown. We stayed out in the anchorage as it slowly became calm, quiet, and regained a hint of the century before this one. The slowly swaying masts darkened into the summer night sky.

Marnie, aboard Nimble, *en route to Edgartown.* (MORTEN LUND)

Edgartown Yacht Club, Edgartown. (BARRY STOTT)

~~~~~~

CHAPTER SEVENTEEN

NANTUCKET SOUND—NANTUCKET ISLAND

~~~~~~

(DAY 23)

We were now leaving Edgartown on day twenty-three of our cruise. Next, Nantucket, our last stop and the high point of our current cruise—of anyone's cruise.

Sid's time with us was over—he had bussed off from Edgartown to take the Vineyard ferry to Woods Hole and the bus to New York. A pity he would miss Nantucket, because it's not like anything else on the East Coast. Historically and in reality, it is a refreshingly different entity.

The tide floods *out* of Edgartown harbor; it comes up from Katama as it rises and goes out the Edgartown entrance. Thus we moved easily out from the anchorage, past the monster yacht still at the town dock,

out the narrow gap between the breakwaters and shore and into the
outer harbor bounded by the Vineyard coast on one side and the long,
low profile of Cape Poge on the other. We had gotten off at nine—
Barry and Marnie, Bernie and Ellen, myself and Bea—and by nine-
thirty we were halfway up Cape Poge, pushed by little whorls of water
urging us in the right direction.

Fessenden Blanchard once wrote of sailing his shallow draft *Mariana*
right through Cape Poge Bay (point 16, map 10) en route to Nantucket.
Cape Poge now has only one entrance open, at the base of the Cape, a
narrow shallow channel that is only three feet deep and best taken on a
rising tide in case you do get stuck.

Nimble is my choice of yachts for cruising these waters because it
only draws two and a half feet. Wilensky's choice was *Pee Gee*, drawing four, and Blanchard's was *Mariana*, drawing two feet eight. We all
have one conviction in common; shoal draft gives one the best of the
cruising between New York and Nantucket.

We were intent on clearing Cape Poge and heading toward Nantucket. As soon as we had turned the corner, we were being set by
the tide that comes north through Muskeget channel between Nantucket and Chappaquiddick. The tide on the flood goes north here for
a while; you will note the effect if you keep track of your position. We
had a northeaster working pretty well for us so we were soon east of
Muskeget Channel, and the tide was now with us, boosting us toward
Nantucket.

The day turned out to be gorgeous, but the northeaster blew itself
out. We simply waited, lolling in the sun, carried on by a favorable tide.
It was too good a day to spoil with an engine.

"Hell of a note for a speed man," said Barry, but he soon subsided
into relaxation. Eventually a southerly sprang up from Muskeget way.
We watched two terns flying low away from us, first with wings beating
in phase, then out of phase, then again in unison. We were soon streaming at Nantucket with wind and tide, sailing a balance of the elements:
the rippling water, the cool delicious breeze, the warm sun, and Nantucket coming on. The water under the stern was a rising, falling stream
and we let civilization drift out of our system.

Abeam, after a while, the island of Tuckernuck (point 17, map 10)
slipped by and then Madaket Harbor (point 18, map 10) at the near
end of Nantucket. We then spotted the bell where we made our turn
inward, at the end of Tuckernuck Shoal. (Over the shoal there are
rocks close to the surface and lots of turbulence.)

This island of Nantucket, "the far away island," as the Indians called
it, was the home of men who truly loved the sea. Nothing undid their
passion; they had to work their will on the sea and wrest their ease

from her. At any given moment half of the Nantucket men were at sea, fishing, whaling, freighting, piloting, sealing, seeking California gold—there was no end to where their mistress led them.

And yet Nantucket started as a farm.

Farmer Thomas Macy and his family sailed down from Salisbury, Massachusetts, in 1659 with Edward Starbuck. They wintered in a shack at Madaket and were joined in the spring by Tristram Coffin, the man who had led the movement to get together enough money from ten families to buy the island. (It cost thirty pounds and two beaver hats, paid to Thomas Mayhew and Mrs. Mayhew of the Vineyard.) The community, which first settled at Capaum Harbor on the north shore, slowly built its way to the west shore of Nantucket Harbor; they raised the same crops the Indians did and got along with them well.

In 1764, history records that the Great Plague killed off the original inhabitants, the Indians; 222 of the remaining 358 died. The very last of them expired, weakened by disease or alcohol, in the next century. Obed Macy, historian of the Nantucket whites, wrote, "Thus, the existence of a tribe of natives terminated and thus their land went to the strangers. In simple charity of nature, they rescued our fathers . . . they opened to them their stores, bestowed on them their lands, treated them with unfailing kindness, acknowledged their superiority, tasted their poison and died. Their only misfortune was their connection with Christians, and their only crime, the imitation of their manners."

In 1672, a scragg, or small whale, showed up in the harbor and the Indians set out after it and killed it with harpoons. The settlers thereafter did the same when opportunity offered. They even became more systematic, erecting whaling stations—lookout posts—around the island. In 1690, they hired a Cape Codder, Ichabod Paddock, to show them advanced whaling techniques. "Whale citching" began to resemble industry, with trypots ashore for boiling the oil out of the blubber and regular expeditions afloat to harpoon coastwise whale.

In 1712, Christopher Hussey, a Nantucket whaler, searching for right whales, ran into a bunch of sperm wales, huge, far more fearsome creatures. Hussey harpooned one, managed to kill it, and brought home a much fatter, oilier carcass than Nantucket had ever tried out before.

By the time the Great Plague had arrived, so had the Quakers. The island had gotten along without any organized religion for nearly a hundred years; now they had one which cut off jollity in favor of sobriety and poured the excess into work. Nantucket was then an island of 4500 people and, more importantly, of 150 vessels skilled in the chase of the whale. Quaker Nantucket was the third biggest town in Massachusetts; man for man, it was incomparably the richest town in America.

Nantucket whalers now sailed as far as the waters of Brazil to capture their monstrous mammals. Nantucket—in those days before oil was discovered in the ground—was as important to England, nearly, as the Near East is today.

Nantucket produced more whale oil than the aggregate of competing colonial whaling ports. Ships went directly to London from Nantucket, traded their oil for goods, carried the goods to Boston. Three Nantucket ships, the *Beaver*, the *Eleanor,* and the *Dartmouth*, carried British tea into Boston Harbor for the Boston Tea Party. Nantucketers took the loss when their fellow colonists dumped the tea in protest against taxes.

The Revolution nearly ruined Nantucket. This island would have joined either side, had either protected her from the other. The colonies ignored her defense. The British sank 134 of Nantucket's ships and killed twelve hundred of her finest men, leaving over two hundred widows and over three hundred orphans on the island.

The ship *Beaver*, which had such a signal part in instituting the Revolution, eventually led the way to healing the scars of the Revolution. Having rounded Cape Horn, *Beaver* came back with the first cargo of Pacific sperm whale oil. The Pacific soon became better known to Nantucket than the precincts of Boston. By 1820, the Nantucket whale ships were bringing back an average of two thousand barrels of oil a trip from the Pacific, with profits up to $150,000 per trip. Nantucket was richer then ever before.

Nimble made it to the old whaling town shortly before eleven. The breakwater took us in to Brant Point where, in 1746, the first lighthouse on the East Coast was built.

Around the point lay Nantucket town, facing the big harbor (point 19, map 10). From the deck of *Nimble*, the town seemed to be heavily bulkheaded at the water. Enroute to the inner harbor, we motored past Steamboat Wharf and Old North Wharf. Here summer residents had built a village of Cape Cods over water and on the water; flowerpots reflected red peonies in the tide, and little sailboats betook themselves seaward from the doorsteps. Very likeable.

We made our way to the belt of wood walls, composed of stout vertical tarred timbers. As we went through the opening, we found three more piers—Straight Wharf, Old South Wharf and Commercial Wharf. They had been refurbished and extended to their original length, we were told, after years of decay. They were designated, respectively, Pier A,B,C, part of the "Beinecke Plan" for Nantucket. The waterfront used to be rundown, gray, salty-looking. ("I liked it that way," said a friend of mine who has been coming to Nantucket for years.) It certainly isn't that way anymore.

The waterfront had been architected within an inch of cuteness, although it has managed to stay on the side of taste. The gray shingle motif has been carried throughout; new little houses (some of them private) on the docks, the waterside restaurants, the Rope Walk Cafe, the showers and the harbormaster's place on Pier A are all done up smartly in salty shingles. It certainly was more dignified than the conglomerate waterfront of Edgartown.

The new breakwater made a safe haven in a harbor that had heretofore been exposed to the north. Nantucket's harbor is so big that yachts were driven to its shores in every big northeaster. Fessenden Blanchard recalled being blown ashore in a fifty-mile-an-hour northeaster while moored here; he saved *Mariana* only by thumping her across the bar into Polpis Harbor (point 20, map 10), thus avoiding the fate of a substantial part of the Nantucket fleet, which ended up on the beach.

Back to Beinecke. While some Nantucketers have taken to wearing buttons labelled "No Man Is an Island," Beinecke has proceeded with his plan. Walter Beinecke is a loyal Nantucket (from boyhood) vacationer. He happened to be lucky enough to inherit part of the S&H Green Stamp fortune—enough to buy up most of the Nantucket waterfront and anything else up for sale on the island. Beinecke defends his plan:

"The town is desperately in need of zoning laws, but efforts failed because a community like this considers itself a diehard bastion of Yankee independence and will forswear any community action. Nantucket's dilemma is that there isn't room here for everyone who would like to come. It is like a great painting. If everybody stands in front of it at once, nobody will ever see it." Beinecke is particularly critical of day tourists, the "trippers."

"To us," he said, "the trippers are people who come on an excursion boat and who leave within four hours or so. As the saying goes, 'They come with a shirt and a five dollar bill and they don't change either one.' "

Beinecke is convinced that no one but the ferry boat company really benefits from the crowds that show up daily on the ferry dock; he has suggested that Nantucket might get rid of the ferry altogether.

Yachting people, of course, are vastly encouraged by the existence of the new marina. It has a particular appeal to the less adventurous power and sail skippers who do not like to hang on a hook overnight.

Just down the line from us on Pier A was a real goldplater, the *Venturosa*. She was a forty-seven foot ketch with a freeboard of about 4½ feet, a 79-hp Mercedes-Benz and a flush deck forward with lots of sit-down space. The owner took us around: *three* ship-to-shore phones, a recording fathometer, deep freeze under one of the bunks, flush toilets, hot and cold running shower, *two* steering stations—one aft and one under the doghouse—ADF, RDF, radar, you name it. I didn't even ask what it might cost to reproduce *Venturosa* for fear it would send me right to Wall Street to become a stock broker, abandoning my life as a free and impoverished writer.

We left *Nimble* at Pier A and walked up beyond the docks to see what else Beinecke had wrought. Cobblestones imported from New Bedford (Nantucket's ancient rival) now pave the big court at the waterfront, the little side streets and the main street. On all sides were immaculate tourist shops.

Nantucket has been called "the Little Gray Lady of the Sea." The gray has survived as a sort of sprightly silver gray, as if the old witch were trying to touch up her hair a bit for the tourists who come by and see her in her front porch rocker.

Once you are off the Beinecke restoration, you have the run of a more naturally aged town, serene and uncrowded, compared with Edgartown. There were lively boys and girls and families foraging up and down the streets, to be sure, but every town has its babies and teenagers.

We wandered to the whaling museum (housed in an old spermacetti candle factory—you can still buy a spermacetti candle) and learned from what we could see and read there the kind of people Nantucketers were. There was David Whippey, who became chief on a Fiji Island after being abandoned by his whale ship; Mayhew Folger, who discovered the remaining crew of the *Bounty* on Pitcairn and so solved that mystery; Capt. Charles Grant's wife, who had one baby on Pitcairn and one in Samoa on the same whaling trip with her husband; the captain of the *Phebe* who lectured his mates on temperance as he himself lay dying of alcoholism on his bunk, and there were the whaling men who went off to the gold fields of California and to Bering Straits for seal, who established the first trade with Australia . . . to quote Melville:

"And thus have these naked Nantucketers, these sea hermits issuing from their ant hill in the sea, overrun and conquered the watery world like so many Alexanders; parcelling out among them the Atlantic, Pacific, and Indian Oceans . . . two thirds of this terraqueous globe is the Nantucketer's. For the sea is his; he owns it, as Emperors own empires . . ."

Nantucket was a civilization, then, unto itself. It was within every man's grasp to make a fortune. Nantucketers were the executives; they hired a troublesome bunch of employees. Melville, writing about his shipmates on *Acushnet*, said, "With very few exceptions, our crew was composed of a parcel of dastardly and mean-spirited wretches divided among themselves and only united in enduring without restraint the unmitigated tyranny of the captain."

But the executives got high pay.

Just go see the captains' homes on Orange Street. By the middle of the 1800's, Nantucket was a town of ten thousand members of the young executive class were out to sea most of their lives, to age thirty, anyway, and could retire in their forties, to a life of ease.

This continual absence of many of its males and the natural disasters of the sea made Nantucket a town where womenfolk were expected to operate on their own while the captain was gone, sometimes forever.

Some of the women became paragons. Maria Mitchell turned herself into a ranking American astronomer, and Keziah Coffin made herself rich in land deals and smuggling (her house down at Polpis Harbor had a handy secret entrance). Lucretia Mott became a leading abolitionist and women's rights crusader. Deborah Chase, tipping the scales at 350 even, was stronger than half the men on the island. (She once ran out on the street and overturned a horsedrawn wagon because it had jolted against her house. She is said to have flipped a 160-pound man up onto a low roof.) A goodly roll call for a small town.

Nantucket produced a bounty of equally redoubtable men: Henry Gardner climbed the mast of John Paul Jones' *Bonhomme Richard* at the height of the engagement with the *Serapis* and dropped lighted grenades down the *Serapis'* main hatch until the ship's ammunition store blew up, turning the tide of the engagement.

One Nantucketer's son became a British admiral, Sir Isaac Coffin. Sir Isaac founded a school in Nantucket for Coffins and their relatives only. This made it practically a public school because *every* family had married at least one Coffin somewhere along the line. (My own favorite Bowdoin College English teacher was Robert Tristram Coffin—colorful, forceful, a Pulitzer Prize poet, the Nantucket genius still strong in him.)

There was Rowland Macy, who started an unpretentious establishment in New York City on Fourteenth Street, known as R.H. Macy's. And there was Walter Folger, self-taught mathematician, who built the most complicated clock ever made in the United States, who had one of the first power looms in the country, who invented a telescope with which he discovered spots on the planet Venus before anyone else saw them. He studied medicine, which he used to help a diphtheria epidemic at bay on the island; he studied law and was elected to Congress.

Your run-of-the-mill whaling captain was just as formidable. He was the doctor (he would amputate), lawyer, skipper, navigator, and disciplinarian. Some of these old captains had remarkable records. Captain Worth of Nantucket sailed one million two hundred thousand miles in forty years at sea, nearly thirty of those years as a captain. He never lost a man, nor had a limb broken aboard, and he brought in twenty thousand barrels of oil, worth well over a million nineteenth-century dollars.

One Nantucket whaling ship, *Essex*, was squarely and deliberately rammed by a sperm whale and sunk (this factual ramming was the inspiration for *Moby Dick*'s climax) in Polynesia. Two of her whaleboats successfully sailed nearly four thousand miles to Chile. The survivors stayed alive by eating those who had died of exposure and, in one case, chose to die by lot so the rest could live. Owen Chase, one of the eight surviving besides Pollard, the captain, wrote and had published an account of their misfortunes. There still remains a copy that Melville got hold of and annotated in the margins.

Five of the *Essex* survivors were from Nantucket. All five, including Pollard, went back to sea and the other four eventually became captains of their own ships. This says a lot about Nantucketers.

Hector St. John Crevecoeur, Frenchman and *emigré*, visited pre-Revolutionary Nantucket and wrote, "Would you believe that a sandy spot of about twenty-three thousand acres affording neither stones nor timber nor meadows nor arable, yet can boast of a handsome town consisting of more than five hundred houses, should possess above two hundreds sail of vessels, constantly employ upward of two thousand seamen . . . and has several citizens worth 20,000 pounds sterling! Had this island been contiguous to the shore of some ancient monarchy, it would only have been occupied by a few wretched fishermen . . . No, their freedom, their skill, their probity and perseverance has accomplished everything. . . ."

Nantucket was then the epitome of America, a condensation, a magnification of the thrust of the young country presaging the shattering roar of the Saturn rocket that sent Americans, first of all human kind, to another body in the sky.

But even as the trail of the Saturn rocket spun its way over a society with some notable weaknesses, in Nantucket there were some notable strains apparent in the fabric. There was a certain cold-bloodedness to an industry that separated men and women for periods longer than those caused elsewhere by war. Nantucketers, particularly the women, as if by compensation, were gourmands—the continual round of meals was as toxic as liquor. There was an incessant and hypnotic socializing between the ladies, who were frequently and lengthily bereft of husbands and sweethearts.

Crevecoeur noted, astonished, that while none of the women flirted, many started the day with a stiff dose of opium and were addicted to it. This was more countenanced among the Quakers of Nantucket than marijuana is among the middle class today. There was a certain strangeness in Paradise.

The embodiment of Nantucket was Melville's Ahab. When Ahab playfully told the ship's carpenter how to fashion a "complete man after a desireable pattern," Ahab specified a being "with no heart at all" and "about an acre of fine brain."

This is Melville's warning to the man and the nation that has no heart: Ahab, as he watched his own ship sink, continued madly after the white whale and throwing the harpoon, ended by perishing in the coil of his own obsession, dragging his men with him.

By 1870, Nantucket was abandoned by her captains. They could not make common cause to dredge the harbor entrance. Rather than do that, they moved their ships—now too deep to come through the entrance—to Vineyard Haven and New Bedford. So ended the Golden Age of Nantucket.

Town square, Nantucket. (BARRY STOTT)

Ship in a bottle, Nantucket. (BARRY STOTT)

Nantucket town, Nantucket Harbor. (BARRY STOTT)

CHAPTER EIGHTEEN

═══════════════════════════════════

NANTUCKET SOUND—SIASCONSET

═══════════════════════════════════

(DAY 23)

"Nantucket!" wrote Melville, ". . . look at it—a mere hillock, an elbow of sand; all beach, without a background. There is more sand there than you could use in twenty years as a substitute for blotting paper. Some gamesome wits will tell you that they have to plant weeds there, they don't grow naturally; that they import Canada thistles; that they have to send beyond seas for a spile to stop a leak in an oil cask; that pieces of wood in Nantucket are carried about like bits of the true cross in Rome; that people there plant toadstools before their homes to get under the shade in summertime; that one blade of grass makes an oasis, three blades in a day's walk, a prairie; that they wear quicksand shoes, something like Laplander

snowshoes; that they are so shut up, belted about, in every way in-
closed, surrounded and made an utter island of by the ocean that
to their very tables and chairs small clams will sometimes be found
adhering, as to the backs of sea turtles. But these extravaganzas only
show that Nantucket is not Illinois."

Indeed it is not.

Outside of Nantucket town, the island is mostly moor, heather and
bracken, having been denuded of trees by the inhabitants well before
Melville saw it. The photographs of the 1800's show Nantucket barren
as Arctic tundra country. But, by the turn of the century, there had
been a sensible comeback. The barren, scalded look of Melville's
time had been softened by planting trees and bushes alongside the
rather bleak roads and in the villages; this is notably so in Siasconset,
one of the most marvelous villages on earth.

Siasconset is on the outer, curved rim of the half-moon of the island;
first a lookout for whales, then a shelter for net and trawler fishermen,
then a place from which to escape from the Quakers of the town of
Nantucket. Nantucketers call it "Sconset"; less touched by progress
than even Nantucket town, it has preserved something unique in American achitecture, in effect a kind of reminiscence of the Middle Ages.
Sconset is a garden town; we saw it after a taxi ride across the big
heath that comprises the middle of Nantucket. Siasconet: cheery, cozy,
nearly overgrown with bushes and plants, a village with small cottages
at its center, some larger places on the outskirts, and undeniably resembling cottage towns of the Middle Ages. Shingled walls peered from
vines and hedges and low trees, like pine cones in a Christmas wreath.

In *Early Nantucket and Its Whale Houses*, H. Chandler Forman
noted that four whale houses were set up on Nantucket in the 1600's:
at Sesachacha, Sconset, and two other points. Sconset's whale house was
built in 1636. It was a rude, solid hut with a tall spar in front,
manned at all daylight hours by a man on watch. When a whale was
spotted, the men below launched a whale boat into the surf. It took
only a few minutes to pull out to the whale in those days; the carcass
could be hauled quickly to shore and boiled down then and there.
By 1726, there were a number of whale houses in Sconset; in that
year the islanders killed some eighty whales off Nantucket's coast.
Seine and trawler fishermen had also built houses at Sconset, following
the pattern of the original whale house.

Wives and children followed, and moved into the houses. Small ells,
or "warts" were tacked on each side of the back of the original rec-
tangle to serve as additional sleeping rooms. A couple of taverns sprang
up; a town was in progress of forming, helter-skelter, in the dunes up
from Sconset Beach.

Later on, Sconset became the let's-get-away-from-the-Quakers place for those who found the broadcloth style of living had a little too much sobriety and industry for their blood. The Sconset "build anchor" parties were the big social occasions; crews about to ship out for the gray seas would gather to "build an anchor" for the cruise, away from the sedateness of the Quaker streets of Nantucket.

A party of seamen could put up quite a noise at a "build anchor" party, bellowing unchaste chanteys and profane doggerel. One of the most celebrated "party verses" in the hell-raising days of Sconset told about the captain who had been to sea so many times he could tell exactly where he was—from Nantucket to Japan—simply by tasting the sounding lead after it had been dropped over and touched bottom. In the bowdlerized version, one of the captain's mates, a jolly fellow named Marden, decided to have a little fun with his captain. Marden took some Nantucket earth aboard and, when well out to sea, dipped the lead into the earth and took it down to the captain's cabin for him to taste:

> The skipper stormed and tore his hair
> Thrust on his boots and roared to Marden
> "Nantucket's sunk, and here we are
> Right over Marm Hackett's garden!"

The road to Nantucket from Sconset was then a pair of ruts; it was said if you take the turn-off to Polpis Harbor by mistake you were forced to continue to Polpis before you could turn around. The Sconset road used to be traversed every day by Capt. Billy Baxter, retired; the captain drove his cart seven miles over the heath in all weather and got to know the look of the country pretty well. On very foggy days, he would stop the cart, look around as if lost, and then plunge the butt of his whip into the dirt by the side of the cart. Savoring his passenger's attention, he would taste the butt and set off confidently in a new direction.

When he entered Sconset, Captain Baxter would produce a horn and blow a great flourish to let the town know that mail was at hand at his "post office"—a window in Mistress Betsy Carey's house, where the Captain lived, married to Betsy Carey's daughter. Over the window hung a sign, "Post Office." Capt. Baxter charged a penny a letter, highly irregular, since the letters were already stamped.

A government postal inspector arrived in Nantucket one morning, boarded Capt. Baxter's stage, and asked if it were true that there was an unauthorized post office in Siasconset. Capt. Baxter said he'd never heard of it, but obliged the stranger by driving him to Polpis Harbor and, having combed the town, satisfied the government man that no such post office existed.

Betsy Carey, Baxter's mother-in-law, kept a tavern in the house, which Baxter gave the name of "Shanunga," for the figurehead of the vessel of the same name, which he had salvaged and stood on end in the backyard. Mistress Carey's likeness has been preserved for posterity by an artist working for *Harper's Magazine* in 1860; she was a fierce old lady, by her portrait—a bottle of rum in each hand and dried codfish hanging on the wall behind her. The article in *Harper's* relates that Mistress Carey first told the artist's party to "Take your traps and tramp!" But, seeing they were all willing to buy food and drink for cash, she became quite agreeable.

Col. Joseph Hart, visiting Sconset in the process of gathering material for the book that became in 1834, *Miriam Coffin* (based largely on the life of Keziah Coffin, Nantucket's lady wheeler-dealer) noted that an unwritten law in Sconset forbade anyone to build better than his neighbor and that no one had the temerity to try. Thus the original fishermen's whale houses with their warts became the pattern for new homes; older ones were preserved intact, if somewhat spruced up.

"For our purposes," wrote Forman in *Early Nantucket and Its Whale Houses*, "the chief value of Sconset is that it forms the only example on Nantucket Island of a surviving settlement of the period of the founding fathers—that is, the seventeenth century."

Forman traces the history of "Shanunga" from whale house to tavern to summer cottage. The original building simply had a front room or hall that went up to the roof. The back of the room was lofted over and, below, divided into two cramped bedrooms, in each of which slept two men used to the narrow quarters of life in the foc'sle.

Above these two rooms on half-floor, reached by a ladder, were two more beds. This kind of construction, Forman says, was the "baulk" or "hanging loft" common in Britain in the 1600's. The design came to Britain with the invasion of the Anglo-Saxons. "The ancestors of the Sconset whale huts," wrote Forman, "go back in time fifteen centuries to the homes of the Anglo-Saxons."

Further, Forman writes, the original village plan of Sconset was "organic and medieval . . . it kept to crooked and meandering roadways, and it was full of walks for pedestrian purposes. It had, as we have seen, two open spaces . . . it possessed also small scaled buildings in true medieval or English medieval fashion."

Forman hoped that somehow a way could be found to preserve the remains of the only medieval country village left in North America.

Nimble's crew walked up and down the lanes between the rose-covered cottages, looking for the old ones, trying to find in them the outlines of the old whale houses, and the simple life.

Edward F. Underhill, in a manuscript on Sconset, has recorded life in an early fisherman's home:

"In the morning, members of the household went, one after the other, to the pewter wash basin or wooden bowl in the main room, or kept on a bench outside and washed their faces and hands in rain water, using home-made soft soap, when soap was needed, and dried themselves with a flaxen towel made on the island and used in common by the household. They arranged their hair with a family comb before the only mirror, a little one, mounted in an antique frame and hung in the living room. Their raiment was not much more than sufficient to fill a small chest. An extra gown for the women made of wool, grown, sheared, washed, carded, spun and woven on the island, and a few underclothes for a change, sufficed."

Crevecoeur visited a family in Sconset in 1722 and noted that the family lived almost entirely by fishing. Their diet was fish, clams, boiled cornmeal and bacon; they had two spinning wheels, which supplied all the cloth for the family. The family, unlike medieval (or even post-medieval) commoners in Europe, could read and write and had a copy of Samuel Butler's poem *Huddibras* and a Bible among their few books.

"New" Sconset is still—in the main—extremely simple and pleasant looking. The roads thrust between the rows of cottages are still sometimes too narrow for cars. In our wanderings, we were invited in to see a "new" cottage, built in the 1800's. The nice older couple said that the going price for a place of modest size on the Sconset bank would be $30,000 to $40,000.

We walked down to the beach; and sat listening and watching as the seas came in from the far oceans that had been the true Nantucketer's home.

It was quite a wrench to go from this, which, in spirit, is the oldest place in the country, back by jet to the city that constantly boasts of the newest.

Yet, the transitional flight over water, during which we could watch, below, the riffles obeying the everlasting wind, strengthened a sense of perspective gained, of time retraced, of our very making revisited.

A house, Siasconset, Nantucket. (BARRY STOTT)

A house, Siasconset, Nantucket. (BARRY STOTT)

Author making notes in Nimble's *forecabin.* (GEORGE WILKINSON)

APPENDIX

≈≈≈

FROM DOWN IN THE GALLEY

≈≈≈

Some guidelines to preparing food while cruising for several weeks on board a twenty-five or thirty-foot boat.

A twenty-five or thirty-footer's cooking facilities are simple: a two-burner alcohol stove, a wood icebox and possibly a picnic-cooler box which cools itself electrically in port, but which is used as a regular block-ice-cooled box during the cruise; plus a simple picnic cooler.

Basically, it all boils down to four things 1) pre-planning, 2) simplicity (ease of preparation), 3) tastiness (satisfying to cruising appetites) and 4) storability (most items should not need refrigeration).

Parenthetically there are a number of "cruising cookbooks" on the market today, most of them utterly useless to the average small boat cruise. They concentrate heavily on recipes and meal suggestions that depend on large quantities of fresh or frozen foods, four burner electrical stoves and generous preparation time. On a 25 footer, you have

160

none of these advantages.

Pre-planning—There are few words as annoying to a skipper as these: "We really *have* to get to a grocery store tonight, I have nothing to cook for dinner." If you pre-plan your menus for the cruise, and stock enough food on board in the beginning so that you *could* cruise continuously without ever stopping, you will never have to confront the captain with such words. You will also gain immeasurable peace of mind when you know that every time you stop in port you won't *have to* be running off to the nearest grocery store before it closes down for the evening—while the rest of the crew sits watching the sunset with drinks in hand. You will have a choice.

Naturally, when the opportunity arises to buy fresh fruits, vegetables, meats and fish, you will probably want to do so, and then relegate some of your canned and dried foods back to the stowage compartment. In addition, remember that pre-planning will mean that when meal preparation time comes, you (who are probably tired out already from serving in your alternate capacity as port winch handler, or what ever) will not have to stand hovering over the stowage hatch, wondering what to cook. You will simply consult your handy "menu for the day" and start cooking. You prepared your menu with imagination and creativity when you were rested and alert—something you rarely are at the end of a cruising day. Finally, should you become ill and unable to function in the galley for an evening, how much simpler to be able to hand someone your menu plan and know that they can find everything they need on board for the meal, and that they won't be messing up the rest of your week's menus by slapdashing together bits of three different days' foods.

Tastiness—Using primarily canned foods does not necessarily mean that all your meals must be of the hot-dog-and-bean variety. Almost everything edible comes canned (or dried), from corned beef to pudding, some good as it comes, some not so good—but a lot better with the addition of something else. Spices can spark up a great many dishes and take up very little space on board. As a bare minimum (although your selection ultimately depends on what you like to cook with), I would suggest taking along these:

> —minced garlic (dried)
> —minced onion (dried)
> —freeze dried chives
> —whole celery seed
> —dry mustard
> —sweet basil leaves
> —dehydrated mint leaves (A dash added to peas

tastes great, or try some in iced tea.)
—curry powder
—poultry seasoning
—salt and pepper

It also seems on our boat that Worcestershire Sauce and A-1 Steak Sauce come in for heavy use; your tastes may differ.

Try heating canned fruit as a side dish with meat. Cranberry sauce and applesauce taste especially good with all sorts of main dishes.

If everything else is canned, a fresh salad can make the whole meal seem fresh.

Canned foods come in all sorts of textures and colors as well as tastes—don't serve three mushy foods at one meal.

Basically, the same rules of cooking that apply on land apply on water; you just have to be a little more imaginative to get tasty meals out of cans instead of out of a refrigerator.

Simplicity—If you've ever cooked on board before, you know that the less time you spend making food the better. If you haven't been a galley captain before, take my word for it: you do not ever want to spend more than 30-45 minutes preparing a meal, and the less time the better. There are a number of reasons for this; some of the more poignant ones: 1) the motion may get you: if you stay below too long, you're liable to get seasick (there is nothing more awful than cooking when you're suffering from mal de mer). 2) Even if the water is calm, there are other possible physical discomforts to be considered—gasoline fumes, motor exhaust, or heat. All of these have the same ultimate effect as a rolling sea when you're below for too long. If you *do* start to feel a little funny, by the way, the best quick cure is a fast turn about the deck, towards the front of the boat, in the wind and the spray. 3) Everyone is usually ravenous, and if you don't feed them quickly, the crew is likely to get roaring drunk, pester you until you *do* feed them, become mutinous and complain a lot. 4) Who wants to spend a lot of time cooking, anyway??? You could be up enjoying the cruise: looking at scenery, acquiring a tan, conversing, reading, taking photographs. Your title is galley chief, not galley slave.

One easy way to start any cruise off as easily as possible is to bring aboard with you some large piece of already-cooked (at home) meat, such as a ham, a corned beef, a turkey, a stew. This will make your first dinner a snap, and should provide leftovers for sandwiches. Also in the name of simplicity I usually bake a large tube-shaped pound cake, which is a versatile base for a number of desserts (add fruit, a sauce, toast it, etc.).

Storability—Remember that a twenty-five-pound block of ice is pretty far gone after two and a half days, especially in summer and especially if it is being chipped away to furnish ice for drinks, no matter how insulated it is kept. Don't take aboard more fresh food than you can eat up in two to three days. Something horrible to avoid is the sight of twenty dollars worth of fresh meat, butter, milk and eggs, all spoiling swiftly as the ice melts down the drain, the sails go slack and the captain announces that he needs the gas he has left to negotiate the entrance to Cuttyhunk so "we won't motor, we'll just have to sit here." Ugh.

Dried foods won't spoil. I have not stressed using dried foods because for a one-to-three week cruise they are rather expensive and harder to obtain than canned items. They *are* lighter and take up less space, so if you're planning to be at sea a long time, you'll want to use them more exclusively.

Foods such as crackers, bread, potatoes, carrots, hard squashes, turnips and onions and fresh fruit (especially if purchased unripe or only partially ripe) will hold up without ice pretty well: at least a week.

Canned foods can really be pretty good, perhaps not up to French haute cuisine standards, but who needs haute cuisine on a cruise? Everyone on board is usually so hungry that even a minor effort in the galley produces raves from the captain and crew. Besides, they all think you're so great to stay below the heaving decks in the haze of heat, cooking odors and pitching seas long enough to cook a meal, they'll be effusively grateful for anything edible. There are great psychological/ emotional rewards for the galley captain which are never proffered the same cook on land!

Keep all of your cold drinks in one ice chest or cooler, the food in another. People will be opening and closing the drink cooler all day long, and it's contents will warm up faster. You will probably need to open the food cooler only three times a day, which will help keep its contents much colder, far longer.

Wrap your foods to be kept cool carefully. Celery, lettuce and other vegetables will become soggy, limp and waterlogged if they are not tightly wrapped in plastic wrap. Butter stays best in an aluminum box with lid—neater, too. Even though not in the cooler, other foods need to be wrapped tightly to stay crisp: crackers, bread, chips, pretzels, rolls.

Store your cans anywhere you can find room as long as they don't get *wet*. Bilges are great unless your boat leaks; at worst salt water will corrode away the cans and, at best, will soak off all the labels so you have to play open-the-can-roulette.

Galleyware—The type of utensils you will need depends on what you plan to serve on your cruise. You would probably want, however, to include the following basics, anyway:

2 Teflon-coated frying pans
1 large stew pot with lid
Teflon-lined saucepans with lids: 1 medium, 1 small
coffee pot
whistling tea kettle (for all water heating)
stainless steel bowls (large for salad, 1 small
        and 1 medium for everything else)
wicker baskets (for crackers, rolls, fruit)
plastic bottles with tops (1 qt., 1½ qt., 2 qt.)
plastic bowls, plates and mugs (for when you
        run out of paper)
stainless steel forks, knives, spoons
Teflon spatulas
pot holders
serrated spoon and cooking fork
ladle (for soups and stews)
two large, extra-sharp carving knives (1
        serrated, 1 plain)
1 wire whisk
wooden cutting board
tray
can opener, paring knives, potato peeler
several beer can openers (They seem to
        get dropped overboard.)
scissors
ice picks (two, in case one breaks)

There are no items more useful to the galley captain than aluminum foil, paper towels, paper napkins, plastic wrap, plastic garbage bags (regular and large trash-bag sized), plastic food storage bags, paper plates, paper cups (hot and cold) and paper bowls. Yes, paper plates are not as elegant as regular ones. No, you should *not* therefore count on using regular ones. If there is something more unpleasant than washing dishes on board a boat, I don't know what it is. I'd rather clean out the bilge, anytime. Remember, you may be using cold water, maybe even cold *salt* water and salt water soap (which, contrary to the promises of its manufacturers, does *not* get things any cleaner in most cases than plain water would) to wash the dishes clean. Also, you will have to boil water to scald the dishes you've struggled to wash clean and then you'll have to dry them and put them away. You'll be below decks with all the discomforts that can entail. It is more than enough to have to wash the pots and pans (remember to have Teflon-coated ones) and silverware.

Paper plates, cups, bowls, etc., are all being made in myriad patterns, weights, textures and sizes these days. The best plates are heavy, coated with plastic and successfully serve hot, wet food; paper plates can be made even stronger by putting them inside wicker holders, which are reusable. You can get plastic click-in disposable paper cups that fit reusable cup holders (these worked out best for me), cold drink cups in various sizes, and sturdy foam cups, as well as the standard hot beverage cups. You might wish to carry enough regular plastic dishes to see you through if you should happen to run out of paper ones, but plan on using them only in such an emergency, unless you wish to become a real galley slave.

Plastic garbage bags are the only way to go to sea. They don't leak, they don't soak open (one session of cleaning wet garbage off the floor after a disaster should cure you of using paper garbage bags). Best of all, the largest trash-size garbage bags will hold two to three days' garbage, all neatly contained and tied up, odorless and away from sight until you reach port.

Aluminum foil is another infinitely helpful and versatile item. It can line a pan, serve as a lid, be fashioned into an extra cooking pot when needed, used to wrap up heavy items, make a top-of-the-stove "oven" for heating rolls and bread. Aluminum foil can be used in pouch form for cooking several types of vetetables in the same pot. Put the vegetables, a little butter, salt, pepper and other seasoning in the foil, seal tightly and pop into the pot of boiling water; the pouched vegetables cook beautifully and there is only one pan going on the stove—it won't even need washing.

Paper towels have a number of uses, limited only by your imagination: cleaning up spills, draining cooked foods, serving as a disposable dishcloth, drying off wet vegetables, catching fruit and vegetable peelings when you are in the midst of preparation, lining shelves, washing windows, drying dishes. I would leave behind several complete changes of clothing if it came to a choice between taking extra aluminum foil and paper towels or the clothes.

I see no reason to list extensive meal plans, as you undoubtedly prefer to devise your own. I have included only one actual menu plan, which was worked out for a one-week cruise for four people, in the hopes that it might give you ideas of your own. Bon appétit and a happy cruise!

— BEATRICE B. WILLIAMS
Galley Captain, *Nimble*

MEAL PLAN:

EIGHT DAYS, FOUR PEOPLE, EAST HAMPTON TO MARTHA'S VINEYARD

DAY NO.	BREAKFAST	LUNCH	DINNER
1	orange juice (canned) boiled eggs (fresh) toast and jam coffee (w. sugar and pream)	fruit salad plate crackers beer	corned beef (cooked at home) with cabbage fresh cooked carrots coffee, cake (baked at home)
2	orange juice (canned) fried eggs (fresh) toast and jam coffee (etc.)	bacon (canned), lettuce and tomato sandwiches fresh fruit beer	ham steak (sliced off a canned ham) with pineapple rings (canned) candied yams (canned) cole slaw (other half of day 1's cabbage) canned fruit, coffee
3	cereal with canned fruit, sugar, milk melon wedges coffee	corned beef sandwiches (leftover from day 1) pickle and relish tray beer	tuna (canned), hard-boiled egg, tomato salad platter rolls and butter chocolate pudding (canned) coffee
4	toasted leftover cake orange juice (canned) scrambled eggs (fresh) bacon (canned) coffee	cheese (jar), tomato and lettuce sandwiches cookies and fresh fruit beer	ham (from canned), noodles, string beans (canned) and cheese (jarred) casserole salad (fresh lettuce and tomatoes) canned fruit, coffee
5	french toast jam and syrup orange juice (canned) coffee	vegetable salad plate (canned, with lettuce and fresh carrots, radishes) crackers and soup beer	Shrimp, chicken, peas, stewed tomatoes (all canned) plus saffron rice mix; all cooked together in a skillet coffee leftover cake with fruit sauce

DAY NO.	BREAKFAST	LUNCH	DINNER
6	boiled eggs (fresh) melon toast and jam coffee	liverwurst sand- wiches (canned liver spread) pickles and relishes fresh fruit beer	hot dogs and bacon (canned) baked beans (canned) brown bread (canned) canned fruit and cookies coffee
7	cereal and canned fruit with milk and sugar orange juice (canned) coffee	ham (from canned) sand- wiches) hard boiled eggs beer	chow mein with rice and noodles (canned) fresh fruit and cookies coffee
8	melon pancakes (mix) syrup bacon (canned) coffee	tunafish sand- wiches (canned) soup (canned) beer	ravioli (canned) breadsticks salad (fresh) coffee rice pudding (jar)

BIBLIOGRAPHY

- *About Lobsters,* T.M. Prudden; The Bond Wheelwright Co., Freeport, Me., 1967.
- *A Cruising Guide to the New England Coast,* Roger F. Duncan and John P. Ware; Dodd, Mead and Company, New York, 1968.
- *American Heritage,* American Heritage Publishing Co., Inc.; New York—"Oak Bluffs," David G. McCullough; Volume XVIII, Number 6, October, 1967. —"The World and Nantucket," Nathaniel Benchley; Volume XVI, Number 4, June, 1965.
- *Bay and the Sound, The,* John Parkinson, Jr.; Little, Brown and Company, Boston, Mass., 1968.
- *Block Island—Lore and Legends,* Ethel Colt Ritchie; Frederick N. Ritchie, Block Island, R.I., 1969.
- *Block Island to Nantucket,* Fessenden S. Blanchard; D. Van Nostrand Company, Inc., Princeton, N.J., 1961
- *Boating Almanac 1969,* Volume 2, G.W. Bromley & Co., Inc., New York, 1969.
- *By the Wind,* Richard Baum; D. Van Nostrand Company, Inc., Princeton, N.J., 1962.
- *Cape Cod Compass,* Yankee Inc.; Volume 22; Dublin, N.H., 1969.
- *Cape Cod—Where to Go, What to Do, How to Do It,* Julius M. Wilensky; Snug Harbor Publishing Co., Stamford, Conn., 1968.
- *Cruising the Maine Coast,* Morten Lund; Walker and Company, New York, 1967.
- *Dolphin Guide to Cape Cod, Martha's Vineyard, Nantucket,* Frances Blake; Doubleday and Company, Inc., Garden City, N.Y., 1965.
- *Early Nantucket and Its Whale Houses,* Henry Chandlee Forman; Hastings House, New York, 1966.
- *Frail Ocean, The,* Wesley Marx; Coward McCann, New York, 1967.
- *Frontiers of the Sea,* Robert C. Cowan; Doubleday and Company, Inc., Garden City, N.Y., 1969.
- *Great Beach, The,* John Hay; Doubleday and Company, Inc., Garden City, N.Y., 1963
- *Hamptons Guide,* Dan Rattiner; Hamptons Guide, East Hampton, N.Y., 1969.
- *History of American Sailing Ships, The,* Howard I. Chapelle; W.W. Norton and Company, Inc., New York, 1935.

- *Inland Sea, The,* Morton M. Hunt; Doubleday and Company, Inc., Garden City, N.Y., 1965.
- *Lonely Sea and the Sky, The,* Sir Francis Chichester; Ballantine Books, Inc., New York, 1969.
- *Long Island Discovery,* Seon Manley; Doubleday and Company, Inc., Garden City, N.Y., 1966.
- *Long Island Sound,* Fessenden S. Blanchard; D. Van Nostrand Company, Inc., Princeton, N.J., 1958.
- *Long Island Sound—Where to Go, What to Do, How to Do It,* Julius M. Wilensky; Wescott Cove Publishing Company, Stamford, Conn., 1969.
- *Loss of the Essex, The,* Edouard A. Stackpole; The Inquirer and Mirror, Inc., Nantucket Island, Mass., Third Edition, 1958.
- *Macmillan Marine Atlas—Long Island Shore & South Shore,* William B. Matthews, Jr.; The Macmillan Company, 1967–68 Edition, New York, 1967.
- *Macmillan Marine Atlas—New England,* William B. Matthews, Jr.; 1968–69 Edition, The Macmillan Company, New York, 1968.
- *Martha's Vineyard, a Short History and Guide,* Eleanor Ranson Mayhew; Dukes County Historical Society, Inc., Edgartown, Mass., 1956.
- *Martha's Vineyard: Summer Resort After 100 Years,* Henry Beetle Hough; Avery's Inc., Edgartown, Mass. 1966.
- *Moby Dick,* Herman Melville; The New American Library, New York, 1961.
- *Nantucket Holiday,* Nantucket Historical Association; Nantucket Island, Mass., 1969.
- *Nantucket, the Far-Away Island,* William O. Stevens; Dodd, Mead and Company, New York, 1966.
- *National Geographic, The,* The National Geographic Society, Washington, D.C.
  —"Cape Cod, Where Sea Holds Sway Over Man and Land," Nathaniel T. Kennedy and Dean Conger; Volume 122, Number 2, August, 1962.
  —"Man-of-War, the Deadly Fisher," Charles E. Lane; Volume 123, Number 3, March, 1963.
  —"Old Whaling Days Still Flavor Life on Sea-Swept Martha's Vineyard," William P.E. Graves and James Blair; Volume 119, Number 6, June, 1961.
- *Of Whales and Men,* R. B. Robertson; Simon and Schuster, New York, 1969.
- *Outer Lands, The,* Dorothy Sterling; The Natural History Press, Doubleday and Company, Inc., Garden City, N.Y., 1967.
- *Piloting Seamanship and Small Boat Handling,* Charles F. Chapman; Motor Boating Magazine, The Hearst Corporation, New York, 1968.
- *Primer for America,* Robert P. Tristram Coffin; The Macmillan Company, New York, 1945.
- *Scott Fitzgerald,* Andrew Turnbull; Charles Scribner's Sons, New York, 1962.
- *Stalking the Blue-Eyed Scallop,* Euell Gibbons; David McKay Company, Inc., New York, 1967.
- *Story of Cuttyhunk, The,* Louise T. Haskell; Bradbury-Waring Div. of Reynolds-DeWalt Printing, Inc., New Bedford, Mass. 1969.
- *Tales and Trails of Martha's Vineyard,* Joseph C. Allen; Little Brown and Company, Boston, Mass., 1949.

- *The Great Gatsby,* F. Scott Fitzgerald; Charles Scribner's Sons, New York, 1953.
- *Thousand Dollar Yacht, The,* Anthony Bailey; The Macmillan Company, New York, 1967–68.
- *These Fragile Outposts,* Barbara Blau Chamberlain; The Natural History Press, Doubleday and Company, Inc., Garden City, N.Y., 1964.
- *T.R.—The Story of Theodore Roosevelt,* Noel F. Busch; Reynal and Company, New York, 1963.
- *Trans-Atlantic Trimaran,* Arthur Piver; Underwriter's Press, San Francisco, Calif., 1961.
- *Trans-Pacific Trimaran,* Arthur Piver; PI-Craft, Mill Valley, Calif., 1963.
- *Trimaran Third Book,* Arthur Piver; PI-Craft, Mill Valley Calif., 1965.
- *Whale Fishery of New England,* Reynolds-DeWalt Printing, Inc., New Bedford, Mass., 1968.
- *Who Killed Society?,* Cleveland Amory; Pocket Books, Inc., New York, 1962.